THE POLITICS OF TRADE

Anglo-French Commerce on the Coromandel Coast 1763-1793

THE POLITICS OF TRADE

Anglo-French Commerce on the Coromandel Coast 1763-1793

ARVIND SINHA

MANOHAR
2002

First published 2002

ISBN 81-7304-419-8

Published by
Ajay Kumar Jain for
Manohar Publishers & Distributors
4753/23 Ansari Road, Daryaganj
New Delhi 110002

Printed at
Rajkamal Electric Press
Delhi 110033

TO MY FATHER

DR. R.N. SINHA

Contents

Illustrations

MAPS

GRAPHS

PLATES

Tables

Acknowledgements

THE PRESENT WORK is the result of many years of research on the French trading activities in India. I wish to express my deep gratitude to the late Professor P.S. Gupta of Delhi University for initiating me into this area of study. I was also encouraged by Professor R.L. Shukla at every stage of my work to pursue this research with greater vigour. I would like to thank my teacher, Professor Tapan Raychaudhuri for developing the theme, Professor Shahid Amin for his constructive advice in the conceptual stages, Professor Rajeev Verma, Dr. Deepak Kumar, Mr. Suresh Prasad and Mr. Vinod Srivastava for going through the drafts and making useful suggestions, Dr. Yogesh Sharma for helping me locate sources in the French Archives, to Professor S. Bhattacharya, Professor Om Prakash and to the late Professors Ashin Das Gupta and M.P. Sreedharan for suggesting areas of improvement in my work through their comments and helping me overcome certain problems relating to my subject, and to friends and colleagues for their encouraging words.

My sincere thanks to the staff of all the Libraries and Archives that I visited for collecting research material. These include the National Archives of India, New Delhi and Pondicherry, the National Library, Calcutta, the State Archives of Tamil Nadu, Pondicherry and Andhra Pradesh, Bibliothèque Romain Rolland, Delhi University Library and Reference Section, Ratan Tata Library, Delhi, Nehru Memorial Museum & Library, New Delhi, ICHR Documentation Library, India Office Records and Library and British Museum, London, Archives Nationales, Archives des Affaires Étrangers and Bibliothèque Nationale in Paris and Archives D'outre-mer in France. I express my sincere thanks to the helpful staff of these Archives and Libraries and in particular to my well-wishers in the National Archives of India.

In addition, special thanks are due to ICSSR and ICHR that enabled me to go abroad for the collection of material, which was extensive and scattered in the various archives.

I wish to express my deep gratitude to the Maison des Sciences des Hommes, Paris, and in particular, to Professor Clemens Heller and Professor Maurice Aymard, who arranged my visits to France and helped me collect the source material. I would like to acknowledge my debt to the British Council for arranging my visit to England. Also, my sincere gratitude to Dr. Jean-Marie Lafont, Mr. Ramesh Jain and B.N. Varma. I lack adequate words to thank them.

Finally I take this opportunity to acknowledge the cooperation and support extended to me by my wife Akhila and my sons Shambhav and Shantanu, while writing this book.

New Delhi ARVIND SINHA

Introduction

COMMERCE HAS been a major cause of competition and antagonism among the European powers. A clash of commercial interests often led to political contentions and even armed conflicts. This is best exemplified by the intense competition that prevailed between England and France throughout the eighteenth century. Pondicherry and Madras on the Coromandel Coast were no lesser rivals than London and Paris, whose European differences were interlinked and extended to India by their commercial ambitions. They traded in the same articles and sought to grasp the same advantages. This work seeks to examine the nature of Anglo-French commercial activities along the Coromandel Coast, explore the extent of French revival in this region despite the political eclipse of the French power and to study this in relation to the English expansion in India.

The focus of this study is on French trading activities along the Coromandel Coast. As the English East India Company was an expanding power, the French could not remain oblivious to its presence and were forced to come to working arrangements with it to continue trading profitably in this region. The two European powers thus had a peculiar relationship of political and commercial rivalry to control and monopolize centres of production on the Coromandel Coast though privately they joined hands to siphon off profit from the Indian trade.

A word about why the period 1763 to 1793 and the Coromandel region has been chosen for the present study. In 1763, the French suffered defeats in Europe, America and India and were forced to sign the Treaty of Paris. In India, the year saw the end of the three Carnatic Wars between the French and the English. It is generally assumed that this marked the total eclipse of the French in India. However, a scrutiny of available sources suggests that at least in southern India the French challenge continued for almost another three decades till all their settlements were seized by the English in 1793 and retained till the end of the Napoleonic wars. This study aims to ascertain the nature and the extent of French revival during this period and their relationship with the English. From 1763 major shifts and vicissitudes were visible in the French policy towards India. Their dream of revival and re-establishment of the lost fortune persisted till their final annihilation after the Revolution. During the same phase, the British economy underwent major transformation leading to a series of changes in their policy towards India. How these policies interacted in relation to the Coromandel commerce forms the backbone of the present work. It is an attempt to study the Anglo-French relationship along the Coromandel Coast as distinct from the traditional diplomatic, military and political relationship.

Some scholars have questioned the advisability of isolating the Coromandel Coast from the other important Indian commercial zones because a close trade nexus always existed between them. Doubts have been cast on the utility of demarcating a continuous coastal belt stretching from Cape Comorin to Bengal into artificial units and giving them separate names. It is not possible to separate Bengal totally from Coromandel because of strong trade links. Yet, this study has decided to treat the Coromandel Coast as a separate region for two reasons. First, this region had developed a distinct identity over several centuries through its social and political organization, its products and trade structure. Its links to the trans-oceanic and 'country' trade also provided it a kind of homogeneity that other regions did not have. Secondly, though Bengal and Coromandel had a long tradition of trade links, politically the two regions were quite different. While Bengal had come under British rule by 1763, the political balance along the Coromandel Coast was still evenly poised and no single power dominated the scene. Hence the French could compete with the English on equal terms for a considerable length of time. It was only after the French Revolution and the destruction of all monopolies by the Revolutionary government that annihilation of French settlements could be achieved by the British.

The study of the French in India has remained a relatively neglected field for several years. Of course, a number of scholarly works are available which supply a lot of information on the activities of the French companies. Paul Kaeppelin's *La Compagnie des Indes Oriental et François Martin* is useful on the organization of the early French East India Company. His analysis of the achievements and failures of the company in its early stage is of great value.

The period prior to 1763 has received greater attention from the

French historians. Most of their works deal with the political and military triumphs of Dupleix, La Bourdonnais, Bussy and Lally. Cultru's work on Dupleix changed the tone of historical writing from eulogy of Dupleix to criticism and analysis. W.H. Dalgliesh, L. Thompson and Dodwell worked in the same field. Malleson's *Final French Struggles in India and on the Indian Seas* and *History of the French in India* deal mainly with their political and military activities. Alfred Martineau made a noteworthy contribution to historical study by unearthing a store of unexplored material. He made an analytical study of the motives that prompted Dupleix to conceive the idea of a colonial empire. It is indeed a work of permanent value. All these works, however, either concentrate on themes prior to 1763 or deal only with political aspects of the French activities in India.

Of the writings on the post-1763 period, Henry Weber's *La Compagnie Française des Indes (1604-1875)* and J. Conan's *La Dernière Compagnie Française des Indes, 1785-1875* are valuable and standard reference works. However, they treat the French companies as nearly exclusively European in their commercial transactions and are of a general nature, covering a very long period.

Among the not so old writings, the most important work is of S.P. Sen. His book *The French in India, 1763-1816* is considered a pioneering exercise in this field. It is an exhaustive work that deals with the organization of the French Company in detail. It concentrates primarily on the political, diplomatic and military projects and on the history of the different French settlements. In all these works, including that of S.P. Sen, the commercial activities and the relationship of the French traders with the English or with Indian merchants and weavers receive scant, or no attention at all. Nor do they discuss in depth the reasons for the abolition of the French Company in 1769 and the nature of trading activities in the period of free trade till 1785 when another company was formed. Brian E. Kennedy's thesis 'Anglo-French Rivalry in India and the Eastern Seas 1763-1793' takes up the theme of Anglo-French global rivalry. He studies it purely from the point of view of political and military factors. The commercial activities do not find any mention. Indrani Ray tried to unravel the history of French mercantile activities in India but owing to her untimely demise the work undertaken by her could not be completed. Her death is a great loss to this area of study.

Holden Furber's *John Company at Work* and *Rival Empires of Trade in the Orient* and Louis Dermigny's writings, particularly *Cargaisons*

Indienes in two volumes, discuss the European companies and their trading activities, including the 'country' trade. But the French Company forms only a small portion of the study and that too, mainly after 1785. Besides, this work covers a vast region embracing the entire Indian coast with an overall emphasis on Bengal, whereas the present book focuses on the main trading activities in the Coromandel region. Louis Dermigny's two volumes, with an extraordinary presentation of statistical details of the *armateurs* and their cargo, is a valuable reference work on the last French Company's trade. However, the period of free trade between the abolition of one company and the establishment of another, i.e. 1769 to 1785 is beyond the scope of this study. Moreover, in this well-researched work, the focus is chiefly on the French side, not on the Coromandel trade. Herbert Lüthy has examined the role of Protestant bankers in *La Banque Protestante en France* in two volumes. This work gives an insight into the Anglo-French financial cooperation in Europe for the Indian trade. But again the Indian trade and the European interaction with the Indians do not figure in these volumes as they concentrate on the commercial history of France, and not of India.

K.N. Chaudhuri's meticulous and scholarly work on the trading activities of the English Company in *The Trading World of Asia and the English East India Company 1660-1740,* is extremely rich in statistics, with several theoretical models and the more recent but general work covering several centuries—*Trade and Civilization in the Indian Ocean*—furnishes useful background information for the present research. He works on a larger canvas and concentrates on the years preceding those of my interest. However, the former work is of extraordinary value for the scholars of the English Company's trade. Similarly, S. Arasaratnam's assiduous works in the form of articles and his books *Merchants, Companies and Commerce on the Coromandel Coast 1650-1740* and his more recent works *Maritime India in the Seventeenth Century* and *Maritime Commerce and English Power in South East India 1750-1800* provide useful information on the Coromandel trade during the eighteenth century. Though a few of his generalizations have been questioned by historians like Joseph J. Brennig, the strength of these books lies in their discussion of Indian merchants and weavers in relation to the changing sphere of trade towards the eastern Archipelago. Whereas Arasaratnam's work is based on the English and the Dutch sources, the present work mainly draws on the French and the English sources and deals with the late eighteenth century.

Among more recent works, Pierre Haudrere's *La Compagnie Française des Indes au XVIII Siècle (1719-1795)*, in four volumes is an exhaustive study of the French Company. It contains voluminous data on trade, military, administrative and political activities. However, this important work covers vast regions of the globe and the stress is on the French Company rather than India. The Indian trade constitutes only a segment while the Indian social groups are relegated to the background. This well researched work is based on massive documentation. Unfortunately these volumes are available only to the French readers. Among the contemporary scholars on pre-colonial economy and early modern India, the works of Om Prakash, Sanjay Subrahmanyam and C.A. Bayly are of immense value because their writings have led to reappraisal of the earlier views. Om Prakash's work on the Dutch trade is a deposition of enormous data, particularly on metal imports. Subrahmanyam's own writings and his edited works have brought out many revisions to the existing literature on the south Indian economy and society. Bayly is one of the earliest scholars to provide fresh interpretation on eighteenth century India. In his major work *Indian Society and the Making of the British Empire,* he studies the process of social formation under a colonial state. Bayly has concentrated on the Gangetic plain and covers a period of almost a century.

These scholarly works are useful in their own right but they do not provide a clear picture of the French activities in India, particularly in the Coromandel region. A brief and selective survey of the existing secondary works shows that Anglo-French commercial relations of the post-1763 period in India has not been studied at length. From those of the above-mentioned writings the present book is based on entirely different sources and the region of study is also not the same. This work is intended to fill some of the gaps in this field by throwing light on the major shifts in the French commercial policy towards India; the English response to such changes; its impact on the nature of trade in Coromandel; and the Anglo-French dealings with the local merchants and weavers.

One reason which discourages a study of French trade relations in India is the absence of sufficient source material in India. Most of the French records of this period have been transferred from the

Pondicherry Archives to that of Outre-mer in France. Of the remaining records, a number of them are still to be acquired or are in the process of reparation. Some of the records pertain to the shipping and trading activities of the French *armateurs*. The Archives at Pondicherry is better equipped with documents of the nineteenth and twentieth centuries, but these are of no use to my subject. Some valuable published contemporary material was available at Bibliothèque Romain Rolland at Pondicherry. The *District Records* located in the Archives of Tamil Nadu and Andhra Pradesh proved to be very useful for my purpose. They shed some light on the Anglo-French dealings with the Indian merchants for *chay* goods as well as their policy towards the weaver class. I have also consulted the *Public Consultation* volumes, the *Commercial Despatches* and the *Home Despatches*. These proved useful in several ways. A few of these documents are in a brittle state. A visit to the Rare Books Section of the National Library, Calcutta, was disappointing in terms of sources pertaining to my field of study.

I have examined and made use of a variety of material in the National Archives, New Delhi. The microfilms of the *Nouvelle Acquisition Series* of Bibliothèque Nationale, Paris, contain some information on the subject, particularly in the mémoirs of that period. However, most of the microfilms of this series deal with subjects such as military preparations, diplomatic negotiations with the English or with local rulers, controversies over the interpretation of different treaties, restoration of different settlements, etc. Reference to trade and commerce is scanty and sketchy. The *Home Miscellaneous Series* of India Office Library (microfilms) contains a wealth of information on the English trade. Particularly relevant to my purpose are MSS 399 to 401. Some identical information is to be found in the microfilms from John Rylands Library, Manchester, which also has the Melville and Pitt Papers. Going through the microfilms was a painful but rewarding exercise. Besides these, I have examined several other sources such as the Secret Department Records, *Fort William-India House Correspondence*, the abstracts of the proceedings of *Conseil Supérieur* of Pondicherry (printed) and Moracin's correspondence with the administrators at Paris, published and edited by Edmond Gaudart in French.

During a brief stay in England I consulted some important sets of documents. Of these, the *French in India Séries* in 17 volumes and the *Madras Despatches* in India Office Records provided very useful information. Besides, some of the *Additional Manuscripts* that included the Auckland and Liverpool Papers were also examined at the British Museum, London. Despite my strong desire, I was not able to go through the shipping records for lack of time.

The French Archives are rich in source material on India. At Archives Nationales, Paris, two series were of immense value—8 AQ Série (unfortunately some of the important ledgers could not be traced) and Série C^2 of *Fonds des Colonies*—Inde et Compagnie des Indes. Série F^{12} and AD VIII Série also contain documents pertaining to the Indian trade. Of all these, Série 8 AQ was most important as it contains the shipping records of the French Company after 1785.

The sources consulted at Bibliothèque Nationale, Paris, include a number of contemporary writings such as those of Lacrettele, Pierre Louis and Blonde, Abbé Morellet, Necker, Stanislas Fôache, Legoux, etc. The work of Legoux de Flaix is of special significance as it lucidly describes the commercial products of India and their trade in the period preceding the French Revolution. These different sources provide scattered but handy information on Indian textile products, on Indo-French trade and on the state of the French companies. The *Mémoires et Documents* on Asia, preserved at Les Archives des Affaires Étrangères, Paris are particularly useful for the study of formation of the Nouvelle Compagnie des Indes in 1785. The Archives Nationales, Section Outre-Mer at Aix-en-Provence stores diverse correspondence from the different French *loges* and *comptoirs.* Apart from these, I have also obtained copies of documents from Cleveland Library, Ohio, in USA, relating to British India during the late eighteenth century.

However, the information furnished by most of these documents mainly in the form of memoirs, is scattered, fragmentary and uncertain. Hence, it is difficult to construct a very clear picture of trade on the Coromandel Coast. The French sources are silent on the volume of trade with Coromandel, owing to the absence of detailed shipping records prior to 1785. Besides, the French did not have, unlike the English, three virtually independent trading zones in the form of the three Presidencies. In such cases, the English sources have been used to overcome this limitation. This work is entirely based on the records in the English and the French languages. The translation of the French documents has been done by me.

Fernand Braudel through his brilliant and painstaking research has ably demonstrated the relationship between the sea and the people around it. On the basis of this analysis, one can study the rise of European settlements along the Coromandel sea-trade route. The first chapter studies the geopolitics of this region along with the socio-economic condition in the mid-eighteenth century. A brief survey of the prevalent monetary system and banking institutions is included in this chapter.

The second chapter examines the rise of the rival companies, their respective organizations, and changes in the structure of trade and the circumstances leading to the abolition of Compagnie des Indes in 1769. An attempt is made to study the reasons for the shift in the French policy from mercantilism to free trade and the English reaction to such changes in India.

An important dimension of the French free trade period (1769-84) was the Anglo-French cooperation for trade with India among the Europeans in their private capacities and their participation in the 'country' trade in the Indian Ocean. The third chapter discusses all these aspects along with a review of the commodity items of trade.

The fourth chapter is a continuation of the third on the Franco-English interaction. The most notable feature of this 'interaction' was the formation of the Nouvelle Compagnie des Indes in 1785. This was the last serious attempt to re-establish the French commerce in India. The rise of pressure groups in Europe affected the English trade pattern and brought about a significant shift in the Company's approach.

Textiles constituted the bulk of Coromandel exports and the place of weavers and merchants in the Anglo-French commercial transactions constitutes an important aspect of this study. Chapter 5 examines this subject. The last chapter of this book attempts to evaluate the place of textiles in Coromandel's foreign trade. There is a short description of the variety of textiles produced in Coromandel and the official policy of the two foreign governments on cotton piece goods of India, followed by the trade performance.

It is hoped that the present book will bring out some of the neglected aspects of French history in India and would be followed by many new works through fresh research.

Abbreviations

AN	Archives Nationales, Paris
APA	Andhra Pradesh State Archives
Arch. Aff. Étr.	Archives des Affaires Étrangers, Paris
BN	Bibliothéque Nationale, Paris
Br. Mus.	British Museum, London
COD	Court of Directors
CPL	Cleveland Public Library, Ohio, U.S.A.
ICHR	Indian Council of Historical Research
ICSSR	Indian Council of Social Science Research
IOR	India Office Records and Library, London
Mem. et. Doc	Mémoire et Documents
NAI	National Archives of India
TSA	Tamil Nadu State Archives

Chapter 1

Ports, Society and Economy

INDIA HAS always held an important position in the trading world. She maintained regular trade relations with Central Asia and Europe for many centuries, even before the Christian era. This relationship broke down with the decline of the Roman Empire, but was later revived following the rise of the Venetians. They encouraged trade with India through the Red Sea and virtually established their monopoly. In the process, they reaped huge profits. Venice re-emerged as the emporium of Asian manufactures. But soon this monopoly was broken by the Portuguese, who were greatly supported by their monarch in their spirit of enterprise and adventure. The subsequent period witnessed the fluctuating fortunes of the European maritime powers—Portuguese, Dutch, English and French, each establishing its dominance in turn in a particular region, in the coastal trade. They founded extensive settlements along the coastline, especially on the Coromandel. However, in the second half of the eighteenth century, the phase of shifting fortunes of the competing powers ended. The English succeeded in establishing their supremacy in India over their arch European rival—the French.

GEOPOLITICS OF THE REGION

The eastern coast of India, despite being interspersed by a number of streams and broken hills, maintains a geographical continuity, and has come to be known as 'Coromandel'. The term appears to have been a corrupt form of 'Choramandelum' or 'Sheramandelum'.[1] The Coromandel Coast portrays certain specific features which were not to be seen in the other regions of India. The natural geography of this long coastline had rendered anchoring of big ships dangerous, especially in certain months of the year. By the middle of the eighteenth century, a large number of European factories and *comptoirs* arose on this coast, principally those of the English and the French, in close proximity to each other. Several small ports existed along the coastline, where the presence of various European powers made the seaborne trade different from other regions of Asia. This peculiarity saved the French from utter rout in their trading activities despite political debacles. In Bengal, the all-pervasive English expansion had encircled the French settlement of Chandernagar and rendered it an almost non-functional trading centre dependent on the English goodwill. But the situation was different in southern India. The well-populated ports on the Coromandel and numerous pockets of manufacture adjacent to these ports, the presence of commercialized zones; and the existence of a number of communities occupied in trading and manufacturing activities, brought an element of competitiveness in the relationship of European powers. This dispersed and diffused character of trade from various ports, situated close to each other, influenced the Anglo-French relationship during the eighteenth century.

The rivers of the Coromandel had tremendous bearing on the life and economy of the region. Some of the territories were important centres of rice production, which made Bartolomeo describe the coast as giving the appearance of a 'green theatre'.[2] Furthermore, as Burton Stein argues, each of these major streams, besides providing focuses of significant population clusters, served to connect the uplands with other more densely settled tracts, constituting one of the tenuous links between the two coastal plains of the peninsula.[3] Moreover, the water of these perennial rivers favoured the weaving and dyeing industry of the region, which was known all over the world, and promoted some type of socio-economic continuity.[4] The rise of a large number of small seaports facilitated the expansion of sea-trade and enabled India to enter the vast commercial network stretching from South-East Asia and China on the one side to the Arab and Persian states of the West on the other. Besides proving important as trading pockets, these small ports afforded economic and political diversities enabling the European powers to be relatively independent of local authority. The presence of a chain of seaports under rival powers also allowed the French to survive and pose a challenge to the English despite the rapid political rise of the English Company.

The strategic and economic importance of certain territories in the Coromandel guided the political and commercial relationships not only between the English and the French but also determined their attitude towards the states in the region.

The districts of Ganjam, Vizagapatnam, Guntur, Chicacol, Rajamundry and Mustafanagar constituted the most fertile coastal strip of the Nizam's dominions: It was a 'transition zone' as Spate had put it, geographically as well as politically.[5] A region abounding in rice, cotton, plantations, dye-woods and thick forest, it furnished the most beautiful cotton goods—white and painted varieties. Golconda offered a very profitable branch of commerce, especially in respect of diamonds, but by the third quarter of the eighteenth century the mines were nearly abandoned because of their heavy expenses.[6] There was a fair degree of urbanization at its principal trading and political centres. The constant transfer of these districts between the French and the English companies reveals that both the powers were equally aware of its economic and geographical importance. The necessity of procuring a continuous stretch of territory as a passage from Bengal to Madras, was impressed upon the home government of the English Company.[7] It was only feasible by acquiring the Northern Circars and Orissa. Moreover, the immense trade potential must have been weighing in the minds of the Company's officials. Clive was urged upon to obtain a grant for Northern Circars from the Mughal Emperor. This was duly obtained through a *firman* in 1765, keeping the Nizam in the dark. A treaty was forced on the Nizam on 12 November 1766 by which the *circars* of Rajamundry, Ellore, Mustafanagar, Murtizanagar and Chicacol were handed over to the English as free gifts, in return for an annual rent of Rs. 9 lakh. The English objective of the treaty was spelled out in a letter to the Court of Directors, 'The exclusion of the French from the *Circars* had been our principal view in obtaining them. . . .'[8]

After 1766, the Anglo-French diplomacy in the Deccan *suba* centred on the question of Guntur province. This region, which the French sources described as 'la Province de Condavir' formed a continuous link with the other four *circars*.[9] Its retention by Basalat Jung broke the continuity of the line of communication from Madras to Ganjam. Hence, the English Company was keen to acquire it. Its efforts in 1772 failed to yield results but it pursued its design unhesitatingly. The French showed equally keen interest in this region. The English were convinced that the French threat had not ended despite the English political triumph in 1763. This region provided the main ground of employment for French troops. A letter of Conway suggests that the French were taking a lot of interest in obtaining this *circar*.[10] However, the English succeeded in the end in subjugating the *circar*.

The State of Tanjore was considered the 'Garden of Carnatic'[11] before

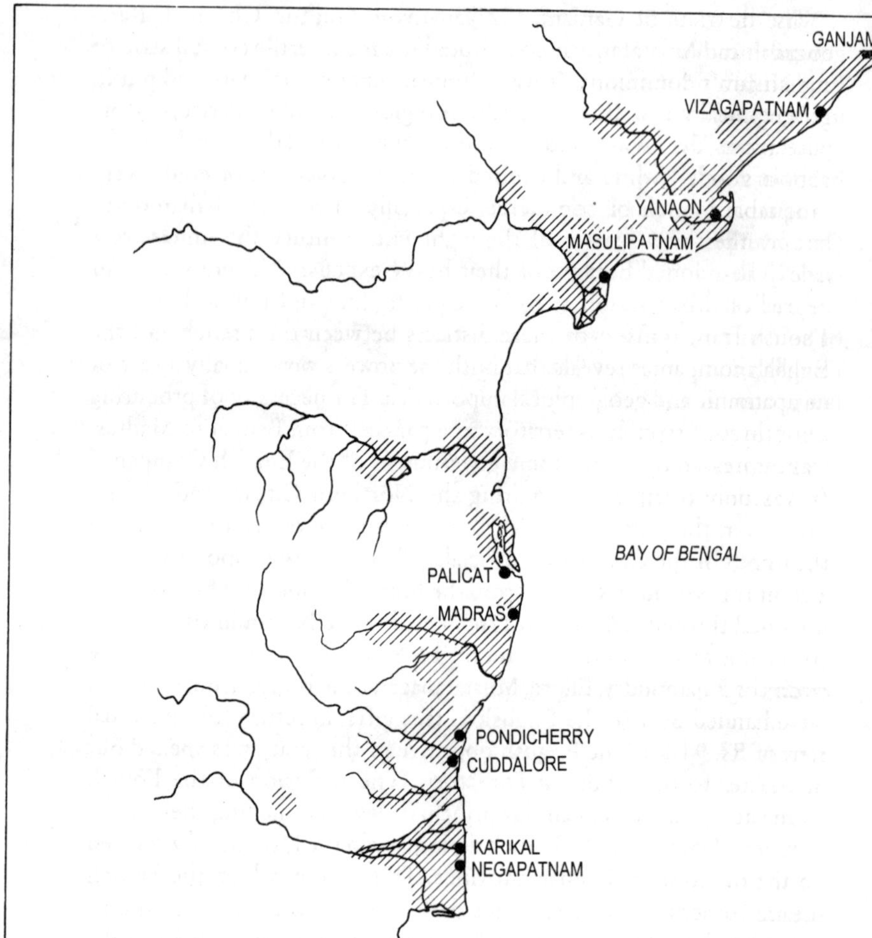

MAP 1.1: COROMANDEL PORTS

it was drawn into the Anglo-French intrigues. Its favourable geographical location and economic strength made it a victim of the English adventurist drives. Its external trade played an important role in the economic life of the people. It was situated on the direct maritime route from Europe to the East Indies, and included a number of harbours or small ports such as Nagapatnam, Karikal, Nagore, Tranquebar and Devikottai. Its wealth attracted the attention of the European powers who began to control the port towns and later their trade. The English Company's expeditions to Tanjore mark one of the earliest European armed interventions in the internal conflicts of south India. The gain of Tanjore, a substantial territory, drew the English increasingly into local politics. They succeeded in obtaining Nagapatnam in 1781 after the Dutch abandoned it, following their political reversal.

The Anglo-French interest in Tanjore was also because of its cotton and textile production. This region abounded in the production of rice and cotton, and also grew some indigo. Its villages were inhabited by a large number of weavers. In the periods of political disturbances or economic troubles, there used to be large-scale migrations of these weavers. The English and the Raja's officials accused the French of causing these migrations through their secret efforts and by their laxity, which the French always denied.[12] In fact, the territorial concessions and alliances embroiled Tanjore in wars which only served European interest. The state was ravaged not only by the armies of the French and the English but also by those of Mysore, Marathas and the Nawab of Carnatic. This ruined its agriculture and handicrafts and destroyed its trade.

The production of cotton and the maritime importance of Madura determined its political relationship with the English. The people of Madura carried on considerable trade with maritime cities on the Coromandel Coast and also transported their cotton stuff to the coast of Malabar. This region grew little rice but produced cotton in abundance.[13] Among the trading cities at the foot of the Ghats was Arampalli, where some years prior to Bartolomeo's visit, about 2,000 looms were employed for weaving cotton stuff.[14] It used to be a mart or a general 'magasin' where all the merchandise was brought. Dindigul was another cotton weaving centre. It rose in importance during the nineteenth century by importing English yarn and silver threads from the French. Madura was not a thickly populated region. It depended probably on the regular demand from its neighbouring markets. The weaving, dyeing and painting industry was located in Pallams around Tinnevelly and Madura.[15] The coming of the English intensified the competition. Their merchants started buying large quantities of coarse cloth and some finer varieties as well. It was their interest in textiles which must have been behind the English moves to eliminate the *poligars*.[16] These rulers were unable to resist the external pressures and succumbed to the English.

Similarly, Carnatic held a position of strategic importance from the viewpoint of the English and French commercial interest. It was a region of great wealth and flourishing trade. As such, it remained a theatre of European and regional warfare. These wars, coupled with lack of foresight on the part of its nawab, resulted in the complete ruination of the state. The constant wars devastated and de-populated the countryside and resulted in large-scale migration of the productive elements, which adversely affected its manufactures and revenues. It enabled the English to establish a firm control over the textile producing villages through political means. The French found the sudden rise of the English power detrimental to their commercial and political interest. The obstacles placed by the English made it difficult for the French to procure their supplies for Europe from the interior regions. The mutual dependence, at the same time, of Nawab Muhammad Ali Khan and the English continued to grow. The Nawab began to depend on the English for his financial loans and the conquest of smaller principalities. In return, the English sought commercial and territorial advantages from him. Describing this relationship between the two, Sulivan wrote, 'Mutual obligation of this nature speedily cemented a connection of necessity into one of friendship. The Nawab has ever acknowledged himself indebted to the English for the unmolested government of his country and they as readily have acknowledged the great benefits, which they have derived from him.'[17]

Commenting on the policy of the European powers towards the Indian states in the late eighteenth century, Bartolomeo wrote, 'such is the manner in which the kingdoms and provinces are acquired there as merchants, imperceptibly endeavour to extend their power, and no longer satisfied with the advantages of trade, . . . until they get possessions of the land which is the object of their ambition.'[18]

The rise of seaports and trade outlets in close proximity to each other along the Coromandel began to govern not only the Anglo-French commercial relationship but also influenced the fortunes of these ports. This is clear from the rapid rise of Madras and Pondicherry.

The rise of these ports and the importance of each port in the eighteenth century was determined not only by geographical reasons but more by political and economic factors.

The rise of Ganjam on the Rukhikulya river was primarily because of its ability to supply large quantities of rice to the southern territories of the Coromandel. Its importance increased soon after the Chicacol *circar* fell into European hands—first under the French Company and then under the English. Ganjam also served as a feeder port for the textile centres, linking them with Madras. It held an important place in the Anglo-French struggle in which the local courts and rulers changed sides along with the success or failure of European powers. After Moracin's failure to make the principal Raja Narayan Dev of Mohiri to enter into an agreement with the French, he abandoned the French settlement at Ganjam in 1759 never to receive it back. The presence of two ports under rival powers in close proximity to each other—Ingeram under the English Company and Yanaon under the French—did not allow them to gain importance despite their several other advantages. In 1784, Ingeram had 10,170 looms under its jurisdiction as ascertained by the Committee of Circuit.[20] The port was mainly used for the export of textiles to Madras for re-shipment. In the same way, Yanaon was primarily used by the French as a feeder port for Pondicherry trade. It consisted of about 8,000 inhabitants, a good proportion of whom were involved in the commerce of cloth.[21] The cotton manufacturers were in a considerable number in that region and could offer goods of the value of 4,00,000 to 5,00,000 *livres*. It was also a good market for disposing of European goods.[22] The trade could have been very lucrative but the presence of the English around it checked its development. Masulipatam, one of the oldest ports of India, had lost its importance to the English and the French ports of the southern region by the middle of the eighteenth century. This port had gained importance by its political links with the kingdom of Golconda and by its proximity to the commercialized town of Hyderabad. As late as 1740, the French officials described the city as 'un gros bourg' or a big market with a population of nearly 40,000.[23] The fluctuating political fortunes in this region affected its trade, and the rapid rise of Madras made the port of Masulipatam lose its preponderance over other ports. The English domination of this region adversely affected the French trade. Although they clung to their limited trade rights and continued to procure cotton and *chay* goods worth 1,50,000 *livres* annually, they could not contest the English who made them pay duties on all their imports and exports. Nevertheless, the region surrounding Masulipatam was still significant as a centre of cotton manufacture, and as late as 1759 this town was described by Orme as 'very extensive'.[24]

Thus, the rapid growth of Fort St. George, which came to be known as Madras, was due to the political rise of the English in this region although it did not have a favourable geographical location. It began to serve as an important centre of international and coastal shipping network. Their influence over Nawab of Carnatic gave the English unmeasured power to procure manufactured cloth and other trade items from the surrounding territories. On the other hand, despite the limitation of not having sufficient political influence, the principal French port of Pondicherry maintained its place in the maritime map of India. The port was favourably placed for the reception of provisions and merchandise from Carnatic, Tanjore and the kingdom of Mysore. Pondicherry developed into a port-city but its trade was closely linked to its political fortune, which continued to ebb and flow. The variable population figures—fluctuating from 60,000 to 28,000—confirm this.[25]

Thus, it was the Anglo-French contest in the Coromandel which set in motion the establishment of the English hegemony. The English hegemony and the economic domination either followed or influenced the political moves as determining agents.

SOCIETY AND ECONOMY

It is difficult to describe the state of the Indian economy in the eighteenth century. Here one may tend to agree with Ashin Das Gupta that there was no India in a political sense in the eighteenth century.[26] Economically and socially the position was even more complex. Some regions went into decline such as Surat, Calicut, Masulipatam, Nagapatnam, Madura, etc., others staggered on, while a few, particularly the seaports controlled by the Europeans and their environs made progress. There was an increasing disparity between the commercially developed regions and the economically underdeveloped zones. There were some commercialized regions where one could observe clusters of ports and trading settlements getting enlarged. The Coromandel was one such region , which witnessed an advanced level of commercial activities. The pull of the market forces was felt more in the coastal belt than in the interior. The trans-oceanic trade and the mechanisms to maintain it touched the lives and the economic activities of the people on this coastal belt. Political breakdown and changes in the trading structure affected certain classes *ad eundem*. In this process of change, the European companies were fast replacing political authority of the local rulers by well-designed moves while European private merchants began to displace the indigenous merchants. Only a few families of local merchants survived by migrating to the new coastal settlements and by accepting a subordinate role as company-merchants in the new trading structure.

During the seventeenth and eighteenth centuries, momentous changes had a profound impact on the commercial sector, on the volume of trade and the investment pattern, on the mechanics of supply and on the social fabric by way of utilization or replacement of local agency. One of the special features of the Coromandel trade was its diffused character. It was not concentrated only at a few major ports but flowed out into different directions from a number of smaller outlets controlled by various European powers. The presence of so many rival ports independent of each other provided a good opportunity to local artisans, workers and merchants to migrate. It made feasible the professional and regional migrations from interior regions to the new port-towns. This demographic shift towards the coastal regions and the increasing control over the producing villages by foreign capital affected social relationships. It also influenced the material basis of those classes, that participated in these activities.

There were certain noteworthy features of the socio-economic life of the Coromandel. Agriculture continued to hold a dominant place in the economic life of the people. The Anglo-French wars devastated agriculture, and frequent making or unmaking of rulers caused political uncertainty. The maximization of revenue, the principle common to both the powers resulted in the neglect of agriculture and caused scarcity of grain. This was accompanied by increasing indebtedness of the producing classes.

Agriculture continued to depend on seasonal rain and weather conditions. We do have sufficient evidence of food-shortages in the port-towns or in the weaving villages caused by wars, famines, or weather conditions.[27]At the same time the development of artificial irrigation was another striking characteristic of that period. Rice cultivation required sufficient water storage and flooding of the field. A number of artificial or natural ponds (*étangs*)[28] existed on the Coromandel and Orissa coasts. Often there were huge reservoirs (*grandes citernes*) constructed to store water, like the one at Pipli, to the north of Cuttack.[29] Throughout the region, particularly in the interior, there were wells in the fields or on the roadside, with wheels to pull out water in leather buckets tied up with ropes. Two methods of irrigation were practised in the Deccan—by inundation of rice fields and by sprinkling or soaking (*arrosage quotidien*).[30] Anquetil refers to the second technique employed in the region of Ginji, to the north-west of Pondicherry. Tank irrigation appears to have been the most common form besides the drain or canal methods near the rivers.

Millet was cultivated around Madura and corn or maize and barley on the coast and in the Deccan. Anquetil also observed palm trees, cocoa cultivation and limited cultivation of cotton in Madura and Marava. The two types of cotton plants were called *paroute* (which was grown in the plains and furnished very fine quality of cotton) and *ilava* (grown on the mountains or hills) but cotton was not cultivated on a large scale.[31]

The cotton textile industry constituted an important segment of the Coromandel economy. Foreign demand must have influenced its functioning. Till the mid-eighteenth century the industry responded well to retain its foreign market by meeting the European demand. The European travellers have often emphasized the highly developed skill and specialization of the Indian spinners, weavers and dyers, but there were other factors as well which contributed to the growth of the textile sector. As K.N. Chaudhuri and Vijaya Ramaswamy suggest, textile production was not a simple affair. It definitely required some specialized knowledge in the preparation and treatment of raw material before the weaving stage commenced.[32] The preparation of thread was a specialized process. The Coromandel textile industry held its ground due to the specialized nature of its products and cost factor advantage. The textile goods had responded successfully to the European demands in normal times. However, the political uncertainties caused by the wars fought by the British and the French against each other as well as with Indian rulers, local chaos and the artificial checks on exports and finally the coming of the Industrial Revolution further affected the fortunes of the textiles centres of Coromandel.

TRADING LINKAGES OF INTERNAL AND EXTERNAL MARKETS

Information on internal trade is quite scanty, particularly in those fields which did not fall within the orbit of European commerce. Much useful information is available on coastal trade in such items as salt, rice, betel, tobacco, etc., because these were consumed in the European port-towns and constituted an important source of revenue. But information on commodities of local consumption is extremely scanty.

Internal trade was usually carried on by a few merchant castes such as Balijas, Banjaras and Coorchivas. The traditional internal market structure was centred at *pettai* and had developed as a permanent market near the rural production centre.[33] *Vara Sante* or the weekly markets existed in different towns on specific days of the week. These markets played an important role in the exchange of goods and at the same time provided revenue to the local rulers. Apart from these fairs, festivals also constituted an important commercial event and facilitated market transactions. These were called *Tirunal Sante*.[34] There appears to have been extensive trade from Arcot to Mysore and in the Nizam's territories. The Banjaras were the wanderers who covered an extensive region and played an important role, especially during the periods of war and scarcity. Such long travels involved a lot of risk. One important feature of the market sector of northern Coromandel's cotton districts was its dependence on the supplies of raw cotton brought by the Banjaras. Bullocks moving in caravans usually of about 10,000 but at times as many as 40,000, provided the major movements of commodities.[35] J.B. Tavernier was amazed to see 10,000 to 12,000 bullock carts moving together to transport rice, corn and salt in these places and exchanging them with various commodities.[36] Even Duperron confirms that the use of oxen was the most common mode of transporting goods. The Banjaras, who were often referred to as lambadies in the south, came all the way from Nagpur in the Berar province[37] in central India, exchanging goods like salt, cotton, betel-nut, pessaloo curry stuff and other commodities of daily consumption, frequently selling and purchasing goods in the course of their long journey of several hundred miles. The Coorchivas traded in salt from the coastal towns to the interior.[38] Cotton was manufactured in almost all regions of the eastern coast and in the interior along some major rivers. Buchanan mentions the revival of internal trade in the early nineteenth century, which must have been dislocated because of local wars and political disturbances. He mentions Silgutta merchants going to Codeal, Nagore, lower Carnatic and to the intermediate towns, taking with them pepper, betel, tobacco, and silk textiles from Bangalore and bringing back raw silk, spices, benjamin, threads, blankets, etc.[39] They also went to Rajawally, a town in the Nizam's dominion and brought in return silk and cotton cloths. The merchants from the Krishna river basin traded in cotton, cotton wool, cotton threads, dark blue cloth, terra japosea, dates, almonds and mailtuta, which was a substance used as a dentifrice. The merchants of Balahari returned with 'three-fourths of sale proceeds in cash and the remainder in castor oil, poplidya and jagory[jaggery]'.[40] There is ample evidence of market exchanges with distant places like Calcutta and Benaras, through the Carnatic and the Nizam's dominions. Grain, salt, spices, dyes, threads, etc., were in constant demand and seem to have been the commodities of routine trade. The use of ready money was a notable feature of internal trade.[41]

There seem to have been several obstacles that worked against the smooth flow of trade. The imposition of customs at every intermediate place and the political enervation caused by wars and rivalry made transportation of goods insecure and expensive. The absence of a comparative rate of exchange and the shortage of silver must have acted as deterrents to internal trade. Banking institutions did exist, but they were not conducive to capital mobilization through small savings nor were they so constituted as to encourage or bring about a radical change in trading operations.

During the eighteenth century, there was a visible shift of trade towards the European ports, situated in northern and central Coromandel. The rapid growth of Madras and Pondicherry reflected this trend. Along with this there was a gradual but definite attempt towards replacing Indian agencies for procuring supplies for the Europeans.

As regards the social composition of the Indians, who were associated with external commerce, weavers, dyers and washermen constituted an important segment of south Indian society. They were much in demand owing to the rise of European trade. There were waves of immigrants of Telugu and Kanarese people from the northern regions whenever any political disturbance or economic dislocation took place. These included Reddiars, Cavarai, Naidus, Balijas, Uppilliars or salt manufacturers and Senians or the Telugu weavers.[42] The artisans constituted an important segment of society and in certain ways supported Coromandel economy. Specialization in crafts existed in many geographical units of Coromandel, based on caste lines. An agglomeration of weaving villages arose which were grouped into territorial units called *paykat* or *payakatts.* Such clusters of villages were more common in the Carnatic and Andhra region.[43] The size of each unit could vary a great deal, 'from Chembaukam with 70 looms to Arnee with 4,000 looms'.[44] A *paykat* had a central clearing house for the sale of woven cloth in those units where sorting and clearing of accounts with merchants or their agents took place. The Northern Division Administrative Report clearly admitted that the weavers in Tripassore in Chingleput district were 'entirely under the control of the Export Warehousekeeper'.[45] In the weaving villages of the north Coromandel, the *copdar* (*kopudarudu*) functioned as a broker mediating between the merchants and the weavers. In certain places *careedar* was an important element in the weaving community; he was more affluent than other weavers and often provided subsistence to unemployed weavers by employing them as 'outdoor' weavers.[46]

It is not easy to estimate the earning of the weavers as it was subject to many factors and variations. Most of the time the family of a weaver joined him to produce two pieces of long cloth a month. According to Dodwell, the Reports of 1790 show that a weaver received Rs. 2 per piece at Vizagapatnam, i.e. about Rs. 4 per month.[47] At Ingeram the time taken for manufacturing a piece was about 18 days for which the weaver received 28 *fanams*. At Cuddalore the payment was the same for 16 days of labour. Thus, a weaver's earning varied from 1 to 1½ *pagodas* or Rs. 3½ to 5¼ a month which was considerably lower than of a sepoy's pay of Rs. 7 per month. Even a peon got half of that amount. It appears that weaving was losing its respectability as a profession. Moreover, weavers were exposed to a variety of imposts like loom tax, forcing of grain on them at a fixed price above market price and road tax on cotton which was needed to prepare thread. Similarly, the dyers also faced numerous problems such as the increasing price of indigo in the market, its non availability in sufficient quantity and the price of the grain, which had profound impact on their earnings. In 1775 the price of indigo had gone up to 24 to 25 *pagodas* per candy from 18 *pagodas* the previous year and 34 to 35 *pagodas* for the variety which was available at 26 to 27 *pagodas* the previous year.[48] This caused enormous difficulty to the dyers who were forced to present a petition to the English officials. They were compelled to borrow a considerable sum of money for indigo which was of poor quality and hence they needed to dye the cloth more than 9 times instead of the usual 6 times at Cuddalore.[49]

The second most important class of Indians associated with external commerce was that of merchants. These included the *Gentues* (as described by the Europeans) and the migrant Muslims.[50] The families of Mudaliars, Chettis and Pillais were some of the most important merchants who were associated with the French. K.S. Mathew describes the relationship between the French and the Indian merchants as one of partnership.[51] But towards the close of the eighteenth century, several elements of early partnership were missing and the domination of the Europeans was becoming quite evident.

In the eighteenth century we notice a rapid shift in the trade zone, described as a 'revolution' by Holden Furber.[52] There was a swift turn from the inter-Asian trade to Indo-European trade. But the revolutionary aspect of the shift was the rapid expansion of trade with China and the linking of India with the Chinese and the European commerce in a triangular trade.

So long as the trade between the Coromandel and South-East Asian countries remained active, the Indian mercantile community participated in it equally with the European private traders, initially independently and later as collaborators. These included members of various castes such as Chettis, Komattis, Balija and Beri-Chettis, and numerous others like Pillais, Mudaliars, Reddis and Naidus.[53] However, from the middle of the eighteenth century, their partnership began to break up. A number of sources suggest that an increasing portion of the external trade was coming into the hands of the Europeans. Writing in the second half of the century, Goddard wrote that the Hindus participated only in the internal commerce of the land whereas the Muslims participated in the maritime activities connected with the coastal trade. Their expeditions were sent to 'the Indian coast, Vietnam, Maldives, Lakshadweep, the African coast, Abyssinia and the whole of Arab and Persian Gulf region'.[54] Another French source of the period explicitly mentions that the external commerce of the Coromandel was in the hands of the Europeans except some Chulias at Naour (Nagore), Porto Novo and on the coast of Orissa.[55] According to Ashin Das Gupta, Chulias, the Tamil Muslim traders, were the main shippers of the south Coromandel port-cities who traded to Achem, Johar and ports of Burma.[56] There were probably four subdivisions of the Chulias—Labbai, Marakkayar, Rawther and Kayalar—though their exact identification is subject to different interpretations.[57] The Marakkayars of Porto Novo had close relations with the French at Pondicherry. The French 'country' ships often carried the freight goods of the Marakkayars. The French also issued them passes at Pondicherry on certain conditions.

Thus, the Indian merchants actually sailing in their own ships was a phenomenon of the pre-European period. In the second half of the eighteenth century most of the oceanic trade had moved into the hands of the Europeans. The Indians, usually Muslims, operated their small vessels to transport cargo and men from the big European ships to the ports to participate in the coastal trade in paddy and salt. On most of the Coromandel Coast, ship communication with land could not be done except by small country crafts called *Chelingue* or *Shilingas*. These were built with high decks to prevent the waves from entering them.[58] The bigger boats could carry up to twenty-five persons and the smallest only five to seven.[59] These were called *tonni* by the Malabos and by the Europeans. These were constructed with light and very flexible wooden planks and their borders or edges, instead of being nailed, were sewn with a strong line, tied to one another and held by a straw, which served to fill up gaps. This construction was less solid than that of the European boats but was better suited to resist the strong violent shocks of sea waves. The violence of the waves, when the boats were thrown up as high as 15 to 18 feet, was withstood by the sewn cords, which were flexible and strong. The European ships, whose edges were fixed by nails and iron-lines, were unable to withstand such powerful currents and there was the fear of nails coming out.[60] There is also the mention of unwieldy vessels for the coastal trading called *donies* or *dhonies* of various sizes and capacities. These varied from 60 to 100 tons.[61] Cocoa and palmyra formed the principal materials for building such vessels. There is also a mention of small Indian vessels called *Shilinga* by the local inhabitants. These *Shilingas* were built with a deck to prevent waves of the sea from entering them.[62] These were mostly used for salt and rice trade between Bengal and the Coromandel. The earlier ship construction centres of Coringa and Narsipore on the principal branches of Godavari were losing their importance. During this period shipbuilding activities had shifted to other regions such as Bengal, Madras, Bombay and Burma. This must have played an important part in ousting the Indian shippers from the coastal trade.

An important feature of the merchants of the Coromandel was their mobility. With the vast coastline trade and the changing fortunes of the local states sprouting foreign settlements, social stability and permanence was generally lacking among the merchants. Arasaratnam also refers to the phenomenon of the absence of continuity in the great families during two hundred years of commercial operation on the Coromandel.[63] The Indian merchant class was heterogeneous in its social composition. The active Muslim merchants of north Coromandel were replaced by Pathans and in the south Coromandel by Chulias. The Hindu merchant families consisted of Chettis,

Balija Chettis, Komattis and Gujaratis. In south Arcot, Komattis or Nattukottai Chettis supplied thread to the weavers, paid them labour and themselves arranged for the sale and export of finished articles.

Another notable feature of the social life of the south was its division into Valangai (Ballagai) or right hand caste and Idangai or the left hand caste.[64] There were frequent disputes between the two castes creating problems for the administrators. Most of their fights were on the issue of privileges. Though superficially the Europeans seemed to have maintained strict neutrality in these caste disputes, yet because of its financial and commercial dominance, the left hand caste received precedence over the right hand caste. Towards the close of the seventeenth century, men of the right hand caste inhabited Pondicherry. It was François Martin who invited the Chettis (left hand caste men) for trade purposes and granted them some privileges.[65] The grant of an equal status was a victory for the Idangais. The men of the right hand caste objected to the Chettis and other sectarians of the left hand entering the town by the Madras street on horseback or in *palanquins* on the ground of long-standing custom. In 1741, the *Conseil Supérieur* abolished all restrictions on the left hand caste in the French settlements.[66] The *arrêt* of 15 July 1768 again upheld the principle of equality between the two groups.[67] There was a serious caste dispute in 1794 in Pondicherry when the city was taken over by the English. A similar outbreak occurred in Madras in 1809.[68]

NOTE ON MONEY SYSTEMS AND BANKING

The European trade along the Coromandel Coast had profound bearing on the monetary system of the region. A large amount of silver and copper influx, the existence of different political authorities, the surplus of exports over imports and the multiplicity of mints producing currencies of different metal contents with different intrinsic value made the monetary system of Coromandel more complex than any other region of India.

Several European sources mention the peculiarity of the monetary system of this region in particular and the Indian system in general. M. Legoux de Flaix observed that all types of money in Hindustan are considered as goods or merchandise.[69] Another French source expresses the same opinion by stating that the gold and silver specie are regarded as goods—the abundance of one material leads to the fall of the value vis-à-vis of the other.[70] Even the English Resident at Tanjore holds the same view regarding the Porto Novo *pagoda*, which he describes as 'an article of trade' due to its scarcity.[71] However, this situation was not something peculiar to India alone. Even the European countries experienced a similar trend whenever bullion was in short supply.

The multiplicity of mints established along the Coromandel Coast and in the interior region is an indicator of the growing volume of trade and the increasing need of money supply. Till the seventeenth century, mints coining the *pagodas* had more or less a uniform standard in the south. After the decline of the Vijayanagar Empire, the emergence of several rival authorities and the import of bullion first by the Portuguese and subsequently by the other European companies began to affect the uniformity of the south Indian coins. Multiplicity of political authority led to the opening up of new mints, thus causing new varieties of coin. The coins reflected regional variations. The premium on the old currency increased manifold.[72] Under the Mughals, coins were minted at Golconda. In the southern Coromandel region, mints were functioning at Alambaram, Sadraspatnam and Devanampatnam. The Dutch began to mint coins jointly with the ruler of Tanjore at Nagapatnam. The Porto Novo mint continued to gain importance during the first half of the eighteenth century due to the quality of coins minted here. The European rival powers also established mints at their respective settlements producing coins conforming to local usage and maintaining a reasonably high standard of finesse.

On the Coromandel Coast, the main currency was the star *pagoda*. It exerted a major influence on commercial transactions between the European companies and the Indian merchants. Traditionally, *pagodas* were made of gold. Its subdivision—the *panam* or *fanams*, as the Europeans called it, gained wide usage during the eighteenth century. *Fanams* were coined from silver that was imported from outside. Most of the transactions with weavers, textile merchants and market functionaries were carried on through *fanams*. It appears that in the course of the eighteenth century there was a steady debasement of the *pagodas* and consequently the demand for *fanam* was growing. A variety of *pagodas* of different purity and value were circulating in the markets of the Coromandel states. The Nawab of Carnatic remained perpetually concerned about the debasement problem because the debased *pagodas* were coming into his treasury in the form of revenue. This implied a definite decline in the real revenue of the nawabs.

The *fanams* were divided into *kasus* or *cash*. The value of a *fanam* varied according to its weight and the region. The standard heavy *fanam* seems to have been worth 24 to a star *pagoda* while the light *fanam* held an approximate value of 46 to a star *pagoda*. The *kasus* or *cash* was made of copper and usually 80 *kasus* formed a *fanam*. The use of rupees became common during the second half of the eighteenth century. Though the relationship between *pagoda* and rupee varied from one place to another and also according to time periods, it usually remained 100:350. Occasionally it could vary from 320 to 390 rupees to 100 *pagodas*.[73] In Arcot and Pondicherry, the rupee was divided into *anas* and *gandas*.[74] Though the exchange rate between the rupee and the *pagoda* was reasonably stable throughout the eighteenth century, the rupee was in greater demand. The major mints of the south were coining rupees in large quantities. The silver import from Europe facilitated this trend. While the Dutch secured the minting rights to coin *pagodas* in Palicat (1647) and Nagapatnam (1676), the Danes secured this right at Tranquebar. The English secured minting rights in Madras in 1639 without any payment of duty and sought its further confirmation in 1682.[75] However, the English *pagodas* could not match the finesse of the Dutch coins. The Dutch *pagoda* enjoyed a higher value by about 2 per cent. The English mint at Madras was dependant to a large extent on the Indian agencies—the shroffs and the goldsmiths and a few merchants who earned commission on the minted coins. Minting of coins was based on a system of contract. The contractor received 6½ *pagodas* on every 1,000 *pagodas* minted and 17½ rupees on every 1,000 rupees minted.

Among the European major powers, the French Company was the last to join the race for territorial settlements in India. The volume of trade with India was growing rapidly with increasing demand for Indian products. The French currency of *livre tournois*[76] was incapable of handling the voluminous trade because the demand for the French currency did not exist in India. In 1719 the Home government issued an edict authorizing the Paris mint to manufacture new types of gold and silver coins. On the representation of the Company officials, the government authorized minting of two types of silver *livres*—the French type and the Indian type.[77] Initially, the rupees of Pondicherry were minted in Arcot, the capital of Carnatic. After almost twenty years of ceaseless and patient efforts and negotiations, the French obtained a letter of authority in 1736 from the Nawab of Arcot, permitting them to mint silver rupee coins in Pondicherry.[78] After obtaining the dye for minting coins, the French authorities gave the work of minting to Indian merchants[79]—Sangu Seshachala Chetti,

Kanakaraya Mudali, Tiruvili Balu Chetti and Gunturi Venkanna Chetti—giving them a share of 3:1:1/2:1/2 respectively. Rs. 16 per thousand were set apart as expenses for running the mint.[80] The French authorities had fixed 100 *pagodas* as equivalent to 320 rupees and a rupee was made equal to 7½ *fanams*. This ratio remained nearly stable for the rest of the century. In 1789, Moracin mentions that a *pagoda* of 24 *fanams* fetched nearly 3 rupees and was worth 7½ *livres*.[81] In Masulipatam, the French minted silver rupees and copper coins called *dabous* where 46 to 48 *dabous* made a rupee. In Yanaon a rupee fetched 60 *dabous*.[82] The regional variation of currency is evident from the fact that while the English divided the three figure *pagoda* into 46 *fanams* with each *fanam* further divided into 80 *cash* or *kasu*, the French divided each *pagoda* into 26 *fanams*.

Among the non-metal and base metal currency *cauries* were the most important. *Cauries* or small shells remained the principal medium of exchange for the poor people. They were brought in large quantities from the Maldives and were a major commodity for both Asian and European traders. A *caurie* was a subdivision of a *poni* or *fani*—60 *ponis* formed half a rupee and each *poni* was divided into 60 *cauries*.[83] The use of *cauries* as a medium of exchange was confined to the local poor population for petty payments and seems to have been more widespread in Bengal than in the Coromandel states.

As in the case of China, foreign investments of Europeans included a large volume of precious metals which were brought to India to purchase Indian goods. The Coromandel trade was no exception to this trend. However, there was a major difference between the Chinese and the Indian situation. Silver coined in Europe or America was accepted in China on the basis of weight and content in commercial dealings while in India it had to be recoined into Indian monetary units before gaining acceptance in the Indian money markets. While the English silver import into India was dwindling in the period of our study with *de jure* control of the territorial revenues in certain regions of India, the French silver import continued. The *piastres* were brought from Cadiz in Spain, as a supplement of *specie*. The Spanish *piastres* were treated like commodities in Asia and, through recoinage, were utilized as money. The usual exchange rate fixed by the Sarafs was 17½ to 17¾ *fanams* to a *piastres*. When converted into rupees the *Sarafs* usually gave Rs. 217 for 100 *piastres*.[84] Legoux writes that 100 Spanish *piastres* were sold for Rs. 213, 11 *fanams* and 4 *cash*.[85] According to Dermigny, 100 Spanish *piastres* were worth Rs. 214.[86] While Legoux suggests that the exchange of *piastres* for rupees gave a profit of about 3½ per cent at Pondicherry,[87] another source maintains that this caused a loss of about 4 per cent to the French.[88] The French loss was a gain for the Indian money changers.[89] The French cargo to Pondicherry included a large quantity of silver weighed in *marcs* which was converted into Indian money. The market price of silver fluctuated from 7 *pagodas* 5 *fanams* to 7 *pagodas* 6 *fanams* per silver *marc*. However, the French trade statistics were usually mentioned in their own currency, i.e. *livres tournois*. A *pagoda* was equivalent to about 8 *livres* 5 *sols* while the rate of exchange of rupee to *livre tournois* varied between 2 *livres* 8 *sols* and 2 *livres* 12 *sols* to a rupee.[90] The *piastres* were brought from Cadiz in Spain where there were several important banking houses linked to the merchant bankers of St. Malo, Bayonne and of Paris. Haudrere mentions the names of Jean Masson of Malboue, a banker at Paris working closely with Cadiz based houses of Masson de Plissay and Jean & Etienne Behic Bros. who played an important role in procuring silver *piastres* for the French Company in India.[91] These *piastres* were sold to the local money agents to be recoined into Indian currency.

The picture of copper money circulation in Coromandel region during the first half of the eighteenth century is not very clear. The English sources, however, provide better information on this subject for the second half of the century. Copper coins were minted in the different mints and were called by different names such as *kasu (cash)*, *doody* or *dubb* and were used for the purposes of daily payment of wages and market commodities in moderate quantities. In the period of our study, copper held a significant place among all the metals sold by the English company in the Coromandel region. The most saleable was the plate copper of about 12 inches in thickness, commonly called 'Brass-wire'. The other forms included copper ship bolts, mixed metal, forged and hardened copper spikes and nails. The greater need for copper for 'country' ship's bottom may explain the expansion of the market for European copper in India in the late eighteenth century.[92]

A substantial quantity of copper imported into India was used for minting copper coins. With the setting up of several new mints, the copper import into India increased gradually. In the Masulipatam port alone, 2,812 maunds of copper were imported between 1776 and 1785 (the period of the American War of Independence when trade was badly dislocated). Of this, the English Company accounted for 750 maunds, the British merchants brought 1,378 maunds and the French 375 maunds.[93] That the major objective of enhancing the copper import was to increase the minted coins is evident from official pronouncements. The Court of Directors wrote, 'In making this purchase our principal object was to throw a large sum into our Treasuries in India, and in some degree to reduce the amount of Bullion which must otherwise of necessity have been sent to Canton.'[94] At another place it was clearly stated that the copper was for coinage at Madapollam, 'We expect to derive double advantages, in the disposal of a large proportion of that metal in such a manner, as will at the same time forward the provision of our investment.'[95]

This policy of bringing large quantities of copper and coining them into '*dubbs*' resulted in the reduction in the value of copper coins. Formerly, a Madras *pagoda* was usually exchanged for 46 copper *fanams* of 4 *dubbs* each, but soon a *pagoda* fetched 72 *fanams*. The value of the copper currency was reduced in the proportion of 7 to 11.[96] This policy of throwing into circulation a large quantity of copper coins not only caused a loss to its own proportional value but deprived the country of its gold and silver currency, particularly silver was becoming increasingly scarce. This must have adversely affected the economic condition of labourers and artisans who were paid in copper coins. Their purchasing power must have diminished in this new situation. The Board of Trade was urged to preserve a constant proportion between different kinds of coin in circulation, and not to increase the coinage of the baser metal, so as to banish those that were more precious.[97] The Company also failed to prevail upon the contractors and merchants to agree to receive part of the advances in copper and broadcloth.[98] Some of the merchants such as Ladeshavah Naick and Ramanah consented to take certain quantity of copper as advance but at the reduced value of 55 current *pagodas* per candy, whereas the average sale price was 66 Madras *pagodas* per candy.[99]

The French also introduced parchment money made in the units of rupee bearing the seal of the Company. Through official order, the people were asked not to refuse this money.[100] To popularize this money the authorities announced that the Company would accept the money at its face value. This currency appears to have consisted of ten-month bonds carrying 12 per cent interest, but due to paucity of funds and regular wars the Company often could not redeem the bonds on maturity. The result was that these were usually exchanged at heavy discounts. Only those persons seem to have bought them who owed money to the Company and wanted to pay off their debts.

As regard the banking institutions, there were two types of bankers among the Indians in the Coromandel region—the rural moneylenders whose dealings included non-commercial lending and the more professional bankers in the urban centres who thrived on business loans and money changing. The banking work was commonly performed by Shroffs and *Saucars* (*Sahukars*). The House of Buccangee was by far the most considerable bank in the Carnatic.[101] It had hitherto transacted the bulk of the Company's exchange throughout the province and had set up agents in Tanjore, Trichinapally, etc. It actively dealt with bills of exchange. *The Private Diary of Ananda Ranga Pillai* also throws light on the system of banking in the French settlements as well as outside. The leading *Saucars* included the names of Goverdhanadas, Kalidasa, Bukhanjee (Buccangee) and Vallaba Sunder.[102] They all carried out their banking operations through their agents or *Gomastas*. The common mode of operation seems to have been drafts, bills of exchange or *hundies*,[103] payable at site or after a prescribed period. These instruments were also transferable.[104] The *Diary* mentions the name of Mehigiri Chetti, Ramalayyan and Guntur Baliachetti as the principal shroffs of that period. According to Anand Ranga Pillai, orders were issued in Godeheu's time, which fixed the rate of interest at 8 per cent for Europeans and 12 per cent for Indians.[105] However, these were not followed strictly. He quotes numerous instances where the interest charged on loans was much in excess of official rates. The indigenous bankers lent money on the security of jewels or property, and the conditions laid down were usually informal. Some moneylenders charged interest at the rate of 18 to 36 per cent.[106] The English Resident of Tanjore frequently transmitted bills of exchange in favour of the Governor of Madras drawn on Rama Chetti of 10,000 star *pagodas* or more usually ten to fifteen days sight at about 25 gold *fanams* per *pagoda*.[107] We also come across references of European moneylenders, lending credit on high interest to Indian rulers. The Nawab of Arcot was a permanent borrower from this source. In the Madurai region, the banking house of Nattukotai Chetti was well known. They functioned as bankers, moneylenders and wholesaler merchants and carried out business activities all over southern India, in Burma, Ceylon and the Strait settlements.[108] This was the most organized banking house among the Indians. It was like a European banking house in respect of its organization, cooperation and business methods.[109] It acquired the theory and practice of banking through family traditions rather than formal education.

During the 1770s a number of new credit organizations emerged.

Known as the Agency Houses, they were based on partnership. These included Chase, Sewell & Chinnery, Tulloh, Connell & Brodie, Roebuck, Abbot, Maitland, etc.[110] Most of them were mixed firms consisting of company servants and merchants and they transacted diverse business by way of advancing money and buying and selling commissions. The best-known agency house was Lautour and the company was founded by Francis Lautour.[111] He came to Madras in 1770. The Carnatic Bank, established in 1788, was the earliest banking house at Madras. The objects of the institution were the receipt of money, issue of bills and notes and discounting of bills, notes and other securities. The initial capital reserve was 1,20,000 star *pagoda*s divided into eight shares.[112] The French were also keen to establish their own banks in India and in Paris but these remained merely suggestions and nothing concrete emerged out of them.[113] For their major commercial requirements, the French had dealings with firms like M.M. Balfour Spalding & Colt, the London based M.M. Charles Herries & Co., having branches all over. M.M. Pelling & Defries and M.M. Samson & Deonna were some other business houses that are mentioned by Moracin.[114] Thus, towards the close of the eighteenth century, with the formation of European agency houses to perform banking and other commercial functions, the role of Indian merchants in foreign trade experienced a steady decline. These European houses increasingly controlled the commercial aspect of the Indian foreign trade.[115] The business of banking among the Indians remained chiefly confined to the issuing and discounting of bills of exchange, moneylending and money-changing while the agency houses began to function as specialized commercial organizations. The French economic transactions in the late 1780s were carried out by the Houses of Andrè Mauvuisse at Madapollam and J.F. Moracin at Pondicherry who dealt with insurance, freight and financial dealings.[116]

Thus, we find that the Coromandel economy in the late eighteenth century presents a picture of increasing monetary transactions and commercialization. The industrial and commercial strength of this region was based on a vigorous trade that received powerful impetus from the existence of various efficient trading circuits. Braudel also hints at the degree of coherence of the Indian subcontinent in which money economy is seen as an essential element.[117] Though there were several limitations to the path of full-fledged capitalism and industrialization, the manufacturing sector had responded well to the challenge of domestic and external markets. Indians had developed their own means of transportation and exchange. As Frank Perlin points out, the credit needs of the foreign merchants were generally met by the indigenous credit facilities and instruments existing in the ports and near the centres of production.[118] The declining silver imports must have contributed to the formation of Agency houses. A wide network of European trade and the presence of numerous banking institutions certainly contributed to the commercialization of the Coromandel economy, particularly in the coastal belt. However, the foreign market structure began to get distorted after the mid-eighteenth century probably owing to the increasing control of the Europeans over trade and manufacture by virtue of their political power.

NOTES

1. The territory from Cape Comorin to the river Ganga has been described by an eighteenth century source as consisting of three kingdoms—Pandimandalum, Choramandalum and Tondamandalum although the limits of this territorial division and its period have not been specified. Éxplication de la carte gèographique de la côte du coromandel—*mémoire*, January 1763, *Indes Orientales*, No. 12, Arch. Aff. Étr.
2. Fra Paolinoda San Bartolomeo, *A Voyage to the East Indies*, London, 1800, p. 2. According to this description, the eastern part of the Indian peninsula was called the 'Chocamandela', i.e. the land of millet, while the western coast was called the 'Malayala' or the land of mountains.
3. Traditionally Tamil land was divided into five types—*kurinji* (mountain lands), *mullai* (forestland), *marutam* (agricultural land), *neytal* (sea coast), and *palai* (arid land).

   Jacques Dupuis, *Madras et Le Nord du Coromandel*, Paris, 1960, p. 18. Burton Stein, *Peasant, State and Society in Medieval South India*, Delhi, 1980, p. 42.
4. On the entire coastal line, particularly around Madras, the terrain was of red soil and pure sand, often saline, and produced very little of rice and cotton. Agriculture was generally neglected as the region began to import a considerable quantity of rice from Bengal and Orissa. Nevertheless, the region had evolved a very well developed network of trade.

   The dyeing sector of Pondicherry was served by two small rivers, which provided excellent water for the purpose of dyeing. This port-city was an important centre for bleaching and dyeing of cotton cloth, particularly for blue dye.
5. O.H.K. Spate, *India and Pakistan—A General and Regional Geography*, London, 1954, p. 687.
6. *Mémoire* (anonymous) 20 December 1774, Commerce et colonies de L'Inde, Série-B, *Feulles Volantes*, No. 201, Archives d'Aix-en Provence.
7. *Fort William-India House Correspondence*, Letter No. 19, Vol. V (1767-9), India Record Series, NAI.
8. Record of Fort William-Bombay Correspondence, Secret Political Dept. Diary,

Vol. IX, 28 September 1767, cited by Sarojini Regani, *Nizam-British Relations, 1724-1857*, Hyderabad, 1963, p. 13.

9. *Mémoire*, 20 December 1774, op. cit.
10. Compte rendu pour Mons. le Ministre de la Maring de Conway, 6 February 1788, No. 9, $C^2$184 (microfilm), AN, Paris. This account suggests that the French wanted to make a secret deal with Nizam Ali, who was described as 'le prince le plus adroit de L'Inde et celui qui connoit le mieux ses interests' (the most skilful prince in India who best knows his own interest). It was assumed that the province of Guntur with good administration could immediately pay rupees four lakhs. The rest could be paid from the further revenues. It was expected that a force of 2,000 of the best Europeans and 4,000 *sipahis* could be raised from this new source. It was also thought that by its possession, the French could sever the English communications between Bengal and Carnatic, and lead to the establishment of their own direct relationship with the Nizam and with the Raja of Nagpur.
11. George Smith's observations on the English possessions in India, 20 September 1785, *Home Miscellaneous Series*, MS 392, pp. 1-35 (microfilm), NAI.
12. Resident to Governor and Council, 22 April 1786, *Tanjore District Records*, Bundles 3444-5, TSA.
13. Most of the cotton was grown in Tirumangalam. The crop was usually raised on black soils but also on clayed red-soil. This variety of cotton was greatly valued for its whiteness.
14. Bartolomeo, op. cit., p. 54.
15. W. Francis (ed.), *Madura District Gazetteer*, Madras, 1906, p. 148.
16. The English officials argued that the migration of weavers from Damul district was because the looms were taxed, a heavy customs duty levied on thread and because poligars of that region kept insufficient force to protect weavers from being robbed. Mitford to Alexander Davidson, 20 January 1785, *Public Dept. Consultations*, TSA.
17. Richard Joseph Sulivan, *An Analysis of the Political History of India*, London, 1774, p. 93. A similar description can also be seen in the mémoir of 20 December 1774.
18. Bartolomeo, op. cit., pp. 49-50.
19. G.C. Lemon (ed.), *The Ganjam District Manual*, Madras, 1882, p. 106.
20. John Rowley, Resident of Madapollam to Board of Trade, 8 December 1792, *Godavari District Factory Records*, Vol. 830, Andhra Pradesh Archives (hereafter APA).
21. Mémoire sur la population de Pondichéry, Karikal, Yanaon et leur dependances, 1791, *Nouvelle Acquisition Série*, F.R.8930 (Ariél), p. 363, BN, Paris.
22. Abbé Raynal, *A Philosophical and Political History of the Settlements and Trade of the Europeans in the East and West Indies* (tr. J. Justamond), Vol. II, London, 1777, p. 169.
23. A. Martineau (ed.), *Correspondance du Conseil Supérieur de Pondichéry (1739-42)*, Tome III, p. xxv.
24. Robert Orme, *A History of Military Transactions of the British Nation in Indostan*, London, 1778, Vol. II, p. 478.
25. E. Divien, 'The Development of Tamil Society in Pondicherry, 1706-1898', unpublished Ph.D. thesis, Madras University, 1975, Appendix IV, and in Mémoire sur la population.

26. Ashin Das Gupta, 'Trade and Politics in 18th Century India', in D.S. Richards (ed.), *Islam and the Trade of Asia*, Oxford, 1970, p. 183.
27. Describing the condition of Pondicherry during the Anglo-French war in 1760, Robert Orme mentions that the consumption of provisions exceeded the supplies received. The black inhabitants were turned out. Soldiers were put to an allowance of a pound of rice a day with a little meat at intervals. Lally caused a strict search of the houses of inhabitants and took away all the grains for distribution to military staff. Robert Orme, op. cit., p. 707.
28. Jean-Luc Kieffer, *Anquetil-Duperron: L'Inde en France au XVIIIe Siècle*, Paris, 1983, pp. 197-8.
29. Ibid.
30. Jacques Dupuis, op. cit., p. 30. Rice was the first crop and irrigation was the first agricultural technique seen by Duperron.
31. Jean-Luc Kieffer, op. cit., p. 207.
32. K.N. Chaudhuri, *The Trading World of Asia and the English East India Company, 1660-1760*, London, 1978, p. 238.
33. S. Jeyaseela Stephen, *The Coromandel Coast and its Hinterland, Economy, Society and Political System*, Delhi, 1997, p. 93.
34. Ibid.
35. Joseph J. Brennig, 'Textile Producers and Production in Late Seventeenth Century Coromandel', *The Indian Economic and Social History Review* (hereafter *IESHR*), 23, No. 4, 1986, pp. 333-56.
36. J.B. Tavernier, 'Les Six voyages de J.B. Tavernier en Turkie, en Perse et aux Indes', Paris, 1679, Vol. II cited in Jean-Luc Kieffer, op. cit., p. 226.
37. J. Revell to Anthony Sadlier, 15 December 1789, *Public Consultations*, 160B, p. 129, TSA.
38. K. Rajayyan, *Administration and Society in the Carnatic: 1701-1800*, Venkateswara, 1966, p. 108.
39. Francis Buchanan, *Journey from Madras through the Countries of Mysore, Canara and Malabar*, Vol. I, London, 1807, p. 326.
40. Ibid., p. 302.
41. Ibid., p. 326.
42. Francis Cyril Antony (ed.), *Pondicherry Gazetteer*, Vol. I, 1982, p. 350.
43. The English authorities tried to bring uniformity by creating new administrative units called *Muggams* in 1803.
44. Arasaratnam, op. cit.
45. Roger Darvell to Board of Revenue, 31 August 1793, Vol. 445, *Chingleput District Records*, TSA.
46. P. Swarnalatha and P. Sudhir, 'The Company and the Coromandel Weaver: Structural Change in the Short Term 1790-1820', *IHC Proceedings*, 1987, pp. 461-6.
47. H. Dodwell, 'The Madras Weavers under the Company', *Proceedings of Indian Historical Records Commission*, Vol. IV, 1922, pp. 41-6.
48. Petition of Pollam dyers to Chief and Council, Cuddalore, 8 June 1775, *Public Consultations*, TSA.
49. Ibid.
50. The European writers referred to inhabitants of southern coastal settlements as Gentues. The low caste Hindus were described as Telugu (Gentue) and the Tamil (as Malabars). Together they constituted a large portion of the local population.

51. K.S. Mathew, 'Indian Merchants and the French during the seventeenth and eighteenth centuries—A study of Partnership', in K.S. Mathew and S. Jeyaseela Stephen (eds.), *Indo-French Relations*, Delhi, 1999.
52. Holden Furber, *Rival Empires of Trade in the Orient 1600-1800* (hereafter *Rival Empires*), Minneapolis, 1976, p. 291.
53. S. Arasaratnam, 'Indian Commercial Groups and European Traders 1600-1800: Changing relationships in Southeastern India', *South Asia* (N.S.), Vol. I, No. 2, September 1978, pp. 42-53.
54. Notions sur L'Inde par M. Goddard, *Nov. Acq.* 8930, Série A, Vol. IV, p. 330, BN.
55. 'Le Commerce Extèrieur du Coromandel est absolument entre les mains des Europèeans, exceptè quelques choulias de Naour, Porte Nove et d'Orixa, qui font des expèditions pour achem, mergui, le Pegu, Siam, Ceilon . . .', *mèmoire*, Commerce et Colonies de L'Inde, 20 December 1774.
56. Ashin Das Gupta, 'India and the Indian Ocean in the Eighteenth Century', pp. 131-61, in Ashin Das Gupta and M.N. Pearson (eds.), *India and the Indian Ocean 1500-1800*, Oxford, 1987.
57. For different interpretations of Susan Bayly, Sanjay Subrahmanyam and others, see Bhaswati Bhattacharya, 'The Chulia Merchants of Southern Coromandel in the Eighteenth Century: A case for continuity', in Om Prakash and Denys Lombard (eds.), *Commerce and Culture in the Bay of Bengal 1500-1800*, Delhi, 1999, pp. 285-305.
58. Bartolomeo, op. cit., p. 5.
59. Jean-Luc Lieffer, op. cit., p. 227.
60. 'Ces bateaux, nommés cheingue à la côte de coromandel, sont construits avec des planches d'un bois léger et trés flexible. Leurs bordages, au lieu d'être cloués avec une forte ligne, qui les unit l'un à l'autre . . . qui sert de calfeutrance.' M. Legoux de Flaix, *Essai Historique, Géographique et Politique sur L'Indoustan avec le tableau de son commerce*, Tome II, Paris, 1807, p. 41.
61. William Milburn, *Oriental Commerce*, London, 1813, Vol. II, p. 86.
    Robert Orme also mentions Massoolas. These were the only boats, according to him, which could ply the surf, but were not sufficient to carry off the ammunition. Robert Orme, op. cit., Vol. II, p. 616.
62. Fra Paolino da san Bartolomeo, op. cit., p. 5.
63. S. Arasaratnam, 'Indian Merchants and the Decline of Indian Mercantile Activity: The Coromandel Case', *The Calcutta Historical Journal*, Vol. VII, pp. 27-42.
64. Francis Buchanan writes that there were mainly 18 right hand castes, which included Rungaru (calico printers and tailors), Curubaru (blanket weavers and shepherds), Agasaru (washermen), Chitragaru (painters), etc., *Journey Through Madras*, Vol. I, London, 1807, p. 78.
65. E. Divien, op. cit., p. 108.
66. *The Private Diary of Ananda Ranga Pillai*, Vol. I, Madras, 1904, p. 177.
67. *Pondicherry Gazetteer*, p. 35.
68. Military Sundry No. 88, Record Office No. 4354 in H. Dodwell (ed.), *Report on the Madras Records*, Madras, p. 51.
69. 'Je ferai observer que toutes les monnaies dans l'Indoustan sont considéres comme marchandises', M. Legoux de Flaix, op. cit., p. 23.
70. 'Les Èpeces d'or et d'argent sont regardées comme marchandises dans l'Inde,

l'abondance d'une matiére et fait tomber la valuer à lègard de l'autre', Mémoire (1780) *M.M. Asie, Indes Orientales*, No. 7, pp. 168-214, Arch. Aff. Étr., Paris.

71. Resident's Correspondance, 1755-83, bundle 3441, p. 513, *Tanjore District Records*, Vol. IV, TSA.
72. According to S. Arasaratnam, the premium increased from 25 per cent in 1633 to 90 per cent in 1660, i.e. 100 gold *pagodas* were exchanged for 190 new *pagodas*. See *Merchants, Companies and Commerce on the Coromandel Coast 1650-1740*, Delhi, 1986, p. 297.
73. According to Pierre Blancard, 100 *pagodas* could fetch 390 rupees in Masulipatam due to the rarity of gold *pagodas*. See *Manuel du Commerce des Indes Orientales et de la Chine*, Paris, 1806, p. 265.
74. 40 *gandas* = 1 *ana*; 16 *anas* = 1 rupee
75. Despatches to England, 21 January 1724, p. 24, mentioned in S. Arasaratnam, op. cit., p. 305.
76. *Livre* tournois was a pre-Revolutionary monetary unit equivalent to approximately 10½ to 11 pence of English money or one can say that 24 *livres* were equal to pound 1 of Britain.
77. The French type included the silver *panam*, double *panam*, half *panam* and copper *cash* while the Indian type included rupees and *anas*.
78. Pierre Benoit Dumas, The Governor of Pondicherry announced on 12 October 1736 that the French were granted the right of minting Indian coins by Emperor Mohammad Shah through Dost Ali, for a sum of Rs. 1,20,000 + 8,000 *pagodas* by way of miscellaneous expenses.
79. *Gazetteer of India, Union Territory of Pondicherry*, Vol. I, 1982, p. 642.
80. Notification of the Supreme Council at Pondicherry, 15 July 1739, *Private Diary of Ananda Ranga Pillai*, op. cit., p. 101.
81. Moracin to the Administrators of the Compagnie des Indes at Paris, 10 September 1789, No. 57, p. 33, NAI.
82. Pierre Blancard, op. cit., pp. 265, 269.
83. The Madras rupee was worth 3,040 *cauries* in Bengal. See also Fra Paolino da San Bartolomeo, op. cit., p. 84.
84. Ibid.
85. M. Legoux de Flaix, op. cit., p. 235.
86. Louis Dermigny, *Cargaisons Indiennes soliers et Cie 1781-1793*, Paris, 1960, p. 438.
87. Ibid., p. 285.
88. M. Legoux de Flaix, op. cit., p. 217.
89. 100 *piastres* fetched about 512 *livres* 10 *sol*, according to *Mémoire* 1780, op. cit.
90. 12 *derniers* = 1 *sol*; 20 *sols* = 1 *livre*
91. Pierre Haudrere, *La Compagnie Française des Indes au XVIIIe Siècle(1719-1795)*, Vol. III, Paris, 1989, p. 954.
    According to Haudrere, between 1720 and 1769, 28 ships left Cadiz directly for Coromandel, 21 ships for Bengal and 13 for China.
92. M. Legoux de Flaix, op. cit.,
93. Extract from the customhouse books, 30 September 1786, *Masulipatam District Correspondence*, Commercial No. 2900, APA.
94. COD to President and Council, Fort St. George, 10 March 1790, *Despatches to Madras*, Vol. 16, E/4/876, *Madras Despatches*, 11 April 1792, E/4/878, Vol. 18, p. 619, IOR.

95. COD to President and Council, 10 March 1790, Vol. 16, E/4/876, *Madras Despatches*, IOR.
96. Anthony Sadlier and Council of Masulipatam to Board of Trade, 20 April 1791, *Masulipatam Commercial Consultation*, Vol. 2841, APA.
97. Ibid.
98. Ibid.
99. Samuel Statham to Charles Floyer, 3 October 1786, *Masulipatam District Correspondence*, Commercial, Vol. 2900, APA.
100. *Gazetteer of Pondicherry*, p. 638
101. Robert Orme, op. cit., p. 438.
102. *Diary of Anand Ranga Pillai*, Vol. II, p. 177.
103. *Hundi* is a word derived from *Hindwi* and functioned almost like a bill of exchange. *Hundis* or Indian promissory notes were used to provide credit facilities. These varied according to the mode of payment from Dhanni-Jog, Shah-Jog, Firman-Jog, Dekhavanhar and Miti Hundi.
104. *Diary of Anand Ranga Pillai*, Vol. VIII, p. 430 and Vol. X, pp. 146-7.
105. Ibid., Vol. IX, p. 45.
106. *Gazetteer of Pondicherry*, op. cit., p. 639.
107. Resident's Correspondence, 6 April 1785, 19 April, 1785, 28 May 1785, *Tanjore District Records*, Vol. IV, 3443, TSA.
108. *Madura District Gazetteer*, Madras, 1906.
109. L.C. Jain, *Indigenous Banking in India*, London, 1929, p. 36.
110. Henry Dodwell, *The Nabobs of Madras*, London, 1926, p. 138.
111. Ibid., p. 139, Henry Davison Love, *Vestiges of Old Madras 1640-1800*, Vol. III, Delhi, rpt. 1988.
112. *Mémoire*, 1770, op. cit.
113. Projet d'établissement d'une banque indienne à L'isle de France, 18 July 1788, dossier 956, *corresp.-gén.*, *Inde*, Archives D'Outre-mer, Paris.
114. The agency houses usually had the rates of commission as follows:

Sale or purchase of goods	5%
Sale or purchase of bullion	1%
On procuring freights to Europe, India or any other port	5%
On procuring loans of money	1%
On procuring money on respondentia payable in Europe India or elsewhere	2%
On procuring company's bonds and certificates	1%

115. William Milburn, *Oriental Commerce*, Vol. II, London, 1813, p. 66.
116. Ole Feldbaek, *India Trade under the Danish Flag 1772-1808*, Copenhagen, 1969, p. 23.
117. Fernand Braudel, *Civilization and Capitalism 15th to 18th Centuries*, Vol. III, *The Perspective of the World*, London, 1984, p. 511.
118. Perlin suggests that minting in India was closely linked to supplies from beyond the subcontinent. Frank Perlin, 'Changes in Production and Circulation of Money in Seventeenth and Eighteenth Century India: An Essay on Monetization Before Colonial Occupation', in Sanjay Subrahmanyam (ed.), *Money and the Market in India 1100-1700*, Delhi, 1994.

Chapter 2

The Rise of Rival Companies

THE RAPID growth of foreign trade in India coincided with somewhat similar developments in Europe. The seventeenth century in north-western Europe witnessed the formation of several joint-stock companies and their continual control over the trading activities with foreign lands. The success of a particular company's monopoly, as Braudel suggests, depended on the coming together of three things—the state, the world of trade (capitalism, banking, credit, customs, etc.) and the trading zone.[1]

The rise of European sea power and commercial expansion during the sixteenth century provided a new dimension to trading activities. A new element in the Indo-European trade emerged in the form of joint-stock enterprises. K.N. Chaudhuri sees in the formal constitution of the chartered trading companies the 'emerging principle of capitalism'.[2] It was also an innovation because these companies (both English and Dutch) reflected an incipient separation between the ownership of capitalism and its management by a professional class of merchants and salaried administrators.[3] Later the French, the Ostenders, and the Danes adopted the same means of organizing their trading activities in Asia.

The English East India Company, soon after receiving the royal charter in 1600, started constitutional and operational arrangements of trade with the East Indies. The English entered the field after the Portuguese and the Dutch, and carried on trade under the protection of the Mughal Emperor. They followed an apparently peaceful commercial policy without territorial responsibilities. However, by the beginning of the eighteenth century, their days of fenceless factories were over and they began to elaborate their administrative machinery. The gradual evolution of fiscal and judicial administration along with the growth of the 'three Presidencies' marked the steady rise of English power in India. According to Lucy Sutherland, from the very beginning, the prestige of the Crown was successfully employed by the Company in its relations with the Indian powers.[4] But, in the early eighteenth century a rivalry between two factions developed within the English Company and this played havoc with the English trade. This rivalry was brought to an end by the diplomatic manoeuvres of Lord Godolphin. The Charter of 1709, amalgamated the 'Old' and the 'New' companies, and laid the framework for the future on which the Company's monopoly rights, its powers, its place in the London money market and its relations with the state could develop.[5]

In the seventeenth century, the Dutch were more successful than the English and the French in establishing a flourishing commercial empire in Asia. The joint stock company of Holland called *Vereenigde Oast—Indische Compagnie* or VOC was founded in 1602 and rivalled its English counterpart in Asia, gaining a powerful position in the Indonesian region. The Dutch also enjoyed exclusive trade with Japan and held outposts in China and India. However, during the second half of the seventeenth century, the Dutch had to fight numerous wars with the English and the French in the European seas. These wars led to the emergence of England and France as the two rival European powers to acquire Indian possessions and control her trade. Thus, by the second decade of the eighteenth century, while the Dutch domination of the spice trade continued in South-East Asia, the growing Anglo-French rivalry in India stole the commercial spotlight from the Dutch. The struggle for economic domination, by exploiting Indian cotton industries and controlling the flow of fine and coarse cotton textiles, spices and other products to Europe, could not be fully resolved till the last quarter of the eighteenth century. Both powers adopted political means of acquiring and controlling Indian territories to achieve their economic aims. By the mid-eighteenth century, the English and the French companies appeared more like political rivals than commercial contestants.

As regards the origin of the French interests in India, the commercial success of the Venetians and the Portuguese in Asia forced the French merchants to draw the attention of Francis I to the advantages of trade with Asia. The Edicts of 1537 and 1543 provided for the ships to carry out voyages to India, but an intense rivalry with Charles V led to a war and suspension of the proposed voyage.[6] In fact, as early as 1503, merchants of Rouen are said to have fitted out a squadron but it failed owing to a sea storm in the Indian Ocean.[7] The first French official effort to reach out to the colonial commerce dates from 1604 when the Compagnie des Indes Orientales was chartered.[8] This French Company had exclusive privilege for the commerce of India and was exempted from all the duties on the merchandise that it carried from its first two voyages. It also had the exclusive privilege of navigating to India for fifteen years.[9] This was an attempt to compete with the English and the Dutch in the Indian Ocean and was specifically designed to encourage a type of trade visualized as essential for France. It represented a departure from the pattern of merchant-initiated trading companies of England and the United Provinces of Netherlands, and its history, as Boulle suggests, served as a classic example of the effects of state intervention.[10] From 1624 to 1635, some merchants of Dieppe made a few voyages to India and Madagascar.[11] Captain Lelievrie D'hon fleur, Rigault and Beaulieu performed journeys and earned rich profits.[12] Captain Regimont, along with others, formed a company in 1635 (without exclusive privilege) and sent a ship to India which returned richly charged with merchandise. Wishing to prosper from this commerce, Richelieu accorded it exclusive privilege for 10 years. However, his hopes remained unfulfilled. By 1650, the company had ceased all its expeditions. Louis Dermigny has significantly underlined the geopolitical circumstances that tended to hinder French participation in the East Indian trade. He has emphasized in his article the size of the country in which the economic unification lagged behind the political, with the continuation of numerous customs barriers and the regionalism of traditional France hindering economic progress as well as the emergence of a 'cohesive merchant community'. Paris, despite being the political centre, could not develop as an economic centre, since it was far away from the sea, and as such from commercial activity. London, on the contrary, was not only the political capital but also the main seaport where three-fourths of the national commercial activity was concentrated. Hence, its Company was explicitly called 'The Company of Merchants of London Trading into the East Indies'.[13] These circumstances, together with a natural tendency to defer to Dutch and Flemish expertise and the desire for settling in Madagascar, prevented the French East India trading from really getting off the ground before the days of Colbert.[14]

The creation of Compagnie des Indes Orientales in 1664 was a direct consequence of the new state mercantilism of France, also described as 'Colbertism'. During this period, several monopolistic companies were created—such as Compagnie des Indes Occidentales (to trade in West Indies; it possessed monopoly over the African slave trade) and

Compagnie du Nord (for Baltic trade). In each case the crown paid a substantial capital at the initial stage as incentive to other investors (mostly officials and a few merchants) and then controlled and regulated the company's administration and operations. The Compagnie des Indes Orientales was reorganized several times before it was abolished in 1769. L'Orient remained the chief port in France for oriental products. It was located near the industrial areas of Nantes, etc., which produced *Indiennages* and had immense storage capacity.

La Compagnie des Indes Orientales was established, like several other French companies when the French capitalist structure was still fragile. Several scholars have described this Company as an over-regulated and under-financed institution. It failed to generate enthusiasm among the merchant class and it utilized other safer and socially attractive sources of investment in land and official posts. Explaining the factors hindering French enterprise, Braudel has discussed the merchants' distrust of the royal government, the comparative inadequacy of the means at their disposal and the immaturity of what might be regarded as French capitalism.[15] Braudel argues that it was difficult for the French to penetrate the existing trade networks. He quotes Jean Menvret who believes that the circumstances had changed at the time of the French entry in the Asian trade; that the French had chosen the wrong moment and that Colbert had arrived on the scene rather too late.[16] It is, however, difficult to agree on the last point. One can argue that the French had achieved an amazing success in the 1730s and 1740s despite their late entry. It was probably the economic strength at home and political power outside that determined to some extent the success of these colonial powers.

It is obvious that the French Company faced a perpetual shortage of ready capital. It had full advantage of government protection and patronage, yet as Parry contends, it was to all appearance a more formidable affair, but in the first half century of its life, its financial situation was precarious.[17] It seems that in the first decade of the eighteenth century, the privileged position of the French within the Spanish empire drew much French commercial capital away from the Indian Ocean into the Pacific Coast trade. The government persisted with the impractical marriage of Eastern and Western trade.[18] In fact, a major crisis was earlier averted by Colbert in 1683 when the commercial operations of the company practically came to an end for want of funds.[19] Private traders were given permission on 10 per cent commission, to take part in the eastern trade on certain specific conditions designed to raise funds for the company. It proved to be a ruinous policy, for in the long run the company began to depend on the easy methods of commissions and freight charges paid by outsiders.

During the War of Spanish Succession, the finances of the French Company suffered so much that it was on the verge of collapse. Some merchants of St. Malo redeemed the situation in 1708. They used the trading rights and privileges of the company by paying commissions. In 1715, on the expiry of fifty years (as specified in the original charter) the company's monopolistic privileges were extended for another 10 years.

The period after the Spanish War was followed by a speculative mania in Europe. The South Sea Bubble Crisis in England reflected a similar trend. In France, John Law was responsible for creating a speculative craze, which resulted in a serious economic crisis. In May 1719 the 'Edict of Reunion' merged Colbert's Compagnie des Indes Oriental with Law's enterprise, along with the Compagnie Royale de Chine and Compagnie de 1'Occident. The new unified institution was called the 'Compagnie des Indes'. It was to direct all the colonial commerce of France.[20] The failure of the Company was attributed to bad administration, insufficient capital, premature payment of dividends and a ruinous borrowing policy.[21] This period marked the gradual take-over by the state of the company's remaining possessions and the consequent diminution of its privileges. The period was also significant because the new system placed on the Company a financial burden totally unrelated to its commercial role. Boulle described the situation after Law's reforms as follows:[22]

> . . . once the financial burden of the Government became too vast for the state to support, the tendency was to reverse the flow of capital and to push back some of the costs of the Government on the commercial companies. . . .

Thus, the Compagnie des Indes was saddled with a financial burden by way of financing military and political wars that made it difficult to function as a commercial venture. The Company's dependence on the government destroyed all spirit of initiative. Yet, the company managed to do well by way of commercial expansion till the beginning of the Seven Years' War. During the period from 1725 to 1759, it spent 27,24,26, 392 *livres* for the purchase of goods in India and the same it sold in France for 53,20,00,000 *livres* with a profit of 25,30,69,631 *livres*.[23] The Seven Years' War dealt a mortal blow to it from which recovery became very difficult and just when it began to show some signs of recovery, it was abolished.

ORGANIZATION OF THE RIVAL COMPANIES

Although the French and the English companies were monopolistic institutions in the nature of joint-stock organizations, their set-up and working differed radically. Though the English East India Company was formed by a royal charter (in 1600), the initiative came from business groups. The Board of Proprietors consisted of shareholders and their stock qualifications were rather high, varying from £1,000 to £ 4,000. The Board's deliberations also reflected public opinion and on an average 200 to 300 proprietors attended its meetings.[24] The Court of Directors was a well-organized body and reflected the city, shipping and unorganized Indian interests.[25] The deliberations of the proprietors exercised considerable influence on the decisions of the directors, particularly till 1784.

In contrast to the English Company, the administrative link between the Compagnie des Indes and the French state was more closely knit. The French government was keen on preserving the Company and helping it in all possible ways. In 1725, all its old privileges were confirmed and simultaneously its past liabilities wiped off.[26] The reorganization led to the Company's close dependence on state support and direction, which considerably hampered its actions. Shareholders could not take initiative in policy matters.

With its large staff and an establishment at L'Orient, the Secretarial set-up of the French Company's headquarters in rue-Neuve des Petite-Champs closely resembled the India-House of the English Company at London.[27] For keeping the Company under proper surveillance, a suitable administrative structure was evolved. 'Conseil des Indes' was set up with members selected by the king from the officers of his Council and the Navy, besides some prominent merchants. Its twelve directors were likewise to be selected by the king. It was not a company in the real sense of the term, rather a syndicate. Only the syndics appointed by the ministers enjoyed the real power in the French Company. There never was any organized body of directors, something corresponding to the English Company's Court of Directors or Dutch Company's 'Seventeen'. No annual meeting of shareholders was called till 1744 when after strong representation from the shareholders, they were granted the right to elect twelve persons, from among whom the king was to choose six syndics. But this concession too was not translated into practice. The shareholders seldom met and when they did, they were prevented from acting by the presence of royal officials. The Assemblée Générale did not bear the slightest resemblance to the

English Company's General Court of Proprietors. The real management of the Company's affairs lay in the hands of the king. In 1730, the king appointed a commissary for its administration. In 1745, the king appointed two, instead of one, commissaries, which led to divisions, intrigues and animosities. Each commissary had his own scheme, and favourites and endeavoured to get his own projects adopted. Abbé Raynal mentions that from this period there was an end to all freedom of debate, 'there was no longer any connection between those who had the management of affairs and the proprietors'.[28]

The English East India Company's overseas administration had assumed a definite shape when the French were still making efforts to establish a foothold in India. The parallel development of the three Presidencies made the English position relatively secure. Their political and geographical placement in the Bengal and Bombay region was superior to that of the French, but on the Coromandel Coast, the latter enjoyed almost equal advantage. It was this factor that prolonged the rivalry between the two in the post-1763 period though everything seemed to have been lost for the French.

Madras was the oldest among the English Presidencies. It was not their earliest settlement but constituted their first territorial acquisition, and for many years, the only fortified possession. The English commenced their trading venture in India with their trading house at Surat in 1612. On the Coromandel Coast their first factory was erected at Masulipatam. The stiff challenge from the Dutch, the oppression by the local governor and officials and Portuguese jealousy, however compelled the English to abandon their factory at Masulipatam. Instead, Armagon was selected as the site for the new factory. This official agent also failed to foster trade and provide adequate supplies. It was in the period of political disturbance and famine that Thomas Clark succeeded in acquiring a site at Madras from the Nayak rulers in 1639. It was here that the English began to expand their territorial acquisitions and then succeeded in establishing their political supremacy.

By the beginning of the eighteenth century, the Madras Presidency rose in importance. The population of Madras rose from about 40,000 in 1670 to about 3 lakhs at the beginning of the nineteenth century, and provided a revenue of 9,45,000 *pagodas* to the Company. It was already a textile centre when the English acquired it and the cotton cloth was about 20 to 30 per cent cheaper in Madras compared to Armagon. According to Krishnaswami Aiyangar in his 'Character and

Significance of the Foundation of Madras', the prosperity of the settlement was linked to its economic success.[29] The English had founded weaving villages at Kaladipettah near Tiruvottiyar and at Chintadripettah, by governors Joseph Collet and Morton Pitt in 1719 and 1734 respectively. Situated very close to the weaving centres and falling on the well-developed sea route from Bengal to Europe and from Malabar to South-East Asian countries, Madras participated actively in this interregional trade. Goods were carried there from China and Malaya, the Archipelago and Ceylon, where they were sorted and repacked before being shipped to Europe. Cuddalore was added in 1690, taken from the Raja of Jingi, followed by a number of grants by the Nawab of Carnatic and the Raja of Tanjore, which extended their territorial limits. Factories were established at Masulipatam, Madapollam, Ingeram, Vizagapatnam and Ganjam—all seaports on the Coromandel Coast. With this, the revenue, judicial, political and military departments were evolved, providing stability and mechanism to the process of colonization.

For the French the Coromandel Coast was the principal centre of commerce and Pondicherry remained all the time their important entrepôt as well as the political-administrative centre in Asia. The original French efforts in India had remained confined to Surat for a long time. As Indrani Ray brought out in her article, it was in 1686, when a total prohibition on the importation of painted cloth and chintz was imposed that the directors were compelled to move out of Surat.[30] It seems that the search for new types of merchandise free from mercantilist prohibition brought the French to Bengal and later to the Coromandel.

The late interest taken by the French in Bengal region was a notable lapse on their part in their colonial efforts in comparison with the English and the Dutch. Part of the explanation could be found in the writings of François Martin. These tend to blame the growing political disorder and recurrent famines and pestilence which ravaged the Coromandel in the last quarter of the seventeenth century. Whenever the French succeeded in establishing their subordinate settlements, it was primarily due to political disturbances or infighting among local rulers, and not because of their economic strength or superior commerce. What Indrani Ray writes about the French in Bengal can also be applied to their activities in the Coromandel. Beset with financial problems, they were not in a position to capture the market by indiscriminate and big purchases, as the English and the Dutch companies were doing.[31] Nor could they, like the Dutch, supplement their funds by means of successful Asian trade.

Divien has classified the French possessions in India into two groups—commercial and political.[32] The latter consisted of chief *lieux* or places owned by the French where councils for administrative purposes were established, and *comptoirs* and *loges,* which were subordinated to one of the councils. In *comptoirs*, the French had proprietary rights but in *loges* they had no such rights and the posts were under local jurisdiction. The political possessions of the French were made up of a large number of *aldées* or villages, e.g. the settlements of Pondicherry, Mahé, Chandernagar, Karikal and Yanaon. Jurisdiction over them was granted by local rulers for financial considerations or when a ruler desired an increase of trade of his region, but mostly in return for military aid.

Pondicherry, Yanaon and Karikal were the three *comptoirs* that served the French commerce on the Coromandel Coast. Pondicherry was the capital town, considerable, well fortified with a garrison, industrially developed and highly populated. It was the seat of power. Whereas Fort William was the seat of the English power in India, fairly safe from the designs of the European powers, the same cannot be said of Pondicherry. In fact, it was the Anglo-French rivalry, which ultimately relegated Madras to a secondary position in relation to the growing port cities of Calcutta and Bombay. The same factor hampered the growth of Pondicherry as one of the prominent port cities of India. The prominence of Pondicherry was chiefly due to its manufactures. The town and its environs produced some of the best cloths—white and painted—and gathered a variety of commercial objects which were stored in town magazines.

The nature of French commerce hardly changed since the beginning of the eighteenth century. A common view is that the commerce carried on by the old Company before Dupleix was average, became immense under his management, decreased after his recall and then was almost destroyed.[33] This view, though generally held, is not true. Dupleix arranged to invite various classes of weavers, Kaikolars, Sedars and Seniyars to settle at Villiyanullur in the vicinity of the town to enable them to build houses and construct looms.[34] The arrival of Dupleix reflected a sudden spurt of trade. He believed that the real prosperity of Pondicherry was not due to commerce. Justifying his action, Dupleix in his Memoir of 1753 showed the insufficiency of commerce, and sought to acquire monopoly of trade through conquered territories.

The steady increase in the number of ships arriving in the East probably reflected this approach.[35] In 1748, the French Company sought 12 million *livres* for their purchases in India, i.e. double the previous year's demand. However, the French failed to find a solution to the problem of coordinating the economic and political aspects of their expansion. Their colonial network in India remained debilitated owing to lack of support and coordination from above and insufficient capital resources from below. The English, on the contrary, commanded considerable local resources and had political means to back them and thus succeeded in subverting the power-fabric of the French. This was amply demonstrated during the Seven Years' War and in the American War of Independence.

The Peace Treaty of Paris concluded in 1763 not only brought an end to the Anglo-French global war but also determined the mutual relationship of the two powers for the next two decades. The Treaty of 1763 regulated the French claims on political settlements. The French Company demanded the exercise of its privileges, which it had obtained from the Indian Emperor and local rulers. However, the augmented power and resources acquired by the English Company not only placed restrictions on the use of the commercial privileges the French claimed but made them dependent on the English goodwill. The French Company was keen to re-establish its commerce to the pre-1749 level but it lacked the means to achieve it. In fact, the developments of the last few years had so altered the balance of forces in favour of the English that they refused to surrender their advantages so easily. Despite the restoration of the Europeans to the pre-1749 state in India, the situation could never be the same.

The French took almost two years to receive back their territorial settlements and *loges* after signing the Peace Treaty in 1763. The war acting as a deterring agent dislocated the economic and demographic pattern of growth. It certainly ruined the principal French settlement of Pondicherry, where population dispersal was frequent. According to Gentil's account, the population of Pondicherry in 1769 was about 60,000, which can be regarded as an optimistic figure.[36] It came down to 28,000 in 1778, the period of the American War. Racine suggests that the quick revival of Pondicherry in between the wars was less due to the French commerce than to the troubles which continued to affect the Carnatic and the neighbourhood.[37] However, one cannot deny the fact that Pondicherry as a town held its place primarily by virtue of its commerce with foreign lands. The French commerce here survived despite wild fluctuations till the beginning of the revolutionary war. At the same time we cannot ignore the efforts of the French administrators to attract the artisan class to augment their exports.

The English Company had also suffered during the Seven Years' War, but they recovered very fast. At this stage, by the time of the Treaty of Versailles, their annual export from India nearly doubled.[38] The establishment of English supremacy in Bengal and their control of the revenues caused a 'double coup'; the control over tax farms provided not only a financial base to their military and administrative establishments but also a solid foundation for the expansion of their power in future. Secondly, the opium of Bengal financed the commerce with China. This covered the trade deficit in India. Yet, the English success did not strangulate the French hopes. From the numerous memoirs of that period it is apparent that they resolved to make efforts to re-establish equilibrium sooner or later.

By 1763, the French Company was on the verge of complete extinction when the liberal grant of their king in August 1764 saved it for a few more years. The number of shares was reduced from 50,268 (fixed in June 1725) to 38,432 in 1764.[39] This was done to raise the credit of the Company. Besides, Article XIII of the Edict expressly secured for the proprietors a settled income independent of all future fluctuations of trade. Sufficient fund was kept apart from the grant which was then free to secure every share of capital of the value of 1,600 *livres*. Neither that capital nor its interest was answerable for such engagements as the Company might enter into in future.[40] Despite these vigorous efforts, the French Company could not be saved in 1769 from extinction when the revival of its trade has just commenced.[41] This is evident from Graph 2.1 showing the import of Indian goods till the abolition of the French Company.

ABOLITION OF COMPAGNIE DES INDES

There were several reasons that led to the abolition of the Compagnie des Indes. A public controversy had developed since the mid-eighteenth century about the desirability of a state directed monopolistic Company which eventually pushed it to extinction. The merchants of the trading cities and town were the first to assert the liberty of commerce against the exclusive privilege of the Company. Several free traders and liberal thinkers also raised their voice against the commerce with India. This group of critics was described by Anquetil Duperron as 'the battalion

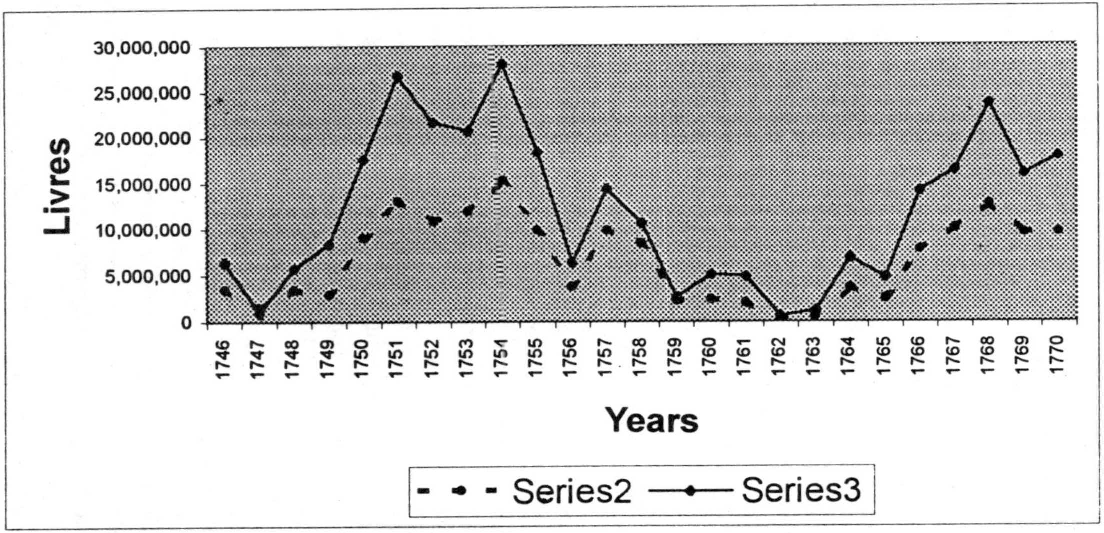

GRAPH 2.1: FRENCH IMPORTS OF INDIAN GOODS (1745-6 to 1770-1) in *livres*

Source: Henry Weber, *La Compagnie Française des Indes, 1604-1875*, Paris, 1904, p. 500.

of the economists placed under the Squadron of Encyclopaedists'.[42] In establishing the liberty of grain trade they attacked the impediments and shackles placed on all types of free enterprise. 'Monopoly' was the word to rally together all the critics and 'Compagnie des Indes' was considered its 'imposing edifice'. The debate that ensued engulfed the very existence of the Company. In this bitter controversy about the question of monopolistic associations, it is apparent that those who thought from the viewpoint of trade were against the *compagnie* and its monopoly, whereas those who saw commerce as a part of general colonial set-up wanted the monopoly structure to continue with its privileged company.

The general mood in France is discernible from several memoirs and pamphlets. Anquetil Duperron forcefully contended that though it was true that the riches of the Compagnie des Indes were acquired by the state, those were banefully distributed amongst the members of the society. His plea was that the Company could never do commerce as profitably as free traders. He asserted that the pursuit of politics by the French and the English companies was opposed to the interest of commerce, for politics led to wars and raised prices inside and outside the kingdom.[43] However, it can be contended that this was not always the case. The Anglo-French commercial relations created conditions for political wars even in those regions where the companies did not operate, e.g. the American Continent. At the same time, one cannot doubt Duperron's inference that because the shareholders had acquired secure profit and exclusive rights, the company lacked the spirit of enterprise and experiment displayed by the 'free traders'.

The first generation of free trade economists saw and considered the colonies as useless, whereas the mercantilists regarded them as a necessity. With the rise of *nouvelle doctrines* and new economic ideas, the concept of empire also underwent an important change, and the means to control the empire—la Compagnie des Indes—was to be replaced by new methods. A systematic attack was launched by new methods. The Encyclopaedists and other writers or public servants launched a systematic attack through memoirs and pamphlets. We also come across a large number of memoirs that try to defend the exclusive status of the French Company by highlighting its useful role.

Among the earliest memoirs against the exclusive monopoly of the Company, were those of De Forbonnais of 1758 and L'abbé Rouband of 1768. [44] Although Montesquieu had also written a memoir in 1749, he had not taken up the subject of exclusive rights of the Company as a debatable issue. He treated these companies purely on the basis of their utility in a particular society and felt that the mode of its operation depended on the nature of its commerce.[45]

The liberty of commerce appeared to be the most advantageous mode for the state and for the private merchants. The judicious economists such as Nickols, Les Vourbonai and Rouband advocated for a long time the advantages that could be derived from free trade after the suspension of the exclusive privilege. Yet, these arguments were not considered sufficient to destroy the privilege of that exclusive association with which the state was so intimately connected in its financial dealings.[46]

An examination of the literature on the suppression of the French Company has brought to light the intrigues and factors other than commerce that played a decisive role in the final decision about the fate of the Company. In the debate which ensued in the French court regarding the future of the Company, M. L'abbé Morellet's arguments proved to be the most effective in the triumph of the free traders.[47] According to Duperron, 'C'est un tableau des crises, des embares, des malheurs de la compagnie des Indes'.[48] Morellet was employed by those who wished to take away the Company's monopoly.

Morellet firmly believed that the cost of maintaining exclusive privilege of the Company had proved burdensome to the state. Free and unregulated trade in place of exclusive commerce of the Company, would provide greater advantages to France.

According to Morellet, from 1756 to 1769 the Company suffered losses to the tune of 8,52,02,702 *livres tournois*.[49] He calculated the dividends on the independent revenue which revealed a steady decline with the passage of time, as is evident from the figures given in Table 2.1.[50]

TABLE 2.1: DIVIDENDS PAID BY THE FRENCH COMPANY TILL 1769

Year	Dividends in *livres*
1725	148
1736	136
1743	135
1756	85
1769	65

Source: L'abbé Morellet, *Mémoire*, 1769, BN.

The China trade of the Company witnessed a similar trend.[51] Morellet warned the Council that despite the assurances by the supporters of the Company, its condition was unlikely to improve in future. He was convinced that the past losses were caused by wasteful expenditures, the administrative structure of the Company and the frequent wars in Europe and in India. He tried to prove the futility of continuing with this exclusive Company at a time when the profits were fast diminishing. Morellet gave a detailed account of the Company's expenses that comprised the increasing sales in France and the cost of purchase in India after the invoice bills—drawn from the books of the Company.

This gradual decline in profit from 1764, as shown in Table 2.2, according to Morellet, could not be regarded as transitory and momentary. The declining profits from the commerce of the Company were caused by the troubles in India, especially in the last phase of the Company's existence and the impressive expansion of British power in India. He felt that these conditions were not going to alter in the near future. He concluded his account by stating that the profits were unlikely to rise, rather one would see them declining.[52] His solutions were radical: liquidating the commerce and the debts of the Company and opening up of the Indian trade to French private traders. To this Gournay added by way of suggestion a 5 per cent tax on all imports from India, 10 per cent on Chinese goods and 3.5 per cent on the goods coming from the Isles.[53]

The only important personality capable of counterbalancing the arguments of Morellet was Necker. He was still to become a minister in 1769 but he had already established his reputation as a financier and an able administrator. The government had utilized his services as a

TABLE 2.2: PROFITS MADE BY THE FRENCH COMPANY ON INDIAN GOODS

(*in livre tournois*)

Years	Sales	Purchase	Profits	%
1725-36	9,99,81,948	5,09,80,429	4,00,01,519	96.5
1736-43	8,85,38,635	4,57,14,320	4,32,24,315	93.7
1743-56	12,08,55,635	6,25,82,825	5,82,69,331	93.1
1756-64	Period of War, hence little returns			
1766	57,87,181	30,70,645	27,16,536	88.5
1767	1,04,67,779	65,71,395	38,96,394	59.3
1768	1,58,80,975	1,00,45,915	5,83,50,605	58.8

Source: L'abbé Morellet, *Mémoire*, 1769, BN.

banker in moments of financial crisis. His ambassador-like qualities and his links with Geneva bankers had carved out a specific role for him. He was a syndic of the Company and was instrumental in pulling it out from a tight situation in 1764.

Necker, Godehu and several shareholders and supporters of the Company found the calculations of L'abbé Morellet highly exaggerated and full of inaccuracies. Necker tried his best, rather belatedly, to defend the Company's performance but by that time it was already on its way out. He presented his arguments in his famous mémoire of 8 August 1769 and tried to demonstrate that the so-called advantage of free trade would exist only in theory and would go against the interest of the state.[54] He criticized Morellet for sacrificing experience for theory and facts for possibilities.[55] It was perhaps for the first time that a mathematical rule played a part in the controversy between the free traders and *negocians* and those who wished the continuation of commerce in the hands of the Company.[56] The main debate which continued even after the abolition of the Company in 1769 was concerned with two questions:

(a) whether the Indian commerce was useful for the state, and
(b) if it was useful, should it be exploited by an exclusive Company or (should it) be rendered open to all the merchants of the nation.[57]

There were as many arguments in favour of the trade with India as there were against it. The Encyclopaedists continued the arguments of Morellet for the defence of free trade.[58] They tried to show that the capital invested in commerce of the Company and its free revenue had constantly diminished since 1725; that the shareholders could not hope to re-establish and conserve their capital to continue with their commerce; that the profits would continue to decline; and that the shareholders were ignorant of the true state of affairs. Beaudeau in his writings demonstrated that the shareholders, through their exclusive Company, could not expect to exploit the commerce in India. This was also because of the relative strength of the English Company, whose purchases were immense and which traded in better quality goods and controlled a variety of merchandise.[59] He argued that despite its powerful position, the English Company could not sell all its goods by itself. It had to depend on the private trade of the French. The English superiority made little difference to them whether the French trade was conducted through a Company or by private means.

The critics of the Indo-French commerce argued that the trade of America and the Levant offered a vast variety of products and provided better market opportunities for the French traders—more useful and more advantageous than that of India. Similarly, it was suggested that the coffee from Moka would be of superior quality if purchased from the Levant.[60] It was also contended that the import of luxury items, such as muslin, in exchange for silver *piastres* was prejudicial not only to the French trade but to her industry as well—for example that of *batiste* (imitation muslin) and of *cambraiys* (imitation lace). The critics pointed out that the import of large quantities of beautiful handkerchiefs from Masulipatam, Madras and Palicat and from several other places in the Coromandel could have been replaced by the red handkerchiefs of Rouen de cholet, Vivares and Bearn by successful imitation and by employing the same thread.[61] The luxury items of the Company such as tea and silk were considered unnecessary and against national interest.

Those favouring close ties with India argued that the trade was as necessary to France as it was to any other nation; that the French Company through its annual sales, in which several foreign buyers participated, brought back more than the total bullion export to India; that it benefited the French manufacturers and producers who sent their goods to Asia; and that the Company offered employment to over 3,000 workers at Port L'Orient and another 4,000 sailors and entrepreneurs through the maritime trade.[62] The supporters of the monopoly believed that the free merchants were ill-equipped to face the obstacles of this long-distance trade; that their extreme greed to outdo one another would result in losses and lowering of the quality of their products; that the shortage of capital and the lack of staff would cause problems in assembling cargoes and that France would lose a vital market.[63] The French government also expected to gain financially by way of customs duties on Indian goods if the trade was thrown open to all merchants.[64] All these considerations were debated aloud and they engulfed the political scene of France throughout the 1760s and 1770s.

In this political debate over the desirability or otherwise of a privileged and monopolistic Company, the over-regulated and underfinanced feature of the Compagnie des Indes was blown up. It was done to prove that no reform short of free trade would mend the situation for France. This structural defect has been regarded by a number of historians as one of the primary reasons for the Company's failure. Marquis de Lally's extreme comment is worth noting. He wrote, 'I think that the state of Compagnie des Indes does not depend on the nature of its commerce. It appears to me that there are in its administration and its constitution, irretrievable abuses and vices.'[65]

Herbert Lüthy, while bringing out important dissimilarities between the structures of the English and the French companies revealed the essential difference in their roles in the politics of their respective countries.[66] The English Company was a commercial corporation of big shipowners of London who were partly bound to their government in the war for naval supremacy. But they knew how to defend their private interests. It was a real reciprocal alliance. The French Company on the contrary was the property of the king and of his administration. The shipowners held no special place. The Company was constrained during the period of war to arm its ships of commerce for facing the British warships. The vessels from L'Orient were placed under two incompatible uses and thus became a victim of military diversion. There is no denying the fact that this shortcoming in the company's organization affected it adversely. In the words of Boulle, it 'stifled private enterprise and encouraged business conservatism'.[67] However, it is difficult to blame the poor performance of the French Company after 1756 on its structural defects. We must keep in view the political state of India at that time while assessing the prospects of the two companies. In fact the trade of the Company had started reviving after 1763 as seen in the graph of the Company's performance.

The cumulative effect of all these developments was the inability of the French Company to defend itself against the mounting criticism. It succumbed to its political opponents when on 13 August 1769 the Compagnie des Indes was declared abolished.[68] The Decree of Council granted to the subjects of France the liberty of navigating and trading beyond the Cape of Good Hope. This Decree only suspended the privilege of the Company, and seemed to leave to the proprietors the power of resuming it but they decided to liquidate their concerns in such a manner as to secure the interest of their creditors. For this they offered to give up to the king all the ships of the Company (numbering 30), all the warehouses and other buildings belonging to them in Port L'Orient and in India, the property of their factories with the manufactures dependent on them, and all the naval and military stores. By the Edict of January 1770 the king created for their benefit a perpetual annuity of 12,00,000 *livres* instead of 4,65,00,000 as demanded by the proprietors.[69]

It is important to note that when the French Company was still debating the importance of Indian trade and the desirable type of relationship with the Indians, the English were providing form and structure to their Indian acquisitions. The English Company was also facing certain difficulties from the time of the Carnatic Wars, but it was not short of funds, for the territorial revenue had already solved that problem. The profit margin was fast decreasing because of a large volume of Indian trade was being carried on account of private individuals. This aspect, along with the Company's assumption of political power drew the attention of the English free merchants, the public and their Parliamentarians. The financial difficulties during the period 1767 to 1769 resulted in a public debate on the East India Company in the context of the deteriorating Indian situation. However, the solutions found to remedy these defects were quite different from those of the French. The British Parliament, through its Acts of 1773 and later of 1781 and 1784 tried to regulate the functioning of the Company and streamlined its administration. As Parry suggests, these Acts were based on the tacit recognition that the Company's purely commercial activities in India had become relatively unimportant.[70] It began to be recognized as a political authority entrusted with administrative responsibilities.

The private trading activities of the Europeans in India expanded enormously during the 1770s. The official response of the English Company to this major shift in the French policy towards India (after the abolition of the Compagnie des Indes) was quite different from that of its servants and traders in their private capacities. At the official level, the Anglo-French relationship was that of rivalry and competition while for the actual commercial operations, it was one of cooperation.

NOTES

1. Fernand Braudel, *Civilization and Capitalism 15th to 18th Centuries*, Vol. II: *The Wheels of Commerce*, London, 1982, p. 444.
2. K.N. Chaudhuri, *Trade and Civilization in the Indian Ocean: An Economic History from the Rise of Islam to 1750*, CUP, 1985, p. 82.
3. Ibid.
4. Lucy S. Sutherland, *The East Indian Company in Eighteenth Century Politics*, Oxford, 1952, p. 4.
5. Ibid., p. 1.
6. *Mémoire*, 9937, *Nouv. Acq.*, BN., Paris.
7. B.A. Irving, *The Commerce of India (Being a View of the Routes Successfully Taken*

by the Commerce between Europe and of the Political Effects Produced by the Several Changes), London, 1858, p. 39.

8. Pierre H. Boulle, 'French Mercantilism, Commercial Companies and Colonial Profitability', in L. Blussé and F. Gaastra (eds.), *Companies and Trade*, The Hague, 1981, p. 100.
9. M. L'abbé Baudeau (ed.), *Encyclopédie Mèthodique—Commerce*, Paris, 1783, Tome I, p. 560, BN.
10. Pierre H. Boulle, op. cit.
11. *Encyclopédie Méthodique*, op. cit., p. 560.
12. *Mémoire*, 9967, BN., op. cit.
13. Louis Dermigny, 'East India Company et Compagnie des Indes', in Michel Mollat (ed.), *Societes et Compagnies de Commerce en Orient et dans l'Ocean Indian*, Paris, 1970.
14. Holden Furber, *Rival Empires*, p. 201.
15. Fernand Braudel, *The Wheel of Commerce*, Vol. II, p. 451.
16. Ibid.
17. J.H. Parry, *Trade and Dominion: The European Overseas Empires in the Eighteenth Century*, London, 1971, p. 63.
18. The French king imposed upon the company a considerable colonizing effort in Madagascar and an expensive series of naval cruises designed to 'show the flag' in the East, in addition to the main task of establishing a commerce full of risks in itself.
19. Besides the character of state enterprise, Kaeppelin also considers this an important factor in its failure. He blames the tentative efforts of colonization at Madagascar causing large-scale dissipation of funds that could have been successfully utilized for the Indian commerce. This loss could never be repaired. Paul Kaeppelin, *La Compagnie des Indes Orientales et François Martin*, Paris, 1908, p. 646.
20. John Law, the Scottish financier, controlled the French economic affairs from 1717 to 1720, as opposed to the dominant Parisian financial circles. He established a direct connection between the colonial scheme that the Compagnie des Indes represented and the Royal Bank, which he created. Colonial commerce was expected to provide the major share of new credit to meet the expanding debt. The failure of Law was bound to affect the chief institution of the colonial trade when the crown assured ownership of Law's bank and the commitment to pay its debt, but it did not repay the principal creditor—La Compagnie des Indes. Instead it greatly undervalued its debt and made it permanent. The crown fixed the minimum dividend at 150 *livres tournois*, to be annually paid, and which could be increased if their profits justified. As the future condition was to prove, such high dividends were not justified.
21. *Arrêt du Conseil d'État du Roy*, 16 July 1719, F.R. 21779 (microfilm of BN at NAI).
22. Pierre H. Boulle, op. cit., p. 116.
23. Barbier, 'La Compagnie Française des Indes', *Revue Historique de L'Inde Française*, Pondichéry, III, 1919, p. 70 cited in S.P. Sen, *The French in India 1763-1816*, Delhi, 1971, p. 43.
24. C.H. Philips, *The East India Company 1784-1834*, Oxford, 1961, p. 3.
25. Ibid., p. 8.
26. S.P. Sen, op. cit., p. 40.

27. Holden Furber, op. cit., p. 209.
28. Abbé Raynal, *A Philosophical and Political History of the Settlements and Trade of the Europeans in the East and West Indies*, Vol. II, London, 1777, p. 120.
29. Susan J. Lawandowski, 'Changing Form and Function in the Ceremonial and the Colonial Port-City in India: An Historical Analysis of Madurai and Madras', *Modern Asian Studies*, Vol. 11, No. 2, 1977, pp. 183-212.
30. Indrani Ray, 'The French Company and the Merchants of Bengal: 1680-1735', *IESHR*, Vol. VIII, 1971, pp. 41-55.
31. Ibid.
32. E. Divien, op. cit., p. 31.
33. Mémoire sur le commerce de L'Inde (1750-1814) et sur la politique à mener envers les anglais et les princes Indiens-Inde, corresp. gén., carton 372, dossier 368, Archives D'Outre-mer.
34. C.S. Srinivasachari, op. cit., p. 162.
35. J.L. Racine, 'Esquisse d'une Histoire Commercial de Pondichérry jusqu'en 1954', *Revue Historique*, Vol. 10, 1972, pp. 1-80. In 1741, 16 ships left for the east, 7 in 1742, in 1743 and 1744 only 9 ships each year, 8 ships in 1745, 7 ships in 1746, 22 ships in 1747, and in 1748, 21 ships. The English witnessed a similar trend. In five years from 1708-9 to 1712-13, they had dispatched an average of 11 ships every year. This increased to 20 ships a year during 1743-4 to 1747-8. H. Dodwell, op. cit., p. 109.
36. Marguerite V. Labernadie, *Le Vieux Pondichéry 1673-1815, Histoire d'une ville colonial Française*, Paris, 1936, p. 335.
37. J.L. Racine, 'Esquisse d'une Histoire Commerce de Pondichéry jusquén 1954', op. cit.
38. Mémoire sur L'Inde à M. De Convoy (1784) C^2 113 (microfilm), p. 17, AN.
39. Mémoire Des Établissemens Française en Asie et Principalement de ceux de Bengale, 1777, F.R. 9367 (microfilm), BN.
40. Abbé Raynal, op. cit., p. 152.
41. See Appendix I.
42. Anquetil Duperron, *L'Inde en Rapport avec L'Europe*, Paris, 1798, p. 404.
43. Ibid., p. 232.
44. L'abbé Rouband, 'La Politique Indien on Considerations sur les colonies des Indes Orientales' (1768), cited in Anquetil Duperron, op. cit., p. 275.
45. Montesquieu, 'En Partie pour les Compagnie de Commerce' (1749), cited in Duperron, op. cit., p. 210.
46. Mémoire Des Établissemens Française en Asia, F.R. 9367 (microfilm), BN.
47. L'abbé Morellet, Mémoire sur la situation actuelle de la Compagnie des Indes (1769), F.R. 9367, BN.
48. 'It is a time of crisis, of difficulty, of bad times of the Compagnie des Indes', Anquetil Duperron, op. cit., p. 278.
49. Morellet, op. cit., p. 120.
50. Ibid., p. 121.
51. Ibid., p. 126. In case of China, the percentage of profit ultimately declined from 104.5 in 1725 to 116.66 in 1743 and 67.66 in 1768. The Indian commerce comprised Pondicherry, the Coast, Bengal, the pepper trade of Malabar and coffee of Moka.
52. Ibid., p. 127.
53. Henry Weber, *La Compagnie Française des Indes 1604-1875*, Paris, 1904, p. 587.

54. M. Necker, Reponse au Mèmoire de L'abbé Morellet', F.R. 9367 (microfilm), BN.
55. 'Il me semble le defenseur de la compagnie d'une partie de votre ouvrage est un attaque continuelle livrè à l'experience par la théorie et aux faits par les possibilités', ibid.
56. From the end of the seventeenth century and throughout the first half of the eighteenth century, mercantilism in France faced opposition from Vauban, Bois Guillebert and d'Argenson. This resistance grew with Gournay and took a definite form under Quesney. Together, they came to be known as the Physiocrats. They included some prominent economists of the period such as Marquis de Mirabeau, Turgot, Abbé Baudeau, Mercier la Rivière, Dupont de Némours, Letrône, Abbé Morellet, etc. They regarded the monopoly of the Compagnie des Indes as a 'monstrous edifice', and believed that its ruin would signify the triumph of a new era.
57. *Mémoire* (undated and anonymous), C[2] 105 (microfilm), AN.
58. M. L'abbé Baudeau (ed.), *Encyclopédie Mèthodique—Commerce*, Tome I, Paris, 1783, p. 635.
59. Ibid.
60. *Mémoire sur la Compagnie et d'Inde*, C[2] 105 (microfilm), AN.
61. Ibid.
62. Réfléxions sur le project de rendre de commerce de l'asie libre et le faire exployer par des armateurs particuliers (1769), C[2] 256 (microfilm), AN.
63. Baudeau, op. cit., pp. 621-5.
64. In the period of free trade, the French government received Droit d'Indult on the imports from India valued a 15,00,000 *livres* (about £ 62,500). Apart from Droit d'Indult, a tax of 25 *livres* (together with an additional tax of 10 sous on each *livre*) was payable in every hundred weight of Indian goods imported directly from India. If the goods were imported through any foreign European nation, the tax rate was doubled.
Reply to the Observations of the French Directors Memorial from the Deputies of the Principal Commercial Towns, Paris, 1787, *Manuscripts on British India*, CPL.
65. Le Comte de Laugragnais, *Mémoire sur la Compagnie des Indes*, Paris, 1786, pp. 80-1, BN.
66. Herbert Lüthy, *Le Banque Protestante en France 1730-1790*, Paris, 1961, Tome II, p. 379.
67. Pierre H. Boulle, 'French Mercantilism, Commercial Companies and Colonial Profitability', in L. Blussé and F. Gaastra (eds.), *Companies and Trade*, The Hague, 1981, pp. 97-117.
68. Arrêst du Conseil d'État du Roi Concernant le Commerce de l'Inde, 13 August 1769, AD XI-41, AN.
69. Abbé Raynal, op. cit., Vol. II, pp. 159-60.
70. J.H. Parry, *Trade and Dominion: The European Overseas Empires in the Eighteenth Century*, London, 1971, p. 171.

Chapter 3

The Period of French Free Trade

IN THE 1760s the English had begun to regulate the vast colonial market through political means. In Europe, they had made rapid strides in the economic and political fields and gained substantial lead in the sphere of industry and technology. In India, they had succeeded in obtaining the rich and fertile trading zone comprising 'Northern Circars' on the Coromandel Coast, established their control over the revenues of Carnatic and then acquired the country's wealthiest province of India—Bengal. These acquisitions not only solved their immediate financial problems but also created private interest groups as a key factor in their future expansion. The endeavours of the French Company gave way to some enterprising private traders. One of the reasons for the continuation of the French trade in India, and its revival to a certain extent, was the collaboration between the private interest groups of England and France.

FRENCH CLAIMS AFTER 1769

The immediate problem, which arose for the English after the dissolution of the French Company, was how to treat the French private traders in India. The French had already demanded from the English their right to establish factories and to station European agents at pleasure, without restraint throughout the provinces; total exemption of their European residents, agents and servants from the jurisdiction of the Country Courts; exemption from all duties without any exception even for prohibited goods on the payment of 2.5 per cent *ad valorem* on articles of commerce; the privilege of issuing '*dastaks*' as free passport for their merchandise to cover it from all duties and impediments; free trade in cloth, sugar, raw silk, salt, saltpetre by express words in their *firmans* and in opium and all other goods and merchandise whatever, under the word '*ghera*'. The privilege of going to and trading at such regions and places as they deemed fit, besides several other privileges they claimed to have possessed in Bengal.[1] In other words, the French desired all those privileges which the English enjoyed before 1765.

The bone of contention was the issue of the rights and privileges granted through 'firmans'. The Dutch had obtained them in 1712. The French also received them in 1730, and that brought them on an equal footing with the Dutch. The French joined the Dutch in claiming that only the person who granted them could recall the *firmans*. By these oppositions, the duties paid by the French, the Dutch and the Danish companies were reduced from 3.5 to 2.5 per cent, whereas the private foreign traders paid 4 per cent. Hence, the doubt arose after the dissolution of the French Company in 1769 whereby the private traders replaced the Company. They were considered to be individual traders by the English Company and thus liable to be charged 4 per cent duty. Mons. Chevalier and numerous French merchants contested the English viewpoint. Law de Lauriston argued that the company had no existence, no right of action except what the nation conferred on it. So the privileges that the Company enjoyed belonged to the nation at large. Even in the Treaty Settlements, it was mentioned that 'England shall restore to France the possessions' and not 'English Company shall restore to the French Company'.[2] They could not use the term 'company' for it was totally uncertain whether the Company existed or not, its annihilation or existence depending merely on the will of the king. Nor could its fate in any degree affect the privileges granted to the nation. On 8 April 1773, the English Board resolved that the French were not entitled to hold any factories or places of trade except what they held in 1749, as restricted by the Treaty of 1763.[3] It was also decided that the French had no right to send European agents or to appoint residents except at their own factories without the leave of the English government. The English also denied the extraterritorial jurisdiction that the French claimed. Later, on 24 March 1777 the English Board of Revenue conceded the point and issued instructions for charging the French with no more than 2.5 per cent duty with a salvo of the right to charge more when it should be found expedient.[4]

In Coromandel, the issue of customs duties arose when the French goods at Yanaon were stopped by the renter of Samal Cotah.[5] Though later he allowed them to pass, yet he sought clarification on it from the English. The English Board was of the opinion that the French were subject to the *Juncan* and other *circar* duties that the English had paid before these *circars* became their property. The French Governor Mons. Law, in his application of 1771 to the Council and to Robert Harland, insisted that French had from time immemorial and ever since their establishment at Yanaon, possessed immunities founded on authentic '*parwanahs*' of Aurangzeb and of the *subas* of the Deccan and of the Rajas.[6] The English tried to ascertain this claim by writing to several zamindars of Rajamundry where the French factory of Yanaon was situated.[7] They came to the conclusion that the French Company's privileges had no better authority than the consent of the zamindars to whom the factory made presents for every privilege they enjoyed, even that of passing the Company's long cloth. By means of these presents they obtained *parwanahs* from the amuldars granting them the privilege of trading duty-free. The English believed that the private traders were never exempted from duties, though sometimes they were excused by making presents to the zamindars. The English further believed that the French combined the trade of their company and their individuals together. The English felt sure that in and before 1749, the French paid duties upon private trade in the *circars* except when exempted by zamindars through presents and by the collectors of the customs. It was obvious that in granting the exemptions, the Indian princes and zamindars wished to increase their own industries and were indifferent to the fact whether the French commerce was carried on by a company or by individuals. They were only concerned with trade in general. The Resident's passport was considered enough to make the goods pass free of duty.

The English argued that they had wrested the place (i.e. Masulipatam) for which the *parwanah* was issued, but the French had forfeited all title to commercial privilege with the abolition of their Company. At the time of making the grants, the end of the Company could not have been foreseen by the country government. These concessions, it was contended, were given to a public company or a collective body of merchants and not to the individuals.[8]

Notwithstanding their official pronouncements against the French claims during 1770s, the English relented, probably to avoid another major rupture, which they could ill-afford at that time. In America, trouble was brewing and in India the political alignments were far from conducive to the English interest. Yet the official disputes had not ended even after the Treaty of Versailles in 1783. The disputed issues were taken up later at the time of the Cathcart-Souillac Convention in 1786.

FOREIGN TRADE (1763-1784)

An immediate result of the Seven Years War and the abolition of the French Company was a sharp decline in the French trade from 1764 to 1771 before it began to pick up again. That the situation started improving from 1773 was evident from their trade performance shown in Graph 3.1 but it was not yet free from the difficulties faced by the French private traders. It was necessary for all the *armateurs* to procure a passport from the *Bureau de la Compagnie* before sending off their ships for India. It could only be obtained at Paris. This caused prolonged delays and proved prejudicial to the trading activities of the French in Asia. The passports also specified the name of the port for fitting out ships. When the commerce was declared free, Pondicherry was too feeble to take an active part in this liberty.[9] On the one hand, Carnatic continued to witness political turmoil affecting the procurement of merchandise, and on the other hand the serious famine in Bengal caused real shortage of funds.

Another problem faced by the French *armateurs* was of assembling good cargo. When the trade was thrown open to the speculators of the cities of Marseilles, Bordeaux, La Rochelle, Nantes and L'Orient, these *negociants* had little knowledge of the market structure of the distant region. There was the usual risk of the long travels and unfamiliar nature of transactions. The cargo was badly assorted and they obtained Indian goods at second or third hands instead of buying them directly from the interior. It was difficult to maintain a systematic correspondence. The biggest problem was of financing the long voyages with sufficient cargo. While the French merchants neglected assorting their cargo of different varieties of cloth, the English, the Dutch and the Danes, were better served by their respective agents. During this period London, Amsterdam and Copenhagen had become the principal centres of sale of the East Indian goods.[10]

It is evident from the trade statistics that in the absence of the Company, the French faced some initial problem. The profits on the articles exported from France remained negligible but then the loading of their ships was merely in wines and *eau-de-vie.* The arrival of French ships in 1771—*Le Massiac, Le Mars* and *Le Pretan,* charged with Indian goods did not signify fruits of the liberty of commerce, as was then believed. In fact, most of the cargo consisted of those articles that had been contracted by the Compagnie des Indes through Mons. Law and Mons. Chevalier. The English houses at Madras had also rendered liberal

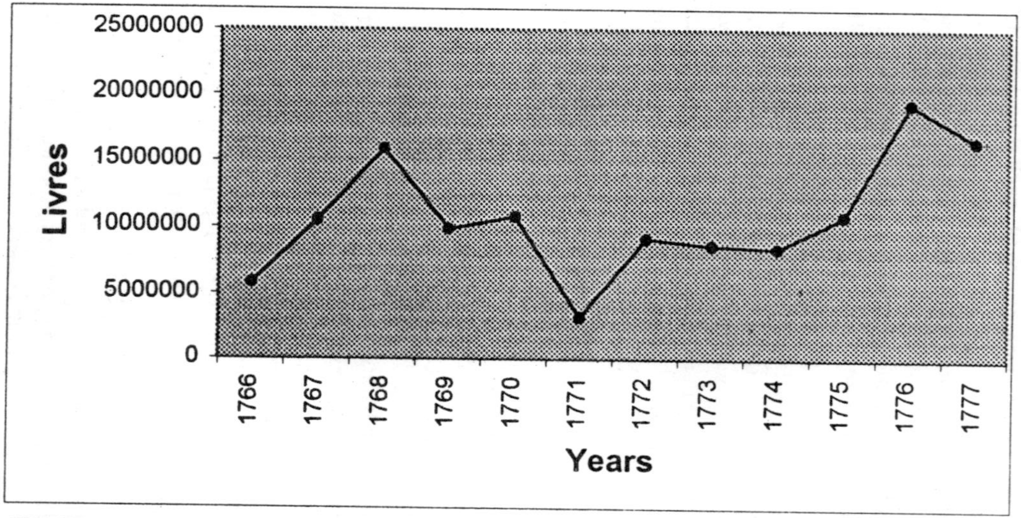

GRAPH 3.1: SALE OF INDIAN GOODS DURING THE PERIOD OF FREE TRADE (1766-77) in *Livres Tournois*

Source: Série 8AQ-377 and Serié $C^{2}56$ (microfilm), AN, Paris.

assistance and facilitated their purchases.[11] The chiefs of different French *comptoirs* were sure that through Chevalier, in association with the English, they would manage complete shipments from Bengal and through Law de Lauriston from Pondicherry. Thus, by 1773 the major problem, that of financing ships, was overcome by extensive borrowings from the British subjects or their banking houses.

Some of the trade voyages turned out to be very successful. The private enterprises between 1776 and 1778 made by M. Grand-Clos-Melè of St. Malo and M. Amiraux of La Rochelle represented phenomenal success.[12] The cargo of their ships was directed by Moracin and La Rochette, both of whom had profound knowledge of the Indian trade. During the period of free trade 340 ships totalling 1,48,945 tons were sent to the East Indies. In the most prosperous period of 1774, 1775 and 1776, 118 ships left for India with a combined capacity of 57,190 tons thus making an annual average of 29 ships. The average for the entire period up to 1784 was 21 ships a year.[13] Thirty-four shipments had been made from Bordeaux between 1769 and 1785, and during the same period 72 ships left Marseilles for the Indian Ocean. According to Paul Butel, the Bordeaux merchants had transferred some of their capital investments from the West Indies to the Indian trade because of decline in profits in the West Indian trade. A vast fund of Spanish *piastres* was available at Bordeaux between 1783 and 1785 from Saint Dominique. This fund was used for investment for their purchases in India particularly in the 'country' trade.[14] At this time the American War of Independence broke out which had global repercussions and it totally dislocated the Indian trade. Yet considering the problems faced by the private traders of France, the extent of trade revival achieved by them appears spectacular.[15] Weber estimates the loss of Coromandel commerce at as much as 20.5 per cent after deducting all the charges, interest on borrowed sum and insurance. However, this situation existed only for a short while. Besides, similar trends are discernible in the English trade as well.

The most important component of the French exports to Coromandel and the East Indies was bullion, which was acquired from Spain. Strong mercantilist views were expressed against the export of silver *specie* to India in exchange for luxury goods. It was regarded as a great financial loss. The defenders of the Indian trade argued that the silver *piastres* brought by France as a fruit of commerce with Spain was not procured from the country silver. Moreover France received back more than what she sent to India.[16]

One does not find separate statistical information of the French commercial activities in the Coromandel region up to 1785, as we find in the case of the English Company. Hence it is difficult to ascertain the exact importance of this region in the French total exports. Yet a rough estimate can be made from the list of merchant ships that sailed from France to different destinations in India. There is some discrepancy in the account provided by William Milburn and the one given by Louis Dermigny. The account of Louis Dermigny suggests that a total of 349 ships left for the East, of which 30 went to the Coromandel.[17] Other point to be noted is that the Coromandel goods formed a portion of the cargo of even those ships that were marked for places other than Pondicherry. Some of these goods could be seen in the cargo of the Bengal ships and even of the ships going to Isle de France.

The French trade, after a steep decline between 1769 and 1771, began to stabilize and showed a significant upward trend from 1773. This is evident from the various notes and information supplied by the British agents. One of the letters to Palk informs him of the arrival of three king's ships and at least eight private merchant ships from France. Together the first three brought about Rs. 7,00,000 worth of silver, 100 soldiers and 1,50,000 dollars for the principal gentlemen of Pondicherry, and a large quantity of European goods sold at Pondicherry and in Bengal.[18] The same source gives information of the arrival of four ships at Pondicherry in 1775. Their cargo included broad cloth, copper, iron, lead, golden thread, wine, brandy and other European goods. They also brought some weapons and firearms. The French trade had revived to such an appreciable extent because of the low tariff duty of 2.5 instead of 4 per cent.[19] The English officials began to complain of the low state of the market in 1776. They charged that the competition of the French in the same articles of trade had been the main cause of its decline as the commodities imported by the French private merchants had an additional advantage of low customs duties compared to the English officials trading in their personal capacity in the Company's ships.[20]

Bartolomeo also refers to the French ships laden with wine, iron, cannons, firearms and French cloths reaching the eastern coast during the period of free trade.[21] They disposed of the bulk of these commodities to the English or to their allies, who employed these very cannons and arms against the French troops. The cargo sent from France usually included iron. India produced only a small quantity of iron made of ore and collected from the upper surface of the mines. However, Indian iron was very soft and flexible, consumed by a few workshops primarily for manufacturing keys, chains and other small instruments.[22] The foreign iron was used in making circles and in binding wheels.[23] The steel (*anciers*) made in India was apparently of excellent quality and was usually made from melted iron. The steel imported from Europe was in the form of small squares, bars and plates and exported by France to the value of 3,00,000 francs. [24]

The French also sold a small quantity of copper (cuivre) but the Indians purchased only red copper for making utensils. The yellow copper did not sell. The Indians, it seems, did not have copper mines in the south, and a few which existed in the northern region produced low quality copper that primarily used for coinage.[25] The price of copper depended upon its demand and the quantity of imports. The French procured part of their copper from the Dutch (who alone traded with Japan, the leading producer of this metal). The French exported a substantial part of their copper to Masulipatam where it was used for coining *doulis*, small coins used in daily business transactions.[26] The English and the Swedes sold their copper at 70 to 80 gold *pagodas* per bar, whereas the French could sell it for as high as 84 *pagodas* 9 *fanams.*[27] The French exported 74,00,000 francs worth of copper to India. Lead also had some demand in the foreign settlements where the profit margin was reasonable but the French did not handle this trade effectively. They also tried to sell clocks but did not succeed. The sale of clocks had really picked up in Europe since the mid-eighteenth century but it was a product of industrialized regions where wages were determined by hours. In India, despite some commercialization, the sense of time had not yet developed. Of all their export items, golden threads (*fils d'or*) were among the most important articles from which the French made some profit. It was used for ornamental purposes (on women's robes and children's dresses). The French exported 38,00,000 francs worth of *fils d'or*.[28]

Table 3.1 clearly reveals that the most prosperous phase of the private trade was from 1773 to 1776. It declined during the American War of Independence but revived from 1783 till 1785 when the private trade gave way to another company.

Wine constituted the most important article of commerce for the French. It was a cumbersome commodity, because of the volume of space it occupied. *Vins de Bordeaux* and *Vins de of Madère*, were the two varieties of wine consumed entirely by the European population

TABLE 3.1: SHIPMENTS FROM FRANCE TO THE EAST INDIES (1769-85)

Years	Mauritius	China	Moka	Bengal	Pondicherry	Various Ports	Mozambique	Mahé	Chandernagar	Satavia	Total
1769	3	–	–	3	–	–	–	–	–	–	6
1770	4	2	–	–	–	–	–	–	–	–	6
1771	5	5	1	2	–	–	1	–	–	–	15
1772	6	3	2	5	–	1	–	–	–	–	16
1773	7	4	2	6	3	–	–	–	–	–	22
1774	13	5	1	4	1	1	–	1	–	–	26
1775	10	6	–	4	3	3	–	3	2	–	31
1776	13	6	–	7	6	3	–	2	1	–	38
1777	13	7	1	6	2	–	–	–	–	–	29
1778	5	3	–	–	–	2	3	–	–	–	13
1779	2	–	–	–	–	–	–	–	–	–	2
1780	17	–	–	–	–	–	–	–	–	–	17
1781	10	–	–	–	–	7	–	–	–	–	17
1782	8	–	1	–	–	3	–	1	–	–	13
1783	8	6	–	4	3	12	–	3	–	2	38
1784	9	6	1	8	4	4	–	–	–	1	33
1785	13	–	–	3	2	1	–	2	–	–	21

Source: William Milburn, *Oriental Commerce*, Vol. 1, London, 1810, p. 402.

living in India.[29] The Indians did not prefer wine and so the market remained limited. '*Vin de caisse*' (wine in bottles) had a better sale than '*Vin de futaille*' (wine in casks). The French also exported a small quantity of '*eau de vie*' but it hardly fetched any profit. The French imported items were mostly bought by six local merchants of the small bazaar located in the 'white town' of Pondicherry. From this bazaar the products were sent to distant towns like Madras, Tranquebar, etc.[30]

Among the Europeans, the French had a special name for selling firearms to the Indians, though very often the quality was bad and occasionally obsolete. According to Flaix these included finished guns of one or two cuts, pistols, bronze cannons of different capacities and service guns without bayonets.[31] The Indian princes and smaller lords desired these weapons but the English never hesitated in placing all kinds of obstacles on their sale through political means. Officials of the English Company urged the authorities to emulate the French and other European nations by exporting military stores for sale. It was argued that the French used to bring 200 to 500 maunds of arms annually besides cannons by which they made 'large purchases of pepper to the prejudice of your (English) investment and by this practice they ingratiate themselves with the country powers and greatly injure your influence with them'.[32] These officials suggested that 'good policy requires that you should interfere in this lucrative branch of commerce'.[33] The French authorities were warned by their own officials to guard against the sale of arms to the various princes in India. It was pointed out that during the period of free trade this sale did not differentiate between the supporters and enemies of the French because of the profit motive and hence proved prejudicial to the French interest in India.[34]

As regards the export of French cloth, their Company or traders never showed keen interest by placing the exact demand or encouraging their export by popularizing them. The semi-finished londrins[35] (imitated cloth) were sold for the same price as the finished ones. The Company charged the same rate for all the colours whereas the red[36] cloth fetched Rs. 2 more.

It is evident from this account that like other European nations, the French faced extreme difficulty in marketing their products in India. The sale of French goods was extremely limited. It was further affected because of the political domination of the English Company, which traded in similar products. Despite a vast variety of commercial items, from Bordeaux wines, firearms and metals to silk stuffs and the gold brocaded fabrics (*dorures*) of Lyon, the French had to depend on the regular supply of silver *piastres* obtained from Spain, and coined into money in their mints, in order to sustain their Asian trade.

The English exports to the Coromandel were as varied and of as small quantities as the French. They also faced a similar problem of marketing their products. For a long period the deficit between the export and import was met by the flow of bullion. Gradually the export cargo consisted of two categories of products: (a) woollens, and (b) metals.

The former included 'broadcloth of fine, double colour (golden and saffron) and ordinary *genre, perpetuanoes* of fine and ordinary types, white serges, camblets, shalloons, jeanets, velvets, casimirs, calamancoes and brocades. There were several types of metals, which the English Company exported to India, though in small quantities, such as copper, lead, sheet lead, iron and steel. The last three items had no demand as commercial products. Woollens constituted the largest proportion of the total export from England. The Company's constant endeavours to find new and wider markets for the woollens and to protect them from foreign competition by means of high protective tariffs failed to yield results. The proportion of woollens to the total merchandise continued to decline from 71 per cent in the period 1708-20, to 66 per cent in 1721-30, and 52.5 per cent in 1731-40, then rose to 59 per cent in 1741-50 before declining to 54 per cent in the period 1751-60.[37]

The decline in the sale of woollens was attributed to several factors by the Select Committee in its report in 1791. It was mentioned in the report that the Company had lost much of this trade owing to the bad quality of the export, rise in price, non-compliance with indents and improper assortments. As a consequence, almost the whole of the finer sorts of broad cloth and a considerable proportion of the coarser variety began to be supplied by other traders. Among the immediate factors which hindered the market for this item was the state of anarchy and confusion which continued uninterrupted for several years not only in India but in Persia and South Asia as well.[38] However, the most important factor, which the English Company ignored, was the unsuitability of this product in warm weather conditions, because of which its demand in the Coromandel remained insignificant.

In the absence of any other commodity which could capture the Indian market and reduce the lopsided trade between England and India, the English Company tried every means to increase the export of metals. However, its volume remained insignificant. In the period between 1751 and 1760, the metal export to India by the English Company was worth £. 9,41,512.[39]

Another interesting feature of the English Company's exports to India was the share of the Madras Presidency in it. In the period between 1708 and 1757, the Madras Presidency received 43.4 per cent of the total exports to India. Of the total bullion imported into India, 49 per cent reached the Madras Presidency, while it received only 27 per cent of the total merchandise exported to India.[40] It seems that the two rival European companies were concentrating their commercial activities in the eastern region after the 1760s because of the disturbed political conditions in the northern and central region, and owing to the rise of Hyder Ali in Mysore and the Maratha ascendancy in the western region. One also notices a significant change in the export trade to India by the English Company after the assumption of the Diwani of Bengal in 1765. Till then, the Company had brought a large proportion of bullion to maintain the trade. It varied from £ 7,00,000 to 1 million annually.[41] After 1765, the Company gained control of the public revenues and utilized the surplus revenues for investment purposes. The flow of bullion shifted into the Chinese channel. The English exports henceforth contained only broadcloth items and metals.

It is evident from Table 3.2 that the English exports to Fort St. George, could never stabilize, and it continued to fluctuate during 1765-84.

An interesting aspect of the English export to India was the virtual absence of its demand among the local inhabitants. Madras was the only Presidency, where some of these goods could be sold on profit. But the volume of unsold goods, as shown in Table 3.3, made it obvious that the English Company, despite its political superiority, was unable to sell its products successfully. In fact, copper was the only item which had some demand in India, but it was broadcloth that provided relatively higher margin of profit though only for a brief period. According to K.N. Chaudhuri, in the 1740s, the sale of Company goods in India was good because of the Anglo-French wars and the expansion of the

TABLE 3.2: INVOICE AMOUNT OF ENGLISH EXPORTS TO FORT ST. GEORGE (1765-84)

Year	Amount in £ St.
1765	1,28,510
1766	1,13,427
1767	1,12,502
1768	1,26,093
1769	1,23,777
1770	55,031
1771	83,781
1772	99,187
1773	1,44,360
1774	99,947
1775	89,150
1776	1,08,689
1777	1,11,443
1778	98,471
1779	1,21,846
1780	88,753
1781	1,30,662
1782	1,39,643
1783	65,662
1784	57,082

Source: Appendix E2, MS 370 (microfilm) Home Misc. Series, IOR.

TABLE 3.3: STATE OF UNSOLD ENGLISH GOODS AT FORT ST. GEORGE (1769-73)

Year	Broad cloth	Perpetuances	Lead	Copper
1769-70	34,234	4,562	160	2,200
1770-1	19,198	4,160	2,393	365
1771-2	13,071	3,662	1,970	124
1772-3	37,393	2,004	612	58

Source: East India House, 21 March 1775, *Add. Ms* 38398 (microfilm), p. 123, Br. Mus.

Company's army. However, there was no marked rise in the selling price of broadcloth.[42] The high expectation in the shipments adversely affecting the future demand.

The imports from Coromandel ports to Europe consisted primarily of textile items. The commodity composition from this region suggests that it differed greatly from the other regions. The luxury items constituted a substantial proportion of the export cargo in the case of Bengal and Malabar. The Coromandel exports, on the other hand, comprised a wide range of products of coarse variety which suited the needs of the south-eastern region, the people around the Red Sea, the African Coast and the plantation labourers of the 'New World'. Ashin Das Gupta's contention that the principal purchasers of Indian cloth or other products were not the aristocrats but the common people of the Middle Eastern towns and that it was their taste and their purse which shaped the market in Western Asia, applies most appropriately to the Coromandel products.[43] This region did produce a few rich and luxurious varieties but the general textile composition was meant for the average or poorer people.

The region between Masulipatam and Nagapatnam produced a variety of cotton cloth, which included the long cloth or *Guinea* cloth, *Salempore* and *Betilla*. The long cloth was usually a low-grade stout cotton cloth sold in bulk and was graded into six varieties. The white *Guinea* cloth of north Coromandel was popular in the Red Sea and the Levant. It was used for printing in Europe. The southern Coromandel region produced blue, red and striped *Guinea* cloth. The English called it long cloth as its each piece was twice the size of other calicoes. It was used in the Guinea Coast and in America by plantation-owners for their slaves. Another category of calico was *Salempore*. There was a wide range of this variety. *Percales* and *Moories* were also calicoes but of different varieties. *Muslin* was a more loosely woven cloth, spun from a fine yarn. In south India it was called *Betilla* or *Beatilla or Betteela*. It was in great demand in South-East Asia and Persia. *Guinea* cloth, *Salempore* and *Betilla* had a special advantage as trade items. They could be sold as manufactured products in the primary market or as a semi-finished item for printing, painting or dyeing. The handkerchiefs, which included red and blue bordered varieties and checks of different sizes, had a special market in Europe, particularly in France.[44]

Another item, which was seen in small quantities in the European ships leaving the Coromandel Coast, was red wood. It was used for preparing dyes. This article was known by the name of *Vartengnen* in Tamil while the Portuguese and the Europeans called it *Sapan* wood.[45] It was found on the eastern coast and was of the same quality as the one from Brazil. However, the Indian *Sapan* wood gave a very dense colour compared to the Brazilian variety. The French called it *bois rouge* and sold it in foreign markets. The English merchants also sent some of the good quality redwood to China.

The extent to which the French trade began to depend on the political condition can be judged by the fact that in ten years from 1776 to 1785, the Armenian merchants had exported from Masulipatam 78,037 pieces of *chay* goods worth Rs.1,60,992, the English and the native merchants exported 1,47,747 pieces valued at Rs. 4,22,612, while the French merchants carried 47,210 pieces of *chay* goods worth Rs.1,76,344.[46] Of this, 14,097 pieces valued at Rs. 59,904 were exported in a single year, i.e. 1785, when the two European powers enjoyed cordial relations.

The trade between India and France can be divided into two branches —one branch gave about 100 per cent gross profit whereas the second branch fetched about 70 per cent only.[47] The former branch included coffee, pepper, cowri or cowrees, while the latter comprised of all types of textiles including linen, handkerchiefs and muslins. Not covered in this description are items like red wood and *rattan*, which constituted a fraction of the total embargo. The second category of goods constituted the bulk of the Coromandel exports. The profit margins varied greatly according to the political-economic situations.

The American War of Independence had a negative impact on the Indian trade. This is evident from Graph 3.1. The two major powers that controlled a considerable part of the external commerce on the Coromandel Coast fought in India on issues totally alien to India. Trade badly suffered during this period when the ships were heavily charged with troops and munitions. The administrative councils were too busy in war preparations and operations to give proper attention to the sale and purchase of merchandise. The additional expenditure entailed on this account had to be recovered from trade profits. Furthermore, these wars resulted in a large-scale migration of weavers and producers. The Anglo-Mysore War brought greater misery to the local inhabitants and in certain districts caused dislocation of the entire production organization. The trade figures of the two European powers clearly demonstrate it. As shown in Tables 3.4 and 3.5 respectively, the sale value of the Indian goods started stabilizing gradually in mid-1770s before the beginning of the American War of Independence.

The French picked up after a complete dislocation from 1784, when out of the sales at L'Orient of 1,69,80,962 *livres* from the East, the Indian share was of 77,07,016 *livres*.[48]

The Anglo-French relationship continued to remain strained at the regional level over the procurement of Indian textile goods. Here the competition was intense. In this sphere, the French offered a stiff challenge despite their obvious limitations. The profit margin on the Coromandel goods was not substantial but they yielded an assured return and provided a stable market to the English, unlike several other products. The annual profits varied from 40 per cent on sale amount

TABLE 3.4: SALE VALUE OF THE FRENCH IMPORTS FROM INDIA AND CHINA (1766-77)

Year	Merchandise from India (*in livres*)	Merchandise from China (*in livres*)	General total
1766	58,31,782.0.0	71,22,399.0.0	1,29,54,181.0.0
1767	1,05,22,030.0.0	44,99,656.0.0	1,50,21,686.0.0
1768	1,59,47,950.0.0	58,41,223.0.0	2,17,89,173.0.0
1769	99,05,021.0.0	48,94,359.0.0	1,47,99,380.0.0
1770	1,08,16,224.0.0	53,54,972.0.0	61,71,196.09.0
1771	32,56,620.2.5	51,73,712.13.4	84,30,332.15.9
1772	91,80,129.17.3	46,99,843.2.7	38,79,972.19.10
1773	87,11,734.9.11	58,22,047.18.0	1,45,33,782.7.11
1774	84,75,691.14.4	85,75,808.7.5	1,70,51,500.1.9
1775	1,09,06,218.17.1	1,09,12,593.12.0	2,12,18,812.9.1
1776	1,94,02,422.1.10	65,04,327.17.6	2,59,06,749.19.4
1777	1,66,16,961.14.6	1,01,10,327.4.0	2,67,27,288.18.6

Sources: *État du produit net d'Escompte des Importations et du droit d'Indult par la compagnie*, 8 AQ 377 (AN) and M. Abbé Baudeau, *Encyclopedie Méthodique—Commerce, 1783-84*, tome II (BN).

TABLE 3.5: IMPORTS DURING THE PERIOD OF FRENCH FREE TRADE (1771-82)

(*in livres*)

Year	Goods from China	Common articles from India & China	Goods from India	Total
1771	76,80,540	19,656	49,02,093	1,26,02,289
1772	44,64,090	11,775	1,26,53,812	1,71,39,677
1773	61,38,928	28,270	1,82,18,438	2,43,83,636
1774	78,23,230	21,054	1,23,60,950	2,02,05,234
1775	1,21,58,096	1,77,010	1,75,49,042	2,98,84,148
1776	17,06,478	1,63,785	3,09,75,963	3,28,46,226
Years of Wars				
1777	1,95,290	2,023	14,21,327	16,18,641
1778	–	–	45,186	–
1779	1,82,336	6,113	63,407	2,51,856
1780	8,46,202	50,984	5,01,626	13,98,812
1781	–	–	–	–
1782	644	7,776	4,04,522	4,12,942

Source: Tableau de 'Importation en France des Marchandises de L'Inde (1771-82), *Mémoire*, Vol. II, Memoirs et Documents, Arch. Aff. Étr.

in 1776, 28 per cent in 1777, 48 per cent in 1779, 61 per cent in 1781, 59 per cent in 1782, a mere 18 per cent in 1784 and 44 per cent in 1786.[49]

It is significant to note that quite often, the purchasing methods of the English and the French in the southern region generated friction between the two. The purchasing mode of the two rival powers was based on a contractual arrangement between the Indian merchants and the company concerned. The local merchants entered into contracts with the Europeans to supply at the respective ports of shipment the stipulated quantity of cotton goods on an agreed price and by a certain date. The Company paid them a certain proportion of the total future investment in advance while the rest of the amount was paid on delivery. The purchasing methods in Bengal could not be adopted in the south owing to a variety of factors. The entire textile producing belt of the eastern coast did not have a direct link with any single major port owing to geographical reasons, whereas the cotton centres were scattered along the Coromandel Coast and fed numerous smaller ports. It was not possible for the same set of merchants to keep proper control over the vast stretch of the eastern coast, where the broken stretches of mountain chains and rivers with their tributaries made communication difficult. So at each principal factory, the respective companies employed a number of Indian merchants who enjoyed financial and social standing in the local market. There was an absence of official brokers on the Coromandel Coast, who usually provided reasonable protection against defaults by individual merchants, as was the case in Bengal.

The system of contract, which served the demand of distant places through the European channel, had arisen out of a list of merchants as suppliers and buyers of those articles in which these companies traded. The merchants had to establish their sound financial base to earn the trust and confidence of the Europeans. Most of them possessed godown space in the settlement. Once the terms were finalized, the merchants received a portion of the advance decided upon, which could be a fifth of the total estimated investment, or a quarter or, sometimes, half. The period of delivery was rigorously observed and was strictly confined to what had been stipulated in the contract. The English Company insisted that the merchants entering into contract with the English were not to accept orders from the foreign companies till the English received their full merchandise. The English and the French did not make substantial advance at the time of the signing of contract and it was necessary for the merchants to have sufficient liquid capital. The creditworthiness and the minimum quotation price for the items to be supplied were the main considerations in the selection of the merchants. It was not very easy to find a new set of merchants. This is evident from the English Company's decision to continue with the previous set of merchants in 1766 for their *chay* goods.[50]

The French also adopted the same method of investment on the eastern coast. Though the form of contract changed or varied with regions and time, the principle of contract continued all through this period. The English Company always stuck to this mode, while the French occasionally deviated from it and resorted to what may be called 'cash purchases'.

ANGLO-FRENCH COOPERATION FOR INDIAN TRADE

The Anglo-French commercial relationship pertaining to Indian trade was not always based on competition and rivalry, as is generally believed. It was often based on the cooperation of the private interest groups during the time of peace. In fact, we notice a close relationship developing between the English and the French trading houses after the abolition of the Compagnie des Indes to finance the Indian trade. This cooperation existed in both, Europe and India.

In Europe such cooperation had existed between the House of Necker of Paris and the House of Bourdieu of London. Their relationship was close and far-reaching. According to Herbert Lüthy, '*Les relations entre la maison de Necker et celle de Bourdieu ont été etroites, etendues et durables, mais il est difficile d'en fixer l'origine*'.[51] Necker had acted as the financier of the Compagnie des Indes after the Seven Years' War. He was merely a shareholder but did not perform any official function. During this period Bourdieu remained close to the Company. Panchaud, another financier, attributed to Necker this new system of financing the Indian trade.[52] Prior to 1784, the role of the House of James Bourdieu and Samuel Chollet, was highlighted in various memoirs, when the delicate negotiations with the English were going on for the formation of a new French Company. In these memoirs the services rendered by this House in Bengal and in the English trade were projected. Even in the days of the old French India Company this London-based House collected over 14 million *livres* in bills of exchange for the French Company. In the era of private trade between 1769 and 1785, they furnished English bills of exchange on India to M.M. Bernier and Perier.[53] Bourdieu and Chollet were also the commissioners of Farmers-General of France for the purchase of tobacco at Maryland and Virginia till the declaration of the American War of Independence. From 1770 they were the commissioners of Necker for the purchase of wheat.[54] During the administration of Terry (1770-4), James Bourdieu advocated the oft-repeated proposal of Anglo-French cooperation in the field of colonial commerce.

The House of Panchaud also had correspondents of international standing, a majority of whom were foreigners—English or Swiss.[55] The most powerful ones were—Samuel Ximenes, a merchant at Amsterdam, Thomas Foley at London, Selwin & Foley at Paris, Charles Reightley and A. & A. Nesbith, Adrien Hope & Co. of Amsterdam, Robert Herries & Co. of Barcelona and Herries & Co. of London.[56] The bulk of the semi-official business was conducted by Ferdinand Grand. In March 1769 Panchaud had proposed to the shareholders that the Compagnie des Indes should follow the example of the English South Sea Company and of Law's Mississippi Company and should resort to credit manipulation to use the Company's funds to float a similar bank. This proposal was finally rejected by Necker and his followers.[57] In

1775 and 1776 a consortium of shipowners formed by Jacques-Donatien, Le Ray de Chaumont[58] included such names as Pierre Bernier and Jacques-Alexandre Gourlads—all associated and guaranteed by Jean Baptiste Chevalier, the king's commander of French possessions in Bengal.[59] The Genevese Bank of Candolle, Lavit & Co. participated with a small investment through Law de Lauriston in expeditions to Isle de France, Pondicherry, Bengal, Sumatra, etc., with a maritime profit of 26 per cent for a voyage of 18 months and 1 per cent of supplement, in place of 0.5 per cent habitual for the delay of each month.[60] Marquis de Mirabeau, a known Physiocrat, lumped together Necker, Panchaud and Le Ray and described them as 'International speculators' and men without loyalty either to the king or to the country.[61]

From the summer of 1777, the Houses of *armateurs* (shippers) for India began to crack. Herbert Lüthy suggests that it occurred because they could not anymore find the necessary credits for supporting their outstanding business at the usual interest rate, where heavy engagements of money for long terms was needed and where each expedition ended with a new shipowners being thrown down with losses.[62] In this negative trend, the Anglo-French war on the issue of American independence must have played an important part.

In August 1777 Pierre-Jacques Lemoine, a shipowner from Rouen, earlier a Director of the French Compagnie des Indes, suspended his payments. The bankers, Necker of Germany, Girardot & Co., were named directors of the group of creditors. Also in August 1777 Le Ray de Chaumont, Bernier and Gourlade, associates and bankers of the consortium in France, were to be treated as joint-creditors of Jean Baptists Chevalier and Jean Law de Lauriston.[63] By a common understanding they were to distribute three million pounds to the security bearers of Chevalier and Law between October and December 1777. Unable to liquidate immediately, Ray, Bernier and Gourlade borrowed three millions pounds from the bank of Girardot, Haller & Co.[64]

The period of free trade revealed to its critics that in order to conduct the trade it was not necessary for companies to have their own warehouses and agents in India.[65]

From the suppression of the old company in 1769 to the establishment of a new company in 1785, 340 vessels were employed in the free commerce to the East Indies, the details are given in Table 3.6.

Messrs Rabaud & Co. had formed a plan for a settlement in India for the manufacture of calicoes and muslins, soon after the return

TABLE 3.6: NUMBER OF VESSELS EMPLOYED BY THE FRENCH IN THE EAST INDIES (1769-85)

Port	Number of vessels	Their tonnage
L'Orient	195	87,335
St. Malo	19	7,720
Marseilles	37	12,950
Bourdeaux	33	14,720
Nantes	16	6,150
Rochelle	18	9,280
Havre	3	850
Brest	4	3,555
In Indies	15	6,585
Total	340	1,49,145

Source: Memorial of the Deputies, 1787, Paris, CPL, Ohio.

of peace. According to Louis Dermigny, Rabaud at first established a subsidiary company at Chandernagar and then transferred it to Calcutta. It was placed under Montpellierains, Eustache Vialars and Fraissinet.[66] Messrs Vialars & Co. of Chandernagar and Messrs Amabrie Michel & Co. of Pondicherry were eager to extend their establishments on the coast of Malabar and in the other parts of India where the French were permitted to have settlements and practise trade.

It is apparent from Table 3.7 that all the expeditions of Raubaud since 1771 gave him a profit of 50 to 60 per cent.[67] In one voyage it was as high as 80 per cent.[68] Where the percentage of profit is not mentioned, it implies a loss. Many voyages were successfully performed by the vessels of such merchants who employed no agents except those who were already found in the country. They loaded their vessels at Coromandel and Bengal ports, and were able to receive back their capital in eighteen to twenty months.

In 1771 *La Conquerant*, a vessel of only 260 tons, was fitted out from Marseilles by the House of Rabaud & Co. with a freight of one-third in silver and two-thirds in merchandise for Pondicherry and Chandernagar. It yielded a profit on a capital of 5,00,000 *livres* (about £ 20,834). In 1776 *La Philippine*,[69] a vessel of 600 tons was fitted out from Marseilles with a cargo of *piastres* and merchandise. It returned to Marseilles in 1778, making a profit of 50 per cent on 9,84,000 *livres* (£ 41,000).[70] Most of its cargo was procured in Bengal and it had to face a competition of 13 other vessels from France. In 1782 the *Victor Amadins* of 500 tons and *Le Compte de Person* of 600 tons left under

TABLE 3.7: SHIPMENTS FROM MARSEILLES TO INDIA AND THEIR PROFITS

(*in percentage*)

Year	Shipowners	Name of the ship	Total value of cargo in *livres*	Profit %
1771	Rabaud	*La Conquerent*	5,00,000	65
	Rabaud	*La Philippine*	9,84,000	50
1782	Rabaud	*La Compte de Perron*	7,33,700	40
	Rabaud	*Le Victor-Arme*	8,07,500	40
1783	Rabaud	*Le Constance Pauline*	5,45,000	60
	Chauvet	*Le St. Charles*	7,00,000	50
1784	Solier Martin Salavy	*Le Consolateur*	11,87,000	55
	Grenier Frères	*Le Felicitè*	10,00,000	80
	Bigand Poulard	*Le Comte d'Artois*	9,30,000	–
1785	Joachim Dallet	*Le Belle Esclave*	4,60,000	–
	Stafforello	*Le Heureuse-Marie*	8,30,000	–
	Peragallo			
	Peragallo	*Le Compte de Noe*	10,20,000	–
	J&D Baux	*Le Chene*	8,20,000	–
	Rabaud	*Le Constance Pauline*	11,09,000	80
		Le Coromandel	10,27,000	60
		Le Malabar	11,06,000	60
		Le Philippine	10,27,000	60
1786	Rabaud	*La Vicomtesse de Besse*	9,15,500	–
	Rabaud	*L'Hedwige Sophie*	7,61,500	–

Source: Louis Dermigny, op. cit., pp. 145-6. Also Memorial from the Deputies of the Principal Commercial Towns, published at Paris, 1787, respecting the exclusive privileges of the French East India Company, *Manuscripts on British India, CPL.*

the Sardinian flag (as it was the period of Anglo-French war over the issue of American independence). These ships returned with cotton piece goods from Coromandel and Bengal and coffee and pepper from other regions and made a profit of about 40 per cent each.[71] In 1783 *La Constante Pauline* was fitted out and with a cargo of seven-eighths of merchandise and one-eighth of *piastres*, and returned in 1784, yielding a profit of over 60 per cent. In 1784 *Le Consolateur* of about 600 tons was fitted out and afforded a capital of about 1,20,000 *livres* (or £ 50,000) and earned a profit of 55 per cent. *La Felicite* on a capital of 10,00,000 *livres* (£ 41,667) produced a profit of about 80 per cent. Similarly, *La Constance Pauline, Le Coromandel, Le Malabar* made a profit of 60 to 80 per cent each on their return to Port L'Orient.[72] The ship *Les Trois Cousins* under Gérard was a relatively small ship in which M.L. Maclean of London was also involved with M. Monneron of Paris.[73] It carried merchandise of the value of Rs. 31,394-1-24 and reached Pondicherry in March 1779. The various letters to Lagrenée at Pondicherry clearly reveal the role of Pelling de Fries & Co. in providing funds to the French traders and in helping them procure cargo material, particularly cloths, handkerchief, white cotton goods, etc. There also seem to be trade dealings between Bourdieu & Chollet, and Maclean of London and Monneron of Paris, with John Macpherson of Fort St. George, and Lagrenée of Pondicherry, in supplying credit and cargo to the French private traders.[74] According to Paul Butel, Charles-Claude Ange, Monneron became a servant of the Tobacco Monopoly after his stay in Pondicherry as an official of the French East India Company.[75] His family was connected with trade and finance. His brothers acted as agents of trade in Isle de France and in India, and one of them—Augustine, was a super cargo on a 'country' trade vessel. Monneron had strong business ties with Lagrenée and Moracin, agent for the French Company of Calonne in the subsequent period. According to Louis Dermigny, Amalric Michel Coulon and Co. was in fact a branch of Rabaud in Pondicherry.[76]

Thus, we find in Europe a wide network of bankers prepared to invest in the Indian trade in the absence of the French Company. They invested liberally when the conditions were conducive for profit making but investments were reduced considerably once the American War engulfed the continent and affected Anglo-French relations. During this short period, Indian commerce became one of the elements of international speculation, involving the activities of borrowings, loans, shares of discounting houses and the frequent transfers of bills of exchange connecting Madras, Pondicherry and Calcutta with London, Paris and L'Orient.

Active cooperation also existed between the English and the French merchants in India. The English East India Company's monopoly structure was seriously challenged by the private traders and by the Company's servants' trade operations with the French and the Dutch. Despite the avowed displeasure of the Director, illicit channels of transfer of wealth and fortunes were devised to the immense benefit of the French trade. The process of this cooperation had started with the acquisition of the Diwani of Bengal by the English Company, but the volume of remittance increased manifold with the abolition of the French Company and the introduction of private trade.[77]

The Agency houses and several individual Englishmen living in Madras or in Bengal had large funds, which they wished to remit to London. The French, on the other hand, were facing a shortage of funds to revive their trade in India. They were operating in Coromandel and in Bengal, and needed cash to supplement their supplies of silver bullion for purchasing goods. So they offered bills of exchange payable in London at 6 to 12 months sight. The French agents through British bankers paid these bills.

From the beginning the Court of Directors was aware of the serious consequences of this method of remittances. As early as 1766 they wrote to the Company government in India alleging that the French were able to procure better and more valuable cargo than the English. The Directors instructed: 'We now inform you that the furnishing the agents of the European companies with money is so evidently detrimental to this Company that there was no further elucidation and you are accordingly hereby directed to discourage and prevent the same to the utmost of your power.'[78] In another letter, they wrote, 'You are to use all the means in your power to prevent our servants and all other residing under our protection, lending their money to the French. . . .'[79] Cornwallis himself was aware of the consequences of these remittances. He wrote to the Secret Committee,

> . . . a foreign commerce, which is carried on, at our expense, supported by funds supplied by British subjects, which tends to lessen the consumption of our native manufacturers, without increasing that of the manufacturers of this country and which diminishes the profits of the company upon the sales of Indian goods in Europe, must be essentially detrimental to the company and to the state.[80]

The English Directors tried all possible means to prevent the French from trading on the capital of their servants. In Bengal they succeeded to some extent but their regulations remained ineffective in the absence of an alternative plan. The Bengal government had raised loans at high interest rates and offered thereby a more attractive field of investment but such measures were still to be tried out in Madras. Moreover, the close trade transactions of the leading men of that time such as Chevalier, the French Governor at Chandernagar, Ross, the Dutch Director at Chinsura with some of the most prominent men of the English Company including Warren Hastings and Charles Grant made it very difficult for the Court of Directors to be effective. It is evident that the cooperation of Calcutta-based English merchants and the French in India was not confined to the region of Bengal but covered the shipments from Pondicherry and Isle de France as well. It is difficult to know the names of the remitters as many of them were fictitious.[81] Chevalier seems to have actively borrowed in 1775 from the British subjects to fill up the cargo of three ships—*Le Boine*, the *Duc d'Aiguillon* and *Duc de Vrilliére.* The bills for the last 2 ships valued at £ 2,34,000 and for *Le Boine* at £ 1,75,000[82] were made through London bankers—Mayne and Needham. A large number of bills seem to have been issued by an Anglo-French consortium which included names such as Chevalier, Samuel Middleton and James Ellis.[83] Several leading agency houses were peddling out their client's money in small lots. These included the houses of Ferguson & Fairlie, Bayne & Colvin, and Paxton, Cockerell and Delisla.[84] The famous British concern Campbell & Anderson also offered bills to the French shipowners. The French concerns such as Louis Tissier acted for Admyrauld & Son of La Rochelle or Bourdieu & Chollet of Paris and London.[85]

There was an important French business family in Chandernagar by the name of Verlée. They were engaged in diverse activities such as indigo and opium plantations, slave trade, salt and cotton goods purchased from the Coromandel region. Louis Lacherey, the French Company's merchant till 1769 and head of the French factory at Casimbazar, maintained close relations with the French agents at Coromandel. From there, they procured piece goods and superfine cotton. There is enough evidence to suggest that Warren Hastings acted as a creditor of Chevalier de Savoarren.[86] This family maintained close commercial dealings with the English through Manick Ray. There appears to have existed some kind of financial arrangement among Messrs Gavin Hamilton, Frimont Arreau, Middleton and Chevalier,[87] and also with Charles Child.[88] Their network of activities extended to Coromandel as well.

At Madras there were several prominent men who helped in large-scale remittances. According to Holden Furber, Moracin, the French agent at Pondicherry directly participated in such business on his own initiative and indirectly through the agency houses of Balfour & Spalding, and of Francis Lautour.[89] The French agents in India also made efforts to win the confidence of wealthy servants of the English Company so that they could use the French bills of exchange. That the French succeeded to a great extent is reflected in the trade revival around 1775, when the number of French ships frequenting Indian coasts increased manifold. The documentary evidence implicate the Governor of Madras Robert Palk in these shady remittances along with M. Lecont of Pondicherry.[90] One of the letters states that Palk in partnership with Adams and Mons. Law bought a ship called *'The Madras Merchant'*, later renamed *'Sarah'*, for Rs. 30,000. It was to carry opium and other goods to China on English or Dutch bills to be procured at Bencoolen and Batavia. The ship was to be insured for £ 24,000 from India to China and for £ 10,000 for its return trip. The share of Elcanoi Adams was one half while Palk and Law divided the rest between themselves.[91]

Furber suggests that between April 1785 and March 1790, bills of exchange up to the value of £ 7,57,177 were presented to the French Company's London agents for payment. It represented remittances from Madras via Pondicherry of £ 6,00,926 and from Calcutta via Chandernagar of £ 1,56,251.[92] The real total, according to Furber, was much higher. In this he did not include the sums spent in India on government account and repaid in Paris. At the same time he did not think that it exceeded £ 10,00,000. This mode of transfer continued to remain popular because it was more lucrative than the official means.

A notable feature in the sphere of economic relationship was the development of new credit organization in the 1770s in the form of agency houses. These were based on rudimentary form of partnership. Dodwell mentions several such houses such as Chase, Sewell & Chinnery, Tulloh, Connell and Brodie, Roebuck, Abbot & Maitland, etc.[93] These were generally mixed forms consisting of company servants and merchants who transacted numerous businesses. They advanced money, bought and sold goods on commission, participated in trade operations and played an important role in remittances through foreign channels. Warren Hastings seems to have participated in similar operations with Jourdan and two other company servants.[94] M.M. Pelling and De Fries & Co. was an important business house at Pondicherry which handled a substantial proportion of the French cargo. A new society (*la Nouvelle Société*) under the marks of L.S. was formed in 1786 that consisted of Moracin, Messrs Sabatiér fils, Desprez Angustine, Pezia and Gourlade.[95] This society actively participated in trade through borrowed money by means of bills of exchange. The usual rate of commission was 5 per cent on sale or purchase of goods and 1 per cent on bullion exchange, 5 per cent on procuring freights, whether to Europe, India or any other part, 1 per cent on procuring loans of money and 2 per cent on procuring money on respondentia, and 1 per cent on procuring company's bonds or certificates.[96] It appears that the British banks in London were prepared to offer money on behalf of clients in Madras and Calcutta, who helped to arrange loans for the French and thus played an important part in these schemes.

Thus, we find that the cooperation between the servants and merchants of England and France prospered whenever the political conditions were favourable, as was the case between 1766 and 1778 and then in the period of Nouvelle Compagnie des Indes. The global war between the two rival powers severed this connection for a few years. It was not the political enmity or the English distrust of the French payments that broke the financial cooperation, rather it was the security reason that compelled the British subjects to remit their fortune through the Dutch, Danish or other sources. The political developments in Europe had repercussions on the Anglo-French remittance. Feldback suggests that Tipu Sultan's embassy to Versailles in 1788 and a general expectation that France would support the ruler of Mysore in case of war with the English made the British reluctant to remit through French channels.[97] The coming of the French Revolution made the situation more uncertain for the investors and thus less attractive.

It can be said that generally those who made good voyages were indebted for their success to specific reasons. Some of them were unconnected with national commerce. Many of them were acting as agents for foreign merchant houses and were being employed by people in the service of the English East India Company to convey their property to Europe. In these transactions, the owners of the ships were only the carriers and agents for the merchandise, which formed the greatest part of their sales. Most of those who did not have that precarious foreign support and all those who pushed into new or unusual channels of trade such as Persia or China, made losing voyages and were completely ruined.

'COUNTRY' TRADE IN ANGLO-FRENCH RELATIONS

Even before the rise of the European settlements along the Coromandel Coast, the Indians had developed a well-marked pattern of oceanic trade. It linked Coromandel with Bengal and further east with Malaya, the Archipelago up to China on one side, and on the other, connected the western coast up to Surat with the African and Arabian coastline through lucrative trade. The Europeans described this as the 'country' trade. The European traders made special endeavours to participate in it. However, the monopolistic nature of the companies and their bureaucratic structure hindered fullest exploitation of this avenue of trade in the initial period.

The fitting out of 'country' ships adopted two principal directions—

(a) Westwards to the coastal ports of the Persian Gulf, the Red Sea and the East African coast, where despite high risk, the profit margin usually varied from 30 to 50 per cent;
(b) towards China and the Archipelago in the east, where bulkier goods were demanded or procured on reasonable profits. Besides, a flourishing coastal trade existed from Bengal in the east to Surat in the west, which included items like rice, sugar and textiles from the eastern coast and cotton and spices from the western. Usually the voyage lasted six months, leaving Bengal in January and returning in June based on the pattern of wind direction. A ship of 500 tons could give a profit of about 2,00,000 *livres*.[98] This profit was used for the investments in the 'country' trade.

Initially, the Dutch were able to exploit the 'country' trade because of their well spread-out settlements with a base at Batavia and a well-supported fleet. The actual rise of European private trade and their increasing participation in this branch of commerce can be traced from the period of the 1750s and possibly earlier.[99] However, by the end of the American War of Independence, the English dominance over the 'country' trade was well established. They had successfully ousted even the Indian merchants and traders. The English capital was derived from the profits, commissions, interests, savings, gifts of individual servants as well as from the agency houses and the large number of bills of exchange.

From the mid-eighteenth century, the control of trade began to be transferred from the covenanted servants to the free merchants and from loosely associated individuals to the well-established trade firms.[100] They practised joint-stock form initially making temporary alliance for specific voyages and shared the profits on return. They adopted another means to reduce the risk by borrowing money on respondentia. These were like loans of bottomry in Europe. The money was borrowed for the duration of the voyage and was entitled to a proportion of any salvage that might be recovered. The rate of interest was very high ranging from 25 to 30 per cent per annum.[101] This form of borrowing was becoming increasingly popular in the Madras Presidency.

The huge profit margins and the vigorous involvement of the English servants and merchants in this branch of commerce, particularly after the acquisition of the Diwani, reflects the growing trend towards mixing up of private and public interests. The fruits of politics and that of trade were received together in such a state of affair. It was the flexible organization of the English Company, which provided plenty of scope to its servants to enter this profitable domain. The presence of a big mercantile fleet, political control of the English over the centres of production, their populous settlements providing ready markets and the development of vast, well-knit and properly administered territorial centres on the two different coasts, separate from each other, producing different sets of natural and manufactured products, were some of the primary factors which led to the English dominance over the coastal trade. Added to these was the efficient credit facility through individuals or associations. The English occupation of Tranquebar and Nagapatnam must have further strengthened their position in the east, as these were important centres of 'country' trade and the principal commercial outlets of Tanjore. Till the American War, the Dutch and the Danish fleet had operated between Nagapatnam and Malaya ports trading in pepper, arrack, sugar and timber in return for piece goods and salt. After the American War, the dominance of the English became well established. According to Furber, 'Whatever be the precise nature of this process [rise of the English], it is perfectly clear that British supremacy in the "country" trade of India was virtually assured after the American War. In the 1760s and 1770s, the British "country" trader had rivals who could pursue an independent existence. In the mid-1780s, he had no rivals who could operate independently of him.'[102]

French participation in the 'country' trade began in 1719 when they began to search for partners—both among the European merchants and the local trading communities having sufficient capital and expertise. This trade was dependent on the family based networks. The first known partnership was with a prominent Armenian merchant—Issac Elias who agreed to undertake voyages to Manila.[103] Carvalho was another famous Portuguese merchant whose name is associated with the French 'country' trade in the initial years.[104] Among the Indians, Balocopal sailed to Manila in 1735 and 1737 while Sanku Rama supplied about half of the Company's textile purchases.[105] Yet the problem of procuring sufficient capital persisted. One name that appears quite often in the French records and in the *Private Diary of Ananda Ranga Pillai* is that of Soucourama. According to Indrani Ray, he was probably Sunka Venkatachalem or Sunku Muthurama Chetti. The French also approached the Muslim trading community specializing in foreign trade with South-Eastern Asia. The Marakkayars were from the Chulia group of wealthy Tamil merchants who had independent links with the elites and with the ruling courts of the south-eastern states of Asia.[106] Imam Sahib was a prominent notable of south Arcot and a Mughal official who also invested vast sums of money in the French ships involved in the 'country' trade. Apart from these names, some of the junior servants of the English Company also invested their small savings with the French or placed their freight on French vessels as they were excluded by the senior officials from the profits of English 'country' trade.[107]

It seems the French had become aware of the importance of 'country' trade in 1730s. A mémoire of 1738 mentions *Commerce de L'Inde en Inde* and refers to Pondicherry's trade with China, Manila, Moka, Persia, Merguy, Pegu and Achem as well as with the Malabar coast.[108] Even Jacques Vincens made a fervent appeal to extend French activities in 'country' trade.[109] He believed that the absence of private merchants was in fact the main reason behind Pondicherry's failure to develop into a prosperous commercial centre like Madras. A French mémoir of 1764 suggested that the 'country' trade was a real advantage for the principal European settlements, and the English Company in ordinary times gathered more than 1,00,000 *pagodas* as taxes on this commerce from Madras alone.[110] Dupleix seems to have actively participated in this branch of trade and amassed a fortune. It was probably he, more than any other French personality, who placed the French on the map of 'country' trade, as an important power. La Bourdonnai, of Isle de France had bought *Le Postillon* in 1731 for 33,500 *livres* and along with Cyril Wiche, an English merchant of Madras and Issac Elias, he bought *Le Pondichèri*, a 400 ton vessel for 28,525 *livres*. Even Dupleix bought *Le Richmond* for 64,800 *livres*.[111] Most of the ships and boats employed in the 'country' trade were of 100 to 500 tons capacity and their price varied from 5,000 to 1,20,000 *livres*. Their cost was quite moderate compared to the European standard as was made of teak wood from Burma.[112]

The French sent a ship *Le Joseph* to China in 1764 that gave a net profit of 5 to 6 per cent, augmenting 30 per cent gain in its European voyage. The English were believed to have lost 30 per cent in the same period. Another ship carried a cargo of 65,000 *pagodas* of which 54,000 were raised by the Company and the rest by city merchants.[113] After the Seven Years' War, French participation in the 'country' trade did not increase as was expected. It was believed that the presence of a privileged Company was detrimental to the French traders' participation in the 'country' trade. The suppression of the monopolistic company was expected to increase the advantages of this trade.[114]

Furber holds the 'commercial revolution' responsible for the major shift in the pattern of 'country' trade.[115] It had important bearings on the commercial life of Bengal, the Coromandel, Bombay and Surat.[116] These changes reduced the exports from Bengal to Bombay and Surat developed a direct 'country' trade between Bengal and China. Initially, based on bullion, this trade began to thrive on opium exports from Bengal. In the process it reduced the importance of Coromandel textiles. At the same time this expansion in the sphere of 'country' trade strengthened the control of the British traders over it.

As the English domination over coastal trading became stronger, their success drew the attention of the French shipowners and merchants. However, they failed to reap huge profits for several reasons. The most important of these was the presence of the English in this arena and their political and economic domination. This field required more resources than the French possessed. In the 1770s, Law de Lauriston, while replying to Bellecombe, wrote, 'The private "country" trade of the French is reduced today to almost nothing and the English have it entirely absorbed for themselves.'[117] Yet, we do find the French ships frequenting the ports of Calicat, Mahé and Surat to supplement their cargo but their participation was far from active. Furthermore, the French faced difficulty in procuring merchandise directly from the producers. They bought goods and merchandise from second and third hands, whereas the English had direct dealings with the suppliers because of their political influence.

One of the major factors that checked French participation in the 'country' trade was the nature of its organization. It was not a strictly private effort, as was the case with the English. According to a contemporary source, those traders or *armateurs* who wished to fit out their ship, had to seek the official support of the Governor and Council. The proposal became semi-official, for the cargo, the place of shipment, the route of the voyage and the feasibility of the enterprise was usually

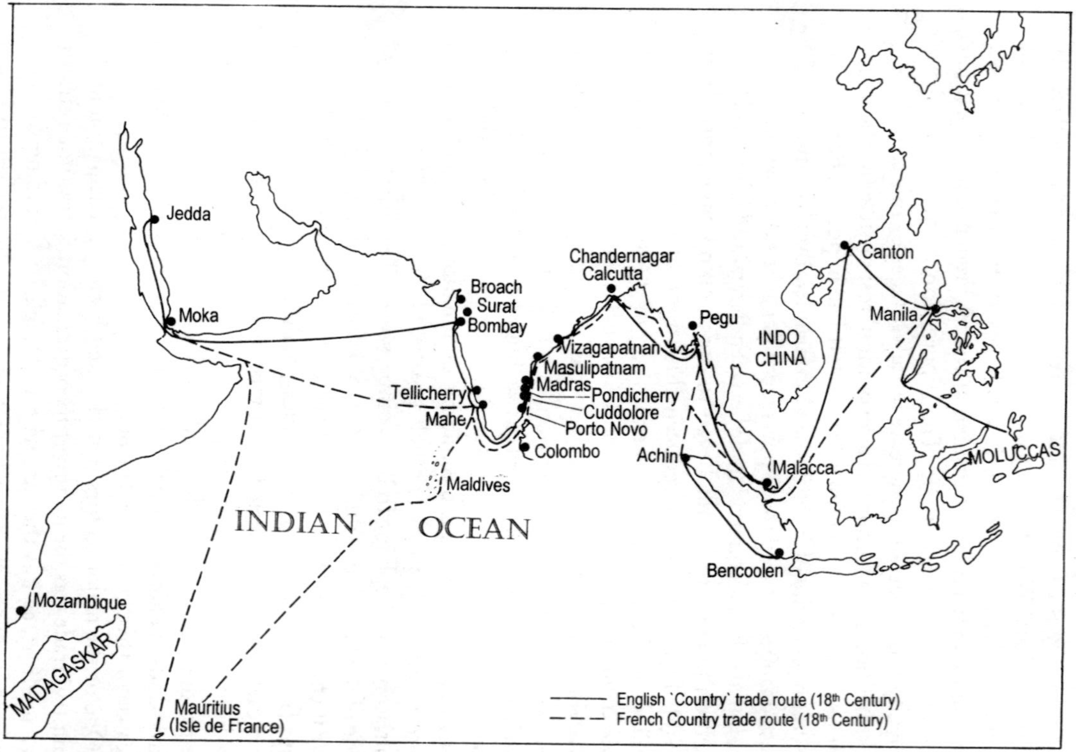

MAP 3.1: 'COUNTRY' TRADE ROUTES IN SOUTH ASIAN REGION

decided at an official level.[118] Whether it was due to the lack of spirit of enterprise on the part of the French *armateurs* (ship-owners) or due to the shortage of funds, or difficulty in procuring goods or because the French officials were genuinely interested in the success of these trade voyages by rendering all possible assistance, it is difficult to say. But the French seem to have suffered in this branch of commerce not because of the lack of settlements or *comptoirs* along the coast, but rather because of the shortage of funds. The situation is aptly described in one of the letters of a French agent. 'Individual French trade within India itself is today reduced to almost nought, and is hardly worth writing a thesis on. The English have assumed entire control over it for themselves and are destroying it by forcing it to its utmost. It has become for them, especially individuals, a cause of bankruptcy. Only fearfully can a Frenchman carry out a loading. Where he loads, he can be sure to pay far more for the goods loaded than paid by the English and moreover the quality of the cargo would be inferior . . . whether one goes to China, Moka, Jeddah, Sumatra or Pegu, in all parts of the "East Coast", one is almost certain to find in abundance wares which one is carrying and at a price which cannot cover the charges of loading.'[119] Isle de France (Mauritius) was also an important part of the French 'country' trade network. The Coromandel goods fetched about 30 per cent profit while those coming from Bengal had a much higher profit margin. One item that was in demand in the 1770s was the golden thread brought from Lyon in France and then reshipped from Pondicherry. Mons. Courier in 1771 placed a demand for golden thread valued at 80,000 to 1,00,000 *francs* from which he expected a net profit of about 5 to 6 per cent.[120] One should remember that the margin of profit was not enormous as the lending rates were very high, there was an acute shortage of capital after the abolition of the French Company, and the assembling of cargo was not an easy task for the private traders as they were still trying to adjust to the new situation. However, the performance of the French in the sphere of 'country' trade was not as dismal as some people believed.

During this period of 'country' trade activity, the French *armateurs* competed well not only because of profits resulting from the purchase and sale but also from the freight that they earned. The margin of profit varied from one region to another. Pierre Blancard asked the French to emulate the English by devoting greater attention to this most assured sphere of profit of the riches of Orient.[121] He suggested that this field of 'country' trade provided an immense possibility of speculation and a vast margin of profit. This is evident from his detailed information on the profit margin on different commodities in various regions, as given in Table 3.8. It could, however, be more of an optimistic impression as he was advocating a vigorous participation of the French in this arena of trade.

The 'country' trade conducted from several European settlements along the Coromandel—from Nagapatnam, Madras, Pondicherry, Yanaon and Masulipatam. It was conducted through numerous

TABLE 3.8: PROFIT MARGIN IN THE 'COUNTRY' TRADE

Year	Commodity	Place of purchase	Place of sale	Profit in %
1774	Calin (tin)	Malacca	Moka	28
	Unbleached		Moka	
	Guinea	Pondicherry	Moka	30
	Cloves	Cochin	Moka	40
	Pepper	Mahe	Moka	48
	Waste Cotton	Surat	Moka	48
	Semi-guineas			
	Blue	Pondicherry	Moka	60
	Eagle wood	Cochin	Moka	69
	Powdered			
	Sugar	Batavia	Moka	145
	Rice	Bengal	Moka	240
1783	Sugar candy	Colombo	Calicut	24
	Powdered sugar	Batavia	Calicut	42
1787	Waste cotton	Bombay	Pondicherry	32
	Calin (tin)	Malacca	China	36
	Common			
	Porcelain	Canton	Malabar	40
	Silk	Canton	Pondicherry	42
	Light pepper	Sumatra (Achem)	Bombay	50
	Pepper	Malacca	China	58
	Waste cotton	Bombay	China	90
	Rice	Bengal	Isle de France	244
1792	Calin	Malacca	China	32
	Pepper	Malacca	China	50
	Waste cotton	Bombay	China	80
	Ebony wood			
	(bois debene)	Isle de France	China	132
	Ratins	Malacca	China	215
	Rice	Bengal	Isle de France	271

Source: Pierre Blancard, op. cit., p. 510.

merchant and trading houses. The Tuifs de Livourne and Gregoire Sheriman who had their correspondents Arutiuns Tacob and Johannes Sciammic at Madras, Marseillean shippers Berard Coulon & Co. at Yanaon, Pondicherry and Porto Novo, we find Gonzebat and Amalric and then Amalric Michel Couton & Co. The last house and possibly the second last too, were the branches of Rabaud.[122] According to Dermigny, the European element on the Coromandel Coast was much bigger and stronger than on the Malabar Coast.[123] An important element of this trade, which is often neglected by the European scholars, was the slave traffic. Though not of the magnitude of the Atlantic world, this did exist.

Slavery existed in the eastern trading world though it was more prevalent in the Malay archipelago and around the Arabian Sea than in other parts of the Indian Ocean. The traffic in slaves also influenced the Anglo-French relations on the eastern coast of India. The French participation in this field appears more intense. S. Arasaratnam points out that in the seventeenth century, the quickening pace of trade across the Indian Ocean led to certain developments in the trafficking in slaves.[124] In the sixteenth and early seventeenth centuries, the Portuguese and the Dutch presence had a major impact on slave traffic, introducing new demand for slave labour in maritime Asia. Though the Mughals sternly checked the slave trade, the eastern coast remained an important source of slaves.

From the fragmentary sources available on slave traffic as a component of eastern trade during the eighteenth century, it is difficult to form a clear picture. However, some idea can be formed about the practices adopted to procure slaves from India. The French colonization of Mauritius (Isle de France) was an important factor in the rise of slave trade. Throughout the century, the Indian slave trade was managed mainly through the French ports on Coromandel and Bengal in which the superior officials played a leading role. Some English officials were also involved in it. Benoit-Dumas, the Governor of Mauritius, Dupleix and Vincens had formed an association for slave trade in the Indian Ocean.[125] By 1761, Indian slaves in Mauritius numbered 870 or 7 per cent of the total slave population there.[126] An estimated 20 to 25 per cent of the Indian slaves died en route to the French islands.[127] M. De Bretel, who lived in Chandernagar on his large landed estate, was a well known supplier of Indian slaves even to the Englishmen.[128] A document on slavery during the 1760s and 1770s mentions the price of slaves bought from Karikal.[129] According to this source, the price usually varied from 3 to 4 *pagodas* (of Porto Novo) per slave. A small child of 2½ years was bought for 3 *pagodas* in January 1767, a girl of 9 years for 4 *pagodas* in March 1774, girls of 8 years were sold for 3 *pagodas* to 3 *pagodas* 3 *fanams*, and there is a mention of two boys aged 12 and 16 years who were bought for 6 and 16 *pagodas* respectively.[130] Another French source mentions the sale of a male slave for 53 Arcot rupees in August 1769 to Nicolas of Madras. These figures suggest that the price of slaves had gone up immensely if one compares these with those mentioned by Arasaratnam.

The slave trade flourished particularly in the period of famines when poor families migrated to coastal towns. At times the children and women were forcibly taken away and sold to slave traders. Ananda Ranga Pillai describes the activities of Paramanandan, a slave dealer in Pondicherry. M. Sonde who worked under M. Cornet, the keeper of the warehouse in the fort, commissioned him to bring slaves on certain commission basis from the neighbouring territories.[131] At times the domestic slaves were kindly treated and provisions for legacies or manumission can be seen in the wills of the Europeans. M. De Bretel had supplied three slaves (two boys and one girl) to Joseph Ward, who lived in Calcutta. The three slaves were set free in December 1793.[132] No doubt, these were rare cases and were seen at a time when the English had abolished slave trade. The fact remains that slavery as an institution in the East could not have been different from that practised in the West.

Though the slaves never formed the major part of the cargo from India, the trade continued in a clandestine manner. The British prohibited the sale of slaves from Bengal in 1789 and extended this to other parts in the next few years,[133] while the French Revolutionary decree of 1794 prohibiting slave trade checked the traffic of slaves. However, illicit trafficking continued.[134]

In the sphere of 'country' trade, we find that the 'Anglo-French' relations remained peaceful and at times harmonious. It was often financed by joint credit through numerous credit and agency *maisons.* The French never challenged the dominance of the English traders as very often they were dependent on them for credit and funds. The French traded in almost the same commodities as the English with the possible exception of white cloths. But this article did not contribute to reasonable profits. The Dutch had found sugar and the English profitably traded in raw cotton and opium but the French commodity composition did not yield sufficient return. The French traders were finding it very difficult to raise funds for their principal trade. Monneron, Rivalz and others formed a society to participate in coastal trade, and were ready to secure credit at as high a rate of interest as 18 to 20 per cent from Crawford or other investors of Madras to buy coffee from Moka and handkerchiefs and *Guinghams* from the coast.[135]

During the 1780s 'country' trade on the Coromandel Coast was quite active, and was supplemented by coastal trade, particularly between Bengal and the Coromandel. It employed a considerable fleet with a reasonably large tonnage. According to Parkinson, the total number of ships employed in this trade was 128 in 1783 with a tonnage capacity of 44,865; the number of ships increased to 575 and their tonnage to 1,75,405 in 1791.[136] The main commodities covered in this region were grains, rice, salt and sugar. The first two articles were worth Rs. 8 lakh in 1793.[137] One-sixth of sugar received at Madras came from Calcutta and the rest was brought from the Dutch settlements.[138] A large number of small boats of 300 to 400 tons each operated along the Coromandel Coast to carry 10,000 to 12,000 sacs of rice at a freight of Rs. 2½ per sac.[139] They took back, besides salt, a small number of products including cotton goods.

The coastal trade in salt caused some differences between the English and the French. Bengal was the principal producer of salt in the mid-eighteenth century, yet it was not self-sufficient. Some salt was manufactured on the Coromandel belt and brought to Bengal by some French shippers and by 'country' traders in their *dhonies.*[140] In return, they took back rice and other items of daily consumption to the rice scarcity zones and for urban settlements. Salt being an essential commodity, control over its manufacture and sale meant a steady source of income for the Company's officials. It was probably this that encouraged Clive to establish the English Company's monopoly through the 'Society of Trade'. A rapidly rising income and its private gains created a vested interest group, which resisted the orders of the Directors aimed at abolishing the salt monopoly.[141]

The attempts to raise revenue by the monopoly of salt, before the American War, were rendered abortive by the vast import of salt both by the local merchants and the French. The Bengal Board tried various oppressive expedients to prevent this influx, but did not fully succeed. During the War, the Board used the opportunity to adopt a new system of management. It caused acute suffering to the salt merchants. The French revived their demand of free salt import on payment of 2.5 per cent duty.[142] The English could not prevent the French from importing salt without involving the state in disputes with France. The English Company tried to minimize the adverse effect on its monopoly by buying up the entire quantity at a fixed price not exceeding Rs.120 per maund. Finally it was agreed by the rival powers through the convention of 31 August 1787 that the French were not to import into Bengal more than 2,00,000 maunds of salt annually.[143] The excess was to be confiscated and sold for the benefit of the English Company, as actually happened in 1790-1. The excess of 4,90,372.20 maunds was confiscated and sold, while the French Company received Rs.20,142.5.8 as freight charge.[144] In 1791-2, the French imported salt into Bengal weighing 3,99,999.20 maunds valued at Rs. 2,39,999.6.4.[145] It shows that it was an important source of income for the French traders, and an equally valuable and considerable source of revenue for the English. In the period after 1782, the English had received over £6 lakhs of revenue from this article.[146]

Thus, we find the English control over this commodity was quite strong and exploitative and in the end their interests triumphed. According to Furber, the English country tonnage increased from 400 tons in 1780 to 25,000 by 1790.[147] The most spectacular growth was in trade with China. But the main factor was the export of opium to China. Louis Dermigny's exhaustive study reveals that the English in 1789 carried to Canton 2,000 chests of opium and 50,000 bales of cotton.[148] However, there was no such product in the Coromandel region which could have transformed the commodity pattern of the 'country' trade. At the same time, there was a steady growth of trade with Coromandel. In 1793 at least 8,000 tons of grain and pulse invoiced at 26 lakh of current rupees were meant for the Europeans.[149] The French, on the other hand, remained content with a few minor concessions in salt importation. Apart from this article, the Anglo-French relationship over the 'country' trade remained free from controversies. Slave trade, though limited in nature, was another field in which the Anglo-French relationship was cordial.

The French participation in the Asian trade showed a phenomenal expansion in the late 1780s while the freedom of trade at Isle de France and Isle de Bourbon remained intact. However, all their ships, according to Furber, were trading between Mauritius, Mahé, Pondicherry, Maldives and Colombo.[150] But we do find several instances of the French Captains also visiting Pegu, Manila, Achem and China in the East and up to Moka (Mocha) in the West.[151] In fact, Moka held a special place for the French in their country trade, which was also utilized to fill up their cargo from India to Europe. The French Company was obliged to hold a *loge* on which the *pavillion* was established. There was another *loge* at Betelfaqui, 40 leagues from there. Coffee shipments were usually made to Pondicherry en route to Mahé and Calicat, to supplement the cargo. This item produced a profit of at least 50 per cent. Besides, some French merchants and agents in their private capacities arranged ships to procure coffee. But Maldives was the only place in the French 'country' trade which they found worth talking about. By the 1770s, that was also on way to destruction. Small French vessels from Bengal, Pegu, and at times from the Coromandel visited Maldives with rice, bales of big merchandise and oil.[152] Occasionally cloths, silk items and potteries were also sold with reasonable profit. The return cargo consisted primarily of *caurie* and *amber* (scent). *Cauries* were the small shells, that served as money unit in Bengal. They fetched a better price than the *cauries* from Manila. By the 1780s this article began to find a new market in Ceylon, which was purchased by the Dutch through a system of contract.[153]

Thus, by 1790 the two European powers had carved out their own spheres of operations as can be seen in Map 3.1. The English operated between the Bengal-China and Bombay-China route encompassing Malaya and the Philippines. The French preferred to operate in the region from Bengal and the Coromandel to Ceylon, Isle de France, Bourbon and Moka, with occasional trips to China and Manila. Together, the private traders of England and France began to penetrate into the traditional Indian structure. From shipowners they became credit suppliers and operated agencies, controlled wholesale trade and managed godowns for grain trade. The large-scale devastation of the south due to wars and political disturbances accompanied by frequent famines and demographic changes caused by the expansion of European settlements raised the prices of rice and other consumer goods. Rising prices and the increasing use of credit instruments, instead of ready cash, marked a new social trend. The Indian merchants and shippers who had dominated the Asian trade as suppliers and carriers were unable to withstand these combined pressures and found themselves ousted from their traditional field. Their role was taken over by the European traders. The latter became not only the actual operators of the 'country' trade but were replacing Indian merchants and *dalals* as creditors, contractors and retailers. The active participation of the French traders in this field and then their quick ouster in the 1790s served the interest of the English private traders and strengthened their control. The

English penetration into Tanjore, Madura and the Guntur Circar in the Deccan and their policy of annexation appear to have been guided by this interest group. The 'country' trade partly compensated the cost of the administration of European settlements, but more significantly the increase of British 'country' trade led to European shipping industry through their links with Burma. By siphoning off the profits from India the European traders contributed to the process of 'drain'.

NOTES

1. *Auckland Papers*—French Claims 1772-6, MS. 34468, Br. Mus.
2. Ibid.
3. Ibid.
4. Ibid.
5. General letter from Alexander Wynch, 24 March 1770, *Public Consult.* No. 56, Fort St. George, TSA.
6. French claims, *Add. Ms.* 34468, Br. Mus.
7. Extract from General Consultation, 8 November 1772 and 5 February 1773, *French in India Series*, Vol. 5, IOR.
8. Observations on the French Memorial, transmitted by the Court of France to English Ministry through Court of Directors, 22 May 1776, *Add. Ms.* 34468, pp. 180-7, *Auckland Papers*, Br. Mus.
9. Panen to Mons. de Lessart, 2 October 1771, *Nouv. Acq.* 8935, BN.
10. Legoux de Flaix, *Essai Historique, Gèographique et Politique sur L'Indoustan avec le tableau de son commerce*, Paris, 1807, Tome II, p. 36.
11. Ibid.
12. M. Legoux de Flaix, op. cit., Vol. I, p. 421.
13. H. Weber, op. cit., p. 619.
14. Paul Butel, 'French Maritime Activities in the Indian Ocean from XVIIIth to XIXth Centuries: The Example of Bordeaux', in K.S. Mathew (ed.), *Shipbuilding and Navigation in the Indian Ocean Region, A.D. 1400-1800*, Delhi, 1996, pp. 98-107.
15. Weber, op. cit., pp. 619-20.
16. Mémoire sur le commerce des Indes Orientles et sur celuy de la Compagnie des Indes en particulier, C^2 247 (microfilm), AN, p. 260.
17. Louis Dermigny, *Cargaisons Indiennes, Soliers et Cie 1781-1793*, Paris, 1960, p. 90.
18. Chopacah to Palk, *Palk Papers*, 29 October 1773 (microfilm from City Exeter Library, London), NAI.
19. 10 October 1775, *Palk Papers*.
20. Letter to Court, 26 September 1776, *Fort William—India House Correspondence*, Vol. II (1773-6), *Public Series*, p. 460.
21. Fra Paolinoda San Bartolomeo, *A Voyage to the East Indies*, London, 1800, p. 11.
22. M. Legoux de Flaix, op. cit., Tome I, p. 399.

23. Ibid.
24. Ibid., p. 400.
25. Ibid., p. 40.
26. Duval de Leyrit and Council to the Administrators of the Company, 3 February 1757, *Correspondence du Conseil Supérieur de Pondichéry*, Tome V, NAI, p. 175.
27. Ibid., p. 172.
28. Ibid.
29. Duvel de Leyrit and Council to the Administrators of the Company, 3 February 1757, A. Martineau (ed.), *Correspondance du Conseil Supérieur de Pondichéry*, Tome V, p. 175, Legoux de Flaix, op. cit., p. 413.
30. S. Jeyaseela Stephen, 'Urban Growth of Pondicherry and the French: A Study of the Town Plans 1702-1798', in K.S. Mathew and S. Jeyaseela Stephen (eds.), *Indo-French Relations*, Delhi, 1999, pp. 109-23.
31. Legoux de Flaix, op. cit., Tome I, p. 416.
32. Dolphin to Weymouth, 21 March 1776. Extract of General letter from Bombay, MS 123 *Home Misc.*, IOR.
33. Ibid.
34. Mons. de Montrivage, 23 July 1771, *Nouv. Acq.* 8935, BN.
35. It was an imitated cloth like the one from London and was made in central France. It was exported to the East Indies for a short period.
36. Duval de Leyrit and Council to the Administrators of the Company, 3 February 1757, op. cit., p. 172.
37. Balkrishna, *Commercial Relations between India and England, 1601-1757*, London, 1924, p. 220.
38. Report of the Select Committee, 7 September 1791, MS 933 (microfilm from Guild Hall Library, Manchester), NAI.
39. Balkrishna, op. cit., p. 218.
40. Ibid., p. 220.
41. Dharma Kumar(ed.), *Cambridge Economic History of India*, Vol. II, Cambridge, 1983, p. 814.
42. K.N. Chaudhuri, *The Trading World of Asia and the English East India Company 1660-1760*, London, 1978, p. 234.
43. Ashin Das Gupta, ' Presidential Address'. Section II, Medieval India Section, *Indian History Congress Proceedings*, 1974, pp. 99-111.
44. These items are discussed in detail in Chapter 6 of this book.
45. M. Legoux de Flaix, op. cit., Tome II, p. 161.
46. Abstract of the General Exports of *chay* goods from Masulipatam, *Masulipatam Consultation—Commercial*, 1786, Vol. 2837, APA.
47. Letter of French agent at Pondicherry to Mons.de Verdiers at Isle de France, 1 October 1770, *Nouv. Acq.* 8935, BN, p. 365.
48. Tableau des merchandises du commerce de I'inde et de la Chine vendues à L'Orient pendant 1784 et 1785, C^2 114 (microfilm), AN. However, the trade figures slightly differ from the ones provided in Tableau de l'Importation en France des Marchandises de l'Inde (1771-82) in a mèmoir, Vol. II, *Mémoirs et Documents*, Asia, p. 16, Arch. Aff. Étr., and by Pierre Louis Lacrettele and Blond in Mémoire à consulter et consultation pour les negociants faisant le commerce des merchandises des Indes contre la Nouvelle Compagnie des Indes, Paris, 1786, BN.

The figures might have been inflated to some extent to prove the success of free trade but the pattern and curves of the trade figures are quite similar.

49. Statement of Investment upon Madras Coast and Sale amount of Coast piece goods, 27 March 1787, *Madras Despatches*, E/4/873, pp. 515-20, IOR.
50. Samuel Statham (Resident at Nizampatam) to Charles Floyers, 26 July 1786, *Masulipatam District Correspondence*, Commercial, 1786-8, Vol. 2900, APA.
51. Herbert Lüthy, op. cit., p. 383.
52. Ibid.
53. Holden Furber, *John Company at Work: A Study of Commercial Expansion in India in the Late 18th Century*, New York, 1970, p. 33.
54. Herbert Lüthy, op. cit., pp. 382-3.
55. This was an Anglo-Genevese financial house. Panchaud was born in London, of Dutch mother and Swiss father. Since 1763, he was a banker in Paris and was described by Horace Walpole as 'an English banker at Paris'.
56. Herbert Lüthy, op. cit., p. 425.
57. Jarett Dereck, *The begetters of Revolution: England's Involvement with France 1759-89*, New Jersy, 1973, p. 157.
58. This was another powerful group of investors who were associated with the family of bankers in Switzerland, Holland and Paris. They were involved in all types of ventures including the financing of Indian trade.
59. Herbert Lüthy, op. cit., p. 452.
60. Ibid., p. 453.
61. Jarett Dereck, op. cit., p. 157.
62. Herbert Lüthy, op. cit.
63. Ibid., p. 455.
64. Ibid.
65. Mémoirs of the Deputies, 1787, Paris, CPL, Ohio.
66. Louis Dermigny, *Cargaisons Indiennes*, p. 118.
67. Macpherson described Rabaud as 'particularly celebrated for the extent and prosperity of his trade to India'. David Macpherson, *The History of the European Commerce with India*, London, 1812, p. 278.
68. Memorial from the Deputies of the Principal Commercial Towns, Paris, 1987, Manuscripts on British India, CPL.
69. Louis Dermigny suggests that *La Philippine* left in 1771 whereas the Memorial from the Deputies mentions 1776, as date of its departure, returning in 1778.
70. Memorial from the Deputies, op. cit.
71. Ibid.
72. Ibid.
73. Lagrenée to Degald Campbell, March 1775, *Lagrenée Correspondence*, No. 358, NAI, Pondicherry.
74. Pelling de Fries & Co. to M. Lagrenée, 7 December 1783 and 1 January 1784, Bourdieu and Chollet to Lagrenée, 11 August 1777, etc., NAI, Pondicherry.
75. Paul Butel, op. cit.
76. Louis Dermigny, op. cit., p. 118.
77. According to one *memoir*, the private trade was nothing but the trade of two officials—Law and Chevalier who made full use of the bills of exchange much to the benefit of the English. Their dealings covered almost three-fourths of the total eastern sale except the China trade. He suggests their removal and replacement

by a council. Mémoire by Chevalier De St. Lubin, 15 March 1775, *Mem. et Doc., Asia*, Vol. 7, Arch. Aff. Étr.

78. Letter from the Court, 21 November 1766, *India House-Fort William Correspondence*, Vol. V, pp. 214-15, NAI.
79. Ibid., 17 May 1766, p. 180.
80. Cornwallis to the Secret Committee of the Court of Directors, 16 November 1786, *Bengal Secret Letter*, First Series, Vol. I, 1778-94.
81. P.J. Marshal, *East India Fortunes: The British in Bengal in the Eighteenth Century*, Oxford, 1976, p. 252.
82. Ibid.
83. Ibid.
84. Holden Furber, *John Company*, p. 49.
85. P.J. Marshall, op. cit.
86. Letter from Chevalier de Savourren to Michel Henry Fabus, 23 September 1783, No. 33. *The Verlèe Collection*, IOR and Larkins to Mons. Bretel, 30 January 1785, *The Verlèe Collection*, IOR.
87. Financial papers of Michel Henry Fabus de Bretel, No. 26 *The Verlèe Collection*, IOR.
88. Rousseaux to John Verlée, 18 August 1789, *The Verlèe Collection*.
89. Holden Furber, op. cit., p. 50.
90. Stone to Robert Palk, 21 February 1776, *Palk Papers*, Serial No. 2 (microfilm from City Exeter Library, London available at NAI).
91. Letter from Adams to Palk, 9 October 1773, Serial No. 1, *Palk Papers* (microfilm), NAI.
92. Holden Furber, op. cit., pp. 50-1.
93. Henry Dodwell, *The Nabobs of Madras*, London, 1926, p. 138.
94. Ibid.
95. Moracin Compte, 31 December 1786, No. 316, NAI, Pondicherry.
96. William Milburn, op. cit., Vol. II, p. 66.
97. Ole Feldbaek, *India Trade under the Danish Flag, 1772-1808*, Copenhegan, 1969, p. 92.
98. Pierre Haudrere, *La Compagnie Française des Indes au XVIIIe Siécle (1719-1795)*, Vol. II, Paris, 1989, p. 812.
99. S. Arasaratnam and Furber trace the enormous growth of private English trade in Asian seas to the 1750s onwards, S. Arasaratnam, 'Trade and Political Dominion in South India, 1750-1790: Changing British-Indian Relationships', *Modern Asian Studies*, Vol. 13, No. 1, 1979, pp. 19-40 and Holden Furber, *John Company*, p. 163. However, the Memoir of Jacques Vericins, as analysed by Indrani Ray, indicates the already established dominance of Madras in this branch of trade. It was realizing as much as 90,000 *pagodas* from export-import duties alone. It was for this reason, Vincens advocated an active French participation in this trade in as early a period as 1730s. This is re-confirmed by the letter of Dupleix to La Bourdonnais of 18 January 1733. Indrani Ray, 'India in Asian Trade in the 1730s—An 18th Century French Memoir', *Indian History Congress Proceedings*, 34th Session, 1973, pp. 271-90.
100. These firms or agency houses played a very important role by providing credit to the 'country' trade and thereby helped the English traders to dominate the coastal trade.

101. Henry Dodwell, op. cit., p. 129.
102. Holden Furber, *John Company*, pp. 160-1.
103. Catherine Manning, 'French Country Trade on Coromandel 1720- 1750', in Om Prakash (ed.), *European Commercial Expansion in Early Modern Asia*, Vol. 10, *An expanding world*, Hampshire, 1997, p. 287.
104. Ibid.
105. Ibid., p. 288
106. W. Francis (ed.), *Madura District Gazetteer, South Arcot District Gazetteer*, Madras, 1906. Ananda Ranga Pillai mentions of a ship *Maure*, belonging to Dumas and Imam Sahib jointly, which left for Mocha in January 1737.
107. Catherine Manning, op. cit., p. 287.
108. Mémoire au sujet du commerce generale des Indes Orientales pour Guillaume Fevrièr, 1738, *Nouv. Acq. Série*, 9354 (microfilm from BN at NAI).
109. Indrani Ray, 'India in Asian Trade in the 1730s—An 18th Century French Memoir', *Indian History Congress Proceedings*, 34th Session, 1973, pp. 271-90.
110. Mémoire sur le commerce des Indes Orientales et Sur Celuy de la Compagnie des Indes (1764?) C^{47}, microfilm, p. 260, AN.
111. P. Haudrere, op. cit., p. 811.
112. Ibid.
113. Dupleix to Messrs Directeurs Generaux, 15 October 1735(?), *Nouv. Acq. Série*, 9334, BN.
114. M. L'abbé Baudeau (ed.), *Encyclopédie Mèthodique—Commerce*, Paris, 1783, Tome I, p. 632.
115. Holden Furber, op. cit., pp. 162-3.
116. The imports from Bengal into Surat went up to the value of Rs. 10 lakh in 1731-2 but dropped to less than Rs. 65,000 annually from 1770-1.
117. Reply of Law de Lauriston, 13 March 1777, *Nouv. Acq. Série*, 8935, p. 382, BN.
118. Mémoire sur le commerce des Indes Orientales (1764 ?), C^{247} A.N.
119. From Mons. de Montrivage, 23 July 1771, *Nouv. Acq. Série*, 8935, BN. A similar expression is to be found in Law's description of private trade in Papiers de Bellecombe et Law (1777), No. 102, NAI, Pondicherry.
120. From to Dumont du Caurier, 7 February 1771, Pondicherry, *Nouv. Acq. Series*, 8935, op. cit.
121. Pierre Blancard, *Manual du Commerce des Indes Orientales et de la Chine*, Paris, 1806, p. 476.
122. Louis Dermigny, op. cit., p. 118.
123. Ibid.
124. S. Arasaratnam, 'Slave Trade in the Indian Ocean in the Seventeenth Century', in K.S. Mathew (ed.), *Mariners, Merchants and Oceans, Studies in Martine History*, New Delhi, 1995, p. 196.
125. The price of slave during the seventeenth century varied from one place to another and also fixed according to the age and sex of the slave. Men aged between 20 to 36 were sold for 24 rupees in Arakan, while women aged 12 to 25 were sold for 12 rupees, boys of 8 to 19 for 15 rupees while children of 3 to 6 years for about 5 rupees. Arasaratnam, op. cit., p. 206.
126. Philip Haudrere, op. cit., p. 809.
127. Marina Carter, 'Indian slaves in Mauritius (1729-1834)', *The Indian Historical Review*, Vol. XV, Nos. 1-2, 1988-9, pp. 233-47.

128. Ibid.
129. Papers concerning slavery, *The Verlèe Collection (1769-1836)*, MSS Eur. F. 193, 6, IOR.
130. *Sale of Slaves, Feuilles Volantes, Karikal*, Série Le-Indes, *dossier nos. 3356, 3422, 3540, 3640, 3657, 3810 and 3871*, Archives d'Aix-en-Provence, France.
131. Accounts of M. Bretel, Aug. 1769, *The Verlée Collection*, op. cit. 'one man said that he was inveigled into the building, on promise of being employed as a cooly to carry a bag, and that when he entered, his head was shaved and fetters were placed on his legs. Another stated that he was offered betel, lightly smeared with lime . . . he was seized with giddiness and was led away . . . the persons engaged in the slave traffic had enticed wood-cutters and grass-cutters into private building, on pretence of buying the articles which they had to dispose of. It further transpired that these kidnappers possessed a house in a village near Tranquebar, and that they were in the habit of alluring thither the people living in the hamlets to the west of that place. Batches of fifty or a hundred individuals were imprisoned, at one time, in the building. They were conveyed, during the night, in a boat to Ariyankuppam, where they were confined in a house belonging to Paramanandam. Here their heads were shaved, black cloths were given to them to wear, and each individual had a fetter placed on one leg. During the night, they were removed again, and brought to the house of M. Soude, where they were put into the slave prison until a vessel came to take them away'. Tuesday, 25 June 1743, Ananda Ranga Pillai, *The Private Diary of Ananda Ranga Pillai*, Vol. I, J. Frederick and K. Rangachari (eds.), Delhi, rpt. 1985, p. 228.
132. The two boys were sent to Rev. Angelus Superior of the Indian Church in Chandernagar to work as monthly-wage workers, while the girl was to receive three *sicca* rupees monthly till she got married or was in a condition to support herself. We do not have any information whether these instructions were actually carried out. The money on the girl was to be spent from a Trust Fund of Rs.160 or 10 gold *mohurs*, which Joseph Ward had deposited with Bretel by means of *hundi*. Joseph Ward to M. De Bretel, 10 Dec. 1793, *The Verlèe Collection*, F. 193, op. cit.
133. Governor to the court of Directors, 28 January 1793, *Madras Public Consultations*, 241/36, TSA.
134. Ibid.
135. Letter of M. Maugin, 13 June 1771, *Nouv. Acq.*, 8935, B.N.
136. C.N. Parkinson, *Trade in the Eastern Seas, 1793-1813*, Cambridge, 1966, p. 336.
137. Louis Dermigny, op. cit., p. 117.
138. Ibid.
139. Ibid.
140. Salt was also manufactured in the Ichapur district of Ganjam but its export was not allowed. Nor were the zamindars and Haveli *parganas* allowed by the English to import salt from outside. As a result salt in these districts was sold 200 to 300 per cent dearer than in their neighbouring territories hardly 40 miles away.
141. Ninth Select Report, 1783, MS 931, John Ryland Library, Manchester (microfilm at NAI, Delhi).
142. Statement of French claims by order of the solicitor—Francis Russell, August 1786, *French in India Series*, Vol. 6, IOR.

143. Extract of letter from the Board of Trade to Governor-General and Council, 5 May 1795, No. 1035, *French in India Series*, Vol. 13, IOR.
144. Tableau du Sel importe par les français dans le Bengale, 22 June 1792, *Verlèe Collection*, No. 102, IOR.
145. Ibid.
146. N.K. Sinha (ed.), *Midnapore Salt Papers, Hijli and Tamluk, 1781-1807*, 1954, p. 6.
147. H. Furber, op. cit., p. 174.
148. Louis Dermigny, op. cit., p. 117.
149. H. Furber, op. cit.
150. Holden Furber, op. cit., p. 186.
151. A letter of 1771 clearly mentions Mons. Law, Martin, Denurs and Montrivage equipping a ship to Moka from a subscription of Rs. 28,000. In fact, the French trade with Moka was quite active. Mons. de Montrivage, 23 July 1771, *Nouv. Acq*., 8935, BN.
152. To M. de Montrivage, 23 July 1771, *Nouv. Acq*., 8935, B.N. Milburn also describes boats from Maldives reaching Indian coasts in fleets of 20 or 30 with their produce such as coir, coconuts, cowries, salt-fish, tortoise shells, and returning with broad cloth, silk goods, sugar, tobacco, etc. William Milburn, *Oriental Commerce*, Vol. II, p. 93.
153. Moracin, op. cit., p. 204; William Milburn, *Oriental Commerce*, Vol. II, p. 93.

Chapter 4

The Birth of Nouvelle Compagnie des Indes and Coromandel Trade 1785-1793

THE PERIOD after the Treaty of Versailles (1783) till the outbreak of the French Revolution (1789) witnessed a steady restoration, and to some extent revival, of trade in India of the two rival European powers. Ever since the English and the French had engaged themselves in a war on the issue of American Independence, their respective trading activities went down to a very low level. Coupled with this, the Anglo-Maratha and the Anglo-Mysore wars in southern India had completely ruined the political and economic life of the region. However, the formation of another French Company in 1785 based on a new spirit of Anglo-French cooperation and the fresh interest of the English directors to develop new commercial products in this area brought about a revival of trade. This period experienced the last serious French effort to re-establish their commercial and political power in India, and the Coromandel was the only region where this revival seemed feasible.

The Anglo-French hostilities caused by the American War of Independence was brought to an end by the Treaty of Versailles. This document was signed on 3 September 1783. It had a specific reference to India, particularly in matters of trade, in Articles 13-16, and 20. Article 13 of the Treaty of Versailles stipulated:

> The King of Great Britain restore to his most Christian Majesty, all the settlements which belonged to him at the beginning of the present war, upon the Coast of Orissa and in Bengal, with liberty to surround Chandernagar with a ditch for carrying off the waters and his Britanic Majesty engages to take such measures as shall be in his power for securing to the subjects of France in that part of India, as well as on the Coast of Orissa, Coromandel and Malabar, a safe, free and independent trade, such as was carried on by the

French East India Company, whether they exercised it individually or united in a company.

Article 14 stated: 'Pondicherry shall be in like manner delivered up and guaranteed to France, as also Karikal and his Britannic Majesty, shall procure for an additional dependency to Pondicherry, the two districts of Valamour and Bahoor, and to Karikal, the four mangans bordering there upon.' These decisions were transmitted to the Fort-William government under the Court's letter of 24 September 1783. The treaty contained two main principles for the restoration of peace: (a) a reciprocal restitution of territories, and (b) a safe, free and independent trade to be carried on by the French in India on the pre-war level.

The first principle was easily, though slowly implemented. The execution of the second principle depended on the formulation of a mutually acceptable agreement, and even after that troubles developed on its interpretation. Articles 13 and 14 were interpreted differently by the two rival powers. The determination of trade relations became a difficult task. The privileges of trade and the mode of ascertaining and realizing the duties by the country government on that trade, were the principal points of dispute.[1] These irritants had existed even before the War of American Independence.

The admission of the French claim to free trade provided in Article 13 was bound to clash with the rights of sovereignty, which the English Company had claimed since 1765. The legal standing of the French was the same as that of the English in their relations with the Mughal emperor. But the practical situation was quite different. The Treaty of Versailles was quite a crucial document in according recognition to the English sovereignty. Yet the recognition of French claims to freedom of trade in India through a European treaty was a substantial achievement for the French. It would not be wrong to suggest that the conclusion of the negotiations for peace with Britain paved the way for the reorganization of French relations with India.

Lt Col. Cathcart, the British minister-plenipotentiary went to Mauritius, to bring about a settlement of the outstanding questions with the French representative—Vicomte du Soulliac.[2] Together they worked out the Anglo-French trade convention at Isle de France. According to the convention:

1. The British accepted in principle to guarantee to the subjects of France a safe, free and independent trade; the guarantee was,

however, not to apply to the territories of the British allies, e.g. Awadh, Carnatic and Tanjore.

2. No manifest of cargoes was to be demanded in future on the arrival of merchant vessels from Europe. But the invoice of goods either imported or exported under the signature of one of the French agents and the seal of the Company had necessarily to specify the kinds, qualities and quantities of such goods with their prime costs so that the Company's collectors of customs might easily determine the duties payable at the rate of 2.5 per cent.[3]
3. The *dastaks* or permits of the French factory at Masulipatam were allowed a free currency in the Northern Circars with a free passage, exempted from all duties, whether on export or import, for goods belonging to the French Company or to French individuals.
4. The British agreed to pay compensation to the French for their loss of *Corvette Experance.*

The Soulliac-Cathcart Convention of Mauritius came under severe criticism from both the sides. The French colonies at Mauritius, Pondicherry and Chandernagar were all unanimous in their condemnation of the convention. It was considered ruinous to the French interests and exclusively favourable to those of the British. On the other side, when the Court of Directors and the India Board received copies of the provisional convention in August 1786, they strongly disapproved of the settlement Cathcart had concluded. They felt that the Fort William Council had overstepped its authority in vesting him with such extensive powers. Most of the Directors were taken aback by the terms of the convention, but they refrained from disallowing it, probably, because Pitt did not wish to embarrass Sir William Eden who was in Paris, carrying on negotiations for the Anglo-French commercial treaty of 1786.

Although both sides tried to abide by the terms of the convention and maintained friendly relations, yet several disputes and controversies arose. Under Cornwallis there was a stiffening of English attitude towards the French, which resulted in the tightening of control on European trade.[4] There were disputes concerning the detention of the French vessels and hoisting of the French flag on their ships and settlements; there were complaints about impediments put on the French trade at several *aurangs* by the English Company and about French boats being seized.[5] The English servants, in their turn, complained that the French agents placed impediments on the English trade[6] and that the French commercial resident at Sylhet had undertaken to supply arms to the local rajas[7] and so acted contrary to the terms of the convention.

The Anglo-French trade convention of 1786, thus, does not seem to have had a major impact on French commerce in India. Though it was called upon to solve all the outstanding disputes there was no spectacular success. Controversies continued to develop on the same issues that had existed in the pre-convention period. The success of the convention depended upon the good faith of both the nations. Superficially it did exist but the English could never accept a situation in which the French traders were to share equal fruits of the trade. Moreover, the results of the convention could not be judged properly, for the Revolution of 1789 dislocated the entire colonial trade, particularly with India.

The strengthening of French relations with India required enhanced funds. This provided an opportunity to the powerful financial houses of France and Britain to collaborate in the Indian trade and directly and indirectly to control it. The French efforts to re-establish their monopolistic structures through a new company was the epitome of this trend. It is interesting to note that even before the formation of the Nouvelle Compagnie, the financial and banking *maisons* were intriguing to establish political contacts with the English government to obtain privileges in order to control the Indian trade.

FORMATION OF THE NOUVELLE COMPAGNIE DES INDES

Throughout the 1770s there had been a growing collaboration between London and Paris based banking houses to finance the eastern trade. A similar cooperation existed in India between the French free traders and the English Company's servants. They operated through the bills of exchange and through different channels of remittances.

Nussbaum refers to a letter which suggests that Bourdieu and Chollet of London and Jacques Necker of Paris were negotiating to provide some kind of cooperation between a reconstituted French Company which was to be established and the English East India Company.[8] In 1772 Bourdieu's efforts did not succeed, nor were they favourably received in the ministry, though the government showed some interest in the political aspect of his scheme and its trade possibilities through organizational changes.

The issue of abolition of the old French Company in 1769 initiated a debate, which was activated each time the question of reforms was raised. In fact, the dissolution of the French Company and the consequent opening of the Indian trade to individual merchants was always regarded a temporary or a stopgap arrangement. The numerous memoirs of this period reflect this opinion. The Estates of Brittany petitioned for the re-establishment of the Company in 1770. It was argued by some that free trade failed to supply the French market adequately. A group of retired judges of L'Orient wrote to Vergennes that attempts of individuals to trade in India had been ruinous to those undertaking it.[9] It was also argued that the trade under *negocians particuliers* had been inadequate and had mostly passed into the hands of foreigners. Despite the attractive profits of the East India trade ranging from 40 to 80 per cent on each turnover of 18 to 24 months' duration, the free traders were unable to provide as much supply of the eastern goods as was demanded.[10] It is evident that the spirit of enterprise of the type we notice in England had not yet developed in France, and the official initiative to involve the government in trade ventures had not ceased.

Thus the peace of 1783 seemed to be an ideal opportunity through which France could promote its commercial revival in India. Soon after it and prior to the formation of another privileged company in France, an experiment was tried out under official direction. An *arrêt* was issued on 21 July 1783 which directed the formation of *une seule et méme association* among the merchants of Marseilles, Bordeaux, Nantes, Saint-Malo, L'Orient and Le Harve, with a capital of 60,00,000 *livres*.[11] Each port was allotted a fixed quota of shares. The king offered three vessels for their trade shipments. The return of the vessels proved fairly profitable. It showed a profit of about 82 per cent.[12] Although no document has been found which could provide results of this experiment, it is apparent that the merchants of the seaport towns had too much of local and personal jealousies and had little cooperative feeling to develop a financial organization that could face the English Company on an equal footing. The experiment suggests that the Indian trade was still profitable but owing to unorganized efforts it was extremely limited. Few individuals made attempts to exploit the profits of the trade. This may have been due to the nature of risk involved in these ventures, but more so because of the scarcity of capital. Even the English sources suggest that despite high profits made from Indian trade, much more than from any part of Europe, there was a scarcity of ready money by means of a central bank. The shortage of money was due to limited circulation. The money channels were too narrow and confined to improper hands.

In this atmosphere, a complex set of factors was driving the French government inexorably towards the recreation of monopoly in the eastern trade. The three most important ministers—Calonne, the finance minister, Vergennes, the minister for foreign affairs, and Castries, the minister of colonies, had some part to play in this venture, though it is difficult to determine their exact role. Montaran had reminded Vergennes that the establishment of foreign trade concerned his department.[13] He received a number of memoirs and suggestions urging him to form a company with a monopoly and well-defined scope. Rayneval justified this on 'political' grounds but advised him to limit it to a purely commercial company without touching the English rights.[14] De Luynes, the deputy of the Nantes association, agreed with Panchaud to confine it to the form of a stock company rather than a closed group of *interèsses.* The famous economic thinker Dupont de Nemours, advised the association to convert Isle de France and Isle de Bourbon into free ports, and to utilize the Indian goods to expand the French industries.[15] It is said that Vergennes during his administration, always had in view the possibility of concluding a commercial treaty between France and England, and he considered it as a point of honour to bring it to a successful conclusion.[16] While Vergennes wished to direct the project of Anglo-French cooperation, Calonne saw in India another opportunity to link the finances of the kingdom with the financiers—new and bold capitalist profit seekers. And for Castries, the redevelopment of the Indian trade meant enlargement of the colonial sphere.

It was neither the projects of the economists nor the ambitions of the politicians that determined the ultimate formation of the Nouvelle Compagnie des Indes. Rather, the Company came into existence because of the well-coordinated effort and influence of the Paris bankers—Girardot, Haller & Co. and the London-based bankers—Bourdieu and Chollet, as leaders of a group of financiers who linked this project with the English Company and politicians. Bourdieu and Chollet established contact with Girardot, Haller & Co. on the proposal of a new French East India Company—a proposal that had been made to Necker as early as 1770 and 1772.

An examination of the factors leading to the formation of the French Company brings out the existence of an intense rivalry among the financial houses. They competed with one another to control the Indian trade even before the actual formation of a company. The entire project envisaged the formation of an exclusive Company to make a treaty with the English Company for purchasing Indian goods. The project was probably backed by Castries.[17] Its four prominent promoters—Bernier, Sabatier, Desprez and Périer visited London in spring 1784 to ascertain from Bourdieu the nature of privileges he was envisaging to and give him authority to negotiate with the English directors and ministers.[18] Bourdieu promptly sent a memoir to the Duke of Portland and to the directors. He tried to appeal to them with his arguments by showing how England would gain by the formation of a company. He seemed to have mentioned that the English Company would prevent the French from establishing direct connections with India, would produce 13 million pounds sterling through new business, and cause the Indian manufacturers to regard the French as the only agents of the Company.[19]

It was at this stage that Calonne established direct contact with Bourdieu, advising him to use his influence with the British government in favour of the formation of a new India Company in France. It is not clear whether Calonne or Castries knew of each other's activities, but Calonne began to direct the future moves of the French government.[20] His letter to Bourdieu took official note of the negotiations and recognized him as an authorized negotiator. Vergennes probably did not know of these developments and was apparently informed by Adhemar, Gourlade and Barthélemy.

In the meantime, Bourdieu succeeded in arousing the interest of the English in the French scheme on the condition that the proper authority officially backed him up. He made a visit to Paris in this connection to obtain an official approval of his negotiations. In his memorial presented to M. De Calonne at Paris, he tried to prove the impossibility of the French East India Company being admitted to a fair participation in the trade of Bengal without immediate protection of the English East India Company and the sanction of the British government.[21] According to Messrs Bourdieu, Chollet and Bourdieu, the Controller-General of France, M. De Calonne gave up the idea of establishing a company unconnected with the English after going through the reasons assigned in the memorial.[22] In December 1784 it was known at Nantes that the government was planning a stock Company to oppose the plan, as it was entirely in the English interest. Vergennes tried to remain non-committal though he wrote to Adhemar suggesting that it would be a financial and political mistake to depend on the English Company. At the same time, the French were compelled to use the services of the English until their own trading ports were restored.

When the French Company was finally formed, it was strongly criticized by the commercial groups of the nation. The stocks did not appear for the ordinary merchants of maritime towns and manufacturers; rather the speculators grabbed those. A series of *arrêts* from February 1785, including an *arrêt* of 14 April 1785, defined the general status of the Company and the lines of its organization.[23] It was authorized as a negotiable share company with a capital of 20 million *livres* and was granted the monopoly of trade beyond the Cape of Good Hope for a period of seven years. Girardot, Haller & Co. was provisionally named cashier at Paris and J.J. Berard & Co. at L'Orient. Two other *arrêts* of 15 May nominated the officials of whom Bernier, Sabatier, Desprez and Périer were the four who lent their support to Bourdieu and Chollet, whereas Simon Berard, who was close to Vergennes, was hostile to this financial house. By 1787 another group, known as Commissaires, appeared as the representative of the stockholders. These included the names of the financiers like Couteulx du Moley, Boyd and Lalance. The 14,000 open shares were immediately purchased by the moneyed speculators of Paris which made the merchants of the seaports complain very bitterly.[24] It proved prejudicial to the Company as it gave the merchants of the seaports a just cause for fresh resentment and complaint. Moreover, during this period a spirit of gambling in the national debts and the stocks of public companies had developed in France to an alarming extent. L'abbé d'Espagnac and his confederates prepared a scheme for getting into their own hands the whole stock of the Compagnie des Indes at whatever price, in order to command a resale on their own terms.[25] As David Macpherson suggests, commercial affairs could not prosper in the hands of a company which purchased shares without any consideration for the benefits arising from the trade but merely in order to sell them again at an enhanced price.[26] The private merchants described the Company as an 'association of stock jobbers' rather than a 'company of merchants'.[27]

The English Company on the other hand was passing through a phase of reorganization by which the private interests of the merchants were being readjusted into a monopolistic structure. The Pitt's India Act of 1784 had given a structure to the Company that lasted almost unaltered till 1858.

Unlike the French, the English enterprise in the East Indies had crossed the stage of experimentation. The Indian possessions had started serving the interests of the English factories. This was clearly brought out in the statement of the Secret Committee of the Court of Directors. It stated, 'The question is not only what system shall be best fitted for the future government of British India, but under what Regulations can the Trade to the East Indies be carried on, so as to increase the Industry of our artisans and manufacturers, the credit of our merchants, and the general spirit of commerce.'[28]

THE ENGLISH RESPONSE TO THE FRENCH PROPOSALS

An agreement with the English Company envisaged a set of arrangements for the procurement of Indian goods from Bengal, the Coromandel and Orissa, and provided a mode of payment by the French Company. According to the proposal, the English Company was to furnish to the new French Company for a term of five years, later reduced to three years by the English, an annual assortment of three or four cargoes, to be settled afterwards by the two parties, and to be delivered at Bengal and Madras, to the yearly amount of 40 lakh of current rupees worth of goods including 30,000 lbs. of raw silk and 400 tons or saltpetre, to be computed at the prime cost.[29] To this was added a profit, which was not to exceed 10 per cent. The French Company was to make payments in bills or drafts at the exchange rate of 2 shillings for each current rupee or 8 shillings per *pagoda*, payable in London with interest, one-fourth at 30 days sight, one-fourth at three months, one-fourth at six months and last one-fourth at nine months sight. The name of Bourdieu Chollet and Bourdieu of London was included in the plan as the guarantor of payment of all the bills.

The initial response of the English directors appeared to be rather cautious. The English were not only watchful but also dilatory in respect to the initial French moves. From the resolution of the Court of Directors it is evident that Bourdieu had communicated the proposal for the formation of the Company to the chairman on 13 January 1784. The directors left the entire subject for the ministers to decide as these proposals seemed to involve many political considerations.[30] At the same time it is clear that the chairman of the Court expressed his eagerness to enter into a treaty. In his letter to Henry Dundas he wrote, 'I think the offer is a good one for us to accept.'[31] In another letter he revealed that Mons. Périer's proposals consisted of two separate agreements—one public and the other private.[32] Devaynes argued that both of them were equally binding.

According to Devaynes, in the first article of Périer's proposals, the French pledged not to be purchasers at the Danish or Lisbon market. At this stage Dundas warned him not to divulge the plan to others. He wrote, 'I must desire you will not communicate the papers to more persons than is absolutely necessarily.'[33] Countering the arguments of Smith, Sulivan and others who felt that the Anglo-French agreement of their respective companies would result in the overloading of markets with their imports and the English would bring home their investments at a loss, Devaynes argued that the agreement would give a profit of 33 per cent and thus facilitate the plan of liquidating the Indian debt.[34] To Devaynes it was considerably advantageous and was weighed in favour of the English.[35] Besides, the proposed agreement offered political advantages by creating harmonious relations abroad between the two companies. It would have made the country powers in India think that the English were supplying the French with their investments. It would also make the English its sole purchasers in Bengal markets.[36] At the same time by this deal the French were not likely to be affected in the Coromandel region.

There were numerous advantages of this proposed agreement, which were brought to the notice of the English Company by Bourdieu and Chollet.[37] The Company had been burdened with expensive wars, which necessitated borrowing under the sanction of an Act of Parliament and to raise the interest of their bonds. It was thought that the implementation of the French proposal would help the English Company discharge the said debt without being detrimental to their self interests. Furthermore, the Company could not have increased its sale in Europe beyond a certain level. The delivery of goods to the French in India was considered a means to remit so much more of the revenues and a help in augmenting the Company's sales in Leaden Hall Street. It was regarded that it would bring a clear remittance from France of £ 5,00,000 annually to the immediate benefit of the Company in particular and to the material advantage of the nation at large without draining India of its *specie*.[38] It was considered good from the point of view of precluding the private channels of transmitting fortunes to Europe, in which the Danes and the Portuguese had made remarkable gains. A regular agreement with the French was likely to put an end to private adventurers. The formal agreement between the two companies was to result in the re-establishment of an exclusive Company in France. It was suggested that in case of failure of the proposed agreement, the private adventurers (for which 47 licences were already granted) assisted by the money of the Company's servants would bring such a glut of goods as would affect the sales of the English Company and discourage the buyers by lowering the price and quality.[39] An exclusive French Company was undoubtedly strong and well secured with seven houses of known fortune and reputation behind its purchases—the premier being the house of Messrs Girardot, Haller & Co. Finally, the common commercial interest of both the companies was expected to become united and inseparable.

There were some persons in the English Company who opposed the idea of any kind of agreement with the French Company. John Manship wrote to the Court of Directors, ' they [the proposals] breathe not a single advantage to us but convey to my mind a heap of the greatest absurdities, against the manifest Interests of Ourselves and Constituents'.[40]

Nathanial Smith and John Manship opposed these French commercial proposals vehemently till as late as December 1785.[41] Both of them considered the treaty highly injurious to the commerce of the English Company without affording them any political advantage in return. The French, on the other hand by this arrangement, had the advantage of procuring Indian goods without facing any kind of investment risk or additional payment of interest on insurance—something they would have paid. The critics of the agreement charged that the white piece goods to be purchased by the French Company were to be received through the influence and authority of the English Company. It also meant that the inferiority of the earlier French investments (the quality of goods procured) were to be overcomed with the English assistance. They pointed out that instead of a proportionate amount of raw silk, a non-profitable item, the French Company was to procure only 380 maunds of it, while the English Company was importing nine to ten thousand maunds.

Warren Hastings also warned the Secret Court of Directors that the proposed treaty would draw the English into future vexatious contentions with the French on the question of quality and quantity of their products.[42] The objects of the proposed measure to sanction the agreement intrigued him. He felt that the aims of the agreement could not be preclusion of disputes and competition. On the contrary, the agreement was likely to add to them. Moreover, it was not expected to provide peace and security because the agreement contained the seeds of future wars and incitements. Nor could it be profit or honour, which, according to Hastings, this agreement could never provide.[43]

The directors had already sought the opinion of William Pitt, who suggested that the Company was competent to consider these proposals but advised that these were to be seen merely in a commercial light.[44] Later, the Court of Directors agreed to abide by the propositions and suggested that these be sent to the Board of Commissioners for the Affairs of India for their approbation.[45] In December 1785 the administrators of the English Company submitted the provisional treaty to the French government. The obduracy of Vergennes, at this stage, brought to an end all the hectic activities of London-based bankers. Calonne's efforts were defeated by Vergennes' refusal to sanction the treaty. Thus the entire negotiations, which had lasted almost two years, took a traumatic turn, and came to an end.

The French businessmen and bankers who combined in 1785 to form the so-called new Company, were aware that their financial success depended on close cooperation with the English Company and its servants. The administrators and political leaders were reviving their Indian interests from the viewpoint of 'power politics' and 'political dominations'. Calonne, in fact, was attempting through the English support, the establishment of an international cartel or a capitalist business organization, joined by the businessmen and bankers with the primary object of profit. It transgressed the traditional mercantilist political line that Vergennes was not prepared to allow. Fredrick Nussbaum had placed the entire responsibility of bringing to an end the efforts for Anglo-French cooperation on Vergennes.[46] The treaty had to be ratified by the French government. This gave Vergennes a chance to avenge the attempts of Calonne and his supporters to ignore him in such important affairs.

Though one cannot disagree with Nussbaum's analysis emphasizing the role of Vergennes in the failure to arrive at a formal treaty with the English, one cannot ignore the pressure of public opinion on him. Not only were his close advisers such as Gourlade, Moracin, Dupont, Adhemar, De Luynes against such an agreement, but innumerable memoirs and pamphlets had also appeared condemning the agreement on national and commercial considerations.

The arguments of Rayneval against the approval of the Anglo-French treaty of their respective companies included all the basic objections that were raised by the free merchants and others.[47] Already a tirade had mounted against the formation of a privileged Company for Indian trade. The secret agreement with the English Company caused a major uproar in business circles. It was argued that the treaty was wholly useless except as a device to ensure profits that came from the pockets of other Frenchmen. It was also argued that the state was enriching a small number of citizens at the expense of others; that the liberty of enterprise had been curtailed; that if Bengal trade could not be carried on without English assistance then the French Company was wholly useless; that the French merchants were adequately protected by the treaty of 1783 to buy eastern goods at Copenhagen, Lisbon and even in England. The import of Indian cloth was considered unnecessary. Instead, Rayneval suggested a Franco-Spanish combination to operate through Manila, which could get supply of silver from South America with well-guarded trading rights in India.[48]

Du Pont described the proposals as 'badly conceived for the company' and 'still worse for the state'.[49] He revealed that it was the English Company which would be the actual seller with assured profit and that all the risks of sea and on advance of borrowings would fall on the French. Whatever profit the French Company reaped was to be from freight and gains on second hand sale or resale. In fact, he suggested formation of a 'society of commerce' like a company of a joint-capital, with proprietors under regular inspection of the government and *commissaires* of the king. It would have the features of a company as well as the liberty of trade. As a company of merchants it would attract foreign capital and would provide gains of commerce to the people which would safeguard it against the English power.[50]

Thus, at home, the French manoeuvres were severely criticized and were regarded with suspicion by the cotton traders of Paris, Versailles, Lyon, Bordeaux, Rouen, Tours, Charlons sur Saône, Troies, Dijon, etc. Lacretelle and Blond in their mémoire contended that the Company with a mere capital of 20 million *livres*, intended to participate in a commerce, which required several times more capital. To them, the monopoly recreated by the government weighed all the time on the nation and to sustain it the Company made pronouncements against the commerce, adopted '. . . the most vigorous prohibitions and followed the most disturbing precautions'.[51]

In short, it can be said that the reaction of the English officials and directors to the French commercial moves was dilatory and cautious in the beginning but later became one of willing cooperation. The attitude of the English officials in India remained watchful and at times hostile. They were ever ready to render abortive any plan of the French that was considered inimical to the British interests in India.

That the French proposals were based on the political reality in India can be gauged by the nature of the demands. Initially the French had asked for two cargoes of goods from Bengal and two from the Coromandel but later agreed only to the Bengal region. The vast acquisitions of the English Company in eastern India placed the French at their mercy. The hurdles in the procurement of goods and the non-availability of funds for investment made the French position weak in Bengal. It was for this reason that they desired the cooperation of the English. On the Coromandel Coast, their position was comparatively safer. The procurement of cargo was relatively easier. Moreover, it was in this region that the French anticipated a political revival with the help of local rulers. So the Coromandel commerce was quietly kept outside the Anglo-French deliberations.

ANGLO-FRENCH TRADE

The end of the American War brought peace in India between the English and the French. The new peaceful condition, the systematic effort of the French to revive their trade, the formation of the Nouvelle Compagnie des Indes for this purpose and the active participation of the French in the cloth trade of the Coromandel created problems for the English as well as for the other European traders. The Danish Company, till then one of the regular trading bodies, discovered in September and October 1786 that the French merchants had almost emptied the entire coast of cloths through their own efforts.[52] When the Madras government had issued repeated prohibitions on private trade, it was being supplied by the French from their production centres around Yanaon. French ships, many of which brought silver and therefore got the best of returns, frequented the Coromandel Coast. According to one estimate, in 1787 and 1788, the French were said to have invested 8,00,000 *pagodas* of Anglo-Indian remittance capital in north coast cloths.[53] The bills were issued by the French agent at Pondicherry—Jean François Moracin—and were carefully honoured in London by Robert Herries and Co. In Calcutta, Fergusson and Fairlie played a major part in managing the financial transactions of the French for such dealings.[54] Besides, the French also operated through Thomas Hinchman, Narsing Nandy, Déonna and Stuart Dickey. Together they handled a considerable portion of procurement and payment of goods.[55]

The revival of English and French trade after the American War was primarily due to the vigorous efforts of their respective administrations. Despite the steady revival of the two companies a common problem faced by them during the 1780s was shortage of funds. The English Company was able to overcome it to some extent by obtaining surplus funds from Bengal. This was used for the purpose of investment. It also used political means to procure piece goods. But the French Company faced a more difficult task. It was mainly the farsightedness and astute dealing of Jean François Moracin and his vast commercial connections, which brought in additional funds for the French Company. He utilized the services of the French business families who resided or traded in the Coromandel region. These included the houses of Delarche, La Maison Coulon e Cie, Bury de st. Fulgence, Lagrenée, Geslin de Chateafeur, etc.[56] Moracin kept open all the possible sources of funds, even from the foreigners. Since 1770 he had been actively trading with foreign merchants. Paul Benfield was one such person with whom he had trade and financial dealings through bills of exchange. At the instance of his friend Wooley, Moracin received 1,02,000 star *pagodas* from Benfield at the exchange rate of 8 shillings per *pagoda*, as the latter was desperate to transfer his funds to Europe.[57] M.M. Balfour, Spalding and Colt were the main names, on which the bills were drawn. Moracin maintained two accounts—C.P. or personal account (*compte personnes*) and C.N. or the new account of the Company (*compte nouveau*)[58]

The revival of French trading activities in the Coromandel cautioned the English authorities, which made strenuous efforts to control and dominate the Coromandel trade. A Board of Trade was formed in the Madras Presidency in 1786.[59] It was to consist of the Governor, a junior member of the Council and three other members from among the senior servants.[60] This Board was to take into immediate consideration the different plans of investment along the coast. It was to constantly acquaint itself with the state of manufactures and the relative position of the English with foreign traders and with the French in particular, whose privileges were expressly defined and secured by the last treaty of peace.

The English exports to India, as discussed in the previous chapter, consisted of two main types of commodities—the woollens and metals. The former had a better market in the Coromandel region. A slight increase in the sale of English goods, particularly woollens, after years of efforts was enthusiastically regarded 'an accomplishment' by the

TABLE 4.1: SALE OF WOOLLENS IN MADRAS PRESIDENCY (1783-4 TO 1788-9)

Years	Value of import in £ St.	Sale price in £ St.
1783-4	25,022	26,983
1784-5	21,525	24,225
1785-6	24,168	25,934
1786-7	18,562	19,537
1787-8	20,683	20,974
1788-9	19,696	21,610

Source: Appendix 7 to the Fifth Report, MS 401, *Home Misc. Series*.

Company officials. It was assumed that this increase would be attended with beneficial consequences to the Company inasmuch as it would afford a considerable aid to their funds for the provision of a returning investment.[61]

There is no doubt that despite these encouraging statements by the English officials, the Indian market failed to respond to the English pressures. They knew that the fine cloths were meant for the use of the Europeans who were small in number and the demand for the coarse cloths was by far the most considerable. This was used for clothing the army. The Select Committee had expressed the fear that no amount of reduction in price would increase consumption in a country where so many substitutes for this, better suited to the climate and more congenial to the customs and prejudices of the inhabitants, were found.[62] It is evident from Table 4.1 that the profit on this item was nominal and that the English gained nothing substantial from it.

Metals constituted the other half of the English exports to India. These included copper, lead, sheet lead iron and steel. Of them the most saleable kind was plate copper of about 12 inches thickness, commonly called 'Brass-wire'. The Company's merchants were required to receive this metal as part of their advance, but this proved to be detrimental to the interest of cotton manufacture and weavers. They were mostly dependent for their advance on the merchants' views of gain on the sale of his copper and his ability to keep it on hand for that purpose. The Company had lately established copper coinage in the south. This created the bulk of demand for copper in the Coromandel and helped the English to tide over monetary problems for their payments. The sale of metals during this period shows a state of loss for the Company, except in the year 1788-9, as shown in Table 4.2.

The other metals, steel, iron and lead, had virtually no demand as commercial products.

TABLE 4.2: SALE OF METALS IN MADRAS PRESIDENCY (1783-4 TO 1788-9)

Years	Value of metals in £ St.	Sale price in £ St.
1783-4	50,129	53,957
1784-5	46,515	45,905
1785-6	79,643	78,665
1786-7	23,028	23,288
1787-8	31,130	32,267
1788-9	40,319	50,886

Source: Report of the Select Committee, 7 September 1791, MS 400, *Home Misc Series*.

The authorities of the Company made serious endeavours to augment the sale of European goods through their political links. Making use of their alliance with the Nizam of Hyderabad, they sought to introduce European goods into his dominions. Richard Johnston had recommended to the Board of Trade that the Nizam could be asked to accept about 100 bales of broad cloth on a regular basis.[63] The Court of Directors also suggested the establishment of warehouses for the sale of copper, broad cloth, etc., in different parts of the Madras Presidency. It directed the Madras government to establish a warehouse in Tanjore. The order was repeated next year, when it stated, 'In our letter of the 12 April 1786 we directed the establishment of a magazine at Tanjore for the vend of such articles and we conceive that similar undertakings may be successfully established at Madura, Tinnevelly and other parts of the coast as soon as it shall be found the situation of the Company affairs will admit.'[64] The object, as spelled out clearly, was not only to promote the sale of English goods but to break the French supplies to Tranquebar and Nagapatnam and other places. Pondicherry had enjoyed this advantage because of its vicinity to these places.[65]

The English authorities were keen to ascertain the potential market for the English products. It was with this objective that they sent to the Nizam cards (samples) containing patterns of several articles manufactured in the towns of Manchester, Halifax and Norwich. But till this time they had not formulated any clear-cut scheme to replace the Indian manufactures with the English products. The sale of English goods in the Madras Presidency did not show any marked increase. The sale of imported goods and stores in this presidency in 1786-7 was worth Rs. 7,45,680. It came down to Rs. 5,91,948 in 1787-8, declined further to Rs. 4,64,058 the next year and then marginally rose to Rs. 5,31,386 in 1789-90.[66] The Company did show interest in exploring new markets for their products. It tried to make a thrust in the kingdom of Mysore. Here they desired to sell its woollen products for the vast military force but the political rivalry and the class of economic and strategic interests did not allow such a development. The English failure to achieve this objective was attributed to the wars of 1780.[67] During the period between the two Anglo-Mysore wars, Tipu Sultan not only prohibited the introduction of British manu-factures but also forbade his subjects to sell the produce of his own country to the English.[68]

In contrast to the English, the French enjoyed an amicable relationship with Tipu. Commercial interests constituted an important factor in the French relations with Tipu. They had asked the latter to allow their merchandise to pass through Salem (Ceilom) and Anantgiri and to instruct the amaldars and *'kilidars'* of those regions not to place duties on them. The French also seem to have demanded the exclusive privilege of buying the products of Mysore, such as pepper and cardamom at a fixed price.[69] Tipu was shrewd enough to know his interests and probably conceded only the first part of their demands. Through Mohamed Hosseman Khan (one of Tipu's ambassadors to France in 1788) the French Company at Pondicherry sent a set of proposals to Tipu. These requested the ruler of Mysore to confer monopoly rights on the French Company for the exports of commercial products like pepper, sandalwood, cardamom, cotton threads, cotton cloths, ivory and some other goods.[70] The Company, in return, offered to furnish all kinds of military equipment such as cannon lead, war materials, artillery, marine products, diverse metals, drapery and woollen goods. The French Company also desired to export some quantity of rice from Mangalore and from a few other ports of Mysore without paying *adlam*—the customs duty. Furthermore, it wished to conduct the entire trade transactions with four principal merchants of the kingdom. These proposals, however, failed to achieve the desired results, as Tipu, it seems, had become disillusioned with the French and realized their political limitation. Still, there was a reasonable exchange of commercial products between Pondicherry and Mysore. The goods brought to the Coromandel included such items as pepper, sandalwood of inferior quality, arracks, gum and small quantities of grains for daily consumption, common cloth, the 'becque' waist belts and loincloth for the inhabitants. These were transported on oxen. Black salt also had a good market in the Coromandel. The Guinea from Salem occupied an important position in the cargo for Europe.[71]

TABLE 4.3: SHIPPING CARGO OF THE NOUVELLE COMPAGNIE DES INDES (FOR INDIA ALONE)

Years	No. of ships	Merchandise in *livres*	*Piastres* value in *livres*	Bills of exchange
1785-6	9	8,72,176	1,20,28,274	11,87,745
1786-7	8	14,03,122	1,15,70,063	1,44,512
1787-8	10	19,21,600	29,28,000	13,25,480
1788-9	6	14,16,362	80,29,034	12,23,000

Source: Louis Dermigny, p. 138.

An examination of the goods exported from France to India by the Nouvelle Compagnie des Indes gives us some idea of how the French tried to revive their trading activities. The contrast in the commodity composition of the French exports with the English exports becomes conspicuous. Whereas the English stopped exporting silver *specie* to Madras, the French had to augment its supply to India. In fact, silver exports constituted the bulk of the French export cargo. This is evident from Table 4.3.

The *piastres* and the bills of exchange constituted 93.81 per cent of the cargo in 1785-6, while merchandise contributed merely 6.19 per cent. In 1786-7, the latter constituted 10.70 while the remaining 89.10 per cent consisted of *piastres* and the bills. In 1787-8, the proportion of cargo changed considerably when the share of merchandise rose to 31.13 per cent while *piastres* and bills made up 68.87 per cent of the cargo. But the next year it rose to 86.72 per cent and the merchandise contributed only 13.26 per cent of the whole cargo.[72] The share of the Coromandel in the French consignments can be seen in Table 4.4.

On the basis of Table 4.4,[73] it is possible to infer that the trade of the Coromandel constituted 42.54 per cent of the French total investments to India and China between 1785 and 1789. The total amount sent to India and China, which included merchandise, *piastres* and the bills of exchange, was to the value of Rs. 6,47,14,308 *livres*, of this the share of the Coromandel was 2,75,34,535.[74] Added to this were bills of exchange drawn on Madras and Calcutta.

It is evident from the list of shipments that the French exports were not composed exclusively of the products manufactured in France. There was English beer, Swedish steel, and brass and tar from Norway. But the French exports were not meant to fetch only profits. They were aimed at providing funds and at reducing the trade imbalance. These were also directed to procure good quality products in sufficient quantity, from which gains were anticipated. And nothing better than

TABLE 4.4: TRADE CONSIGNMENT BY THE NOUVELLE COMPAGNIE FOR COROMANDEL

Name of the ship	Consignment	Total consignment in *livres*
Le Calonne	1785-6	34,29,396
Le Made Castries	1785-6	24,72,798
Le Comte d'Artois	1785-6	25,28,203
Le Ct de Vergennes	1785-6	1,30,785
Total		85,61,182
Le Vesse de Besse (freight for return)		
Le Marechal de Duras	1786-7	37,75,486
Le Duc de Normandie	1786-7	37,75,349
Le Duc de Penthieve	1786-7	1,80,762
Total		77,31,597
Le Comte d'Estaing	1787-8	18,85,070
Le Prince de Conde	1787-8	19,25,093
L' Actionnaire	1787-8	4,18,950
Le Marechal de Segur	1787-8	3,24,950
Total		48,22,394
Le Necker	1788-9	29,53,940
Le Royale Elisabeth	1788-9	34,65,422
Total		64,19,362

Source: J. Conan, Le Derniére Compagnie Française des Indes, p. 95.

silver bullion could achieve it. Unlike the English, the French did not have revenue surplus in India that could be converted into merchant capital.

Since France herself did not produce silver bullion, metals and marine stores which formed the bulk of export cargoes to India, these had to be bought from outside. For its bullion supplies, the French Company depended equally on two houses—Le Couteulx & Co. and Magon Fréres at Cadiz.[75] It appears that in the case of shipments to India, the French gave up attempts to compete seriously with the English and confined themselves to the heavy metals. At the same time they seem to have kept a close watch on the changes in the English export policy by securing information from the local agents.

One noticeable difference between the era of free trade and that of the new French Company was in the availability of silver *specie* for the purpose of investment. The years between 1772 and 1778 were marked by the availability of considerable funds for private trade with which the *armateurs* purchased a huge quantity of cloth from northern Coromandel. According to Moracin, this silver supply had become scarce during the 1780s. The quality of cloth had also declined after the years of disturbances.[76]

The commodity composition of the French export trade to the Coromandel continued to be more or less the same as it was before the formation of the new Company as is evident from Table 4.5.

Besides silver money the items of export from France, it included iron-plates, iron-anchors, pig-lead (*plomb en saumons*), Swedish steel, copper nails, copper sheet, copper plating, cordages, spun yarn (*bitord.*), voile thread, voile cloths, red-wine, liquor, perfumes, sulphur, etc. All these items were exported in small quantities.

TABLE 4.5: SHIPMENTS OF NOUVELLE COMPAGNIE DES INDES TO INDIA

1785-6 (9 ships)		%
In Merchandise	8,72,176	6.19
In silver *piastres*	1,20,28,274	85.38
Bill of exchange	11,87,745	8.43
Total	1,40,88,195	
1786-7 (8 ships)		%
In Merchandise	14,03,122	10.70
In silver *piastres*	1,15,70,063	88.20
Bill of exchange	1,44,512	1.10
Total	1,31,17,697	
1787-8 (10 ships)		%
In Merchandise	19,21,600	31.13
In silver *piastres*	29,28,000	47.41
Bill of Exchange	13,25,480	21.46
Total	61,75,080	
1788-9 (6 ships)		%
In Merchandise	14,16,362	13.26
In silver *piastres*	8,02,934	75.26
Bill of exchange	12,23,000	11.46
Total	34,42,296	
Total 33 ships		
In Merchandise	56,13,260	12.74
In silver *piastres*	3,45,55,371	78.46
Bill of exchange	38,80,737	8.80

Source: Louis Dermigny, op. cit., p.138.

TABLE 4.6: FRENCH EXPORTS TO INDIA (1785-6 TO 1788-9)

1785-6	9,31,480 *livres*
1786-7	17,14,527 *livres*
1787-8	21,48,377 *livres*
1788-9	13,64,071 *livres*

Source: Conan, op. cit., p. 97.

Another remarkable feature of the French exports to India was their steady increase in the first three years. According to Conan, French exports increased steadily as shown in Table 4.6.

The exports maintained a respectable figure all through the existence of the new Company. It was this aspect of trade that drew the widest attention. The Company made reasonable profits, be it in exports or in imports. It is difficult to calculate the gains as it reflected considerable fluctuation.[77] It seems to have varied from 30 to 80 per cent, depending on the manner in which it was calculated. One of the problems in calculating profit was the question of unsold goods. All the merchandise was rarely sold and so it was necessary to take into account the value of the unsold goods. According to Conan, the total exports to Bengal during the period of the new Company was 28,94,807 *livres*. The profit on this represented a ridiculously low figure of 1,12,432 *livres*, i.e. hardly 5 per cent. But if one takes into account 3,16,633 *livres* of unsold goods, one finds a more reasonable figure of 14 per cent. This was true in the case of the Coromandel region as well. The directors of the French Company maintained an average profit of about 30 per cent on the sale of cargo in France.[78] This appears to be a reasonable margin.

The breakdown of the negotiations with the English Company had created some problem of funds, for which sufficient precaution had not been taken. This problem was tackled through the efforts of Calonne, Orleans, Proli, etc., by raising the stock by another 20 million *livres* under the plan of augmenting the funds of the French Company.[79] The interest on the ready sums was paid on the base at 6 per cent per annum in two parts. Besides, the lenders received 4 per cent on the profits.[80] In its exports the French Company performed well by raising all possible resources of the national produce.

Another problem that the French Company faced was the extreme difficulty in marketing its products both in India and Europe. Incidentally, the English also faced a similar situation. The French faced greater difficulty in Bengal in selling their products and procuring bills of exchange because of English political dominance there. Since the appointment of Cornwallis, the French difficulties increased greatly in Bengal. He was very watchful and adopted an aggressive attitude to the French efforts at revival, particularly through English funds. His severe regulations by way of reforms for the English trade threatened those who earlier supplied cloth or goods to the French. However, the French position was strong along the Coromandel Coast, where the English political dominance was not so strong and the French outposts remained independent and well spread out. They still maintained commercial connections with local traders and retained some control over a few weaving centres around Pondicherry and Yanaon. But the most important reason for the French revival was the presence of Jean Moracin, an experienced and enterprising businessman. During the first year of the Company's operation, when sufficient funds were not available, Moracin used all the funds of the Company and authorized nearly Rs. 1,60,000 (4 lakh *livres*) from the account of the king.[81] He had developed his own private system of bills of exchange by accepting principal shipments of cloths on English account. This he did for John Coxe, Hippisley, John Call, Robert Ewing, etc., whose consignments were sold at L'Orient. By these means and such transactions Moracin received personal commission and the French Company got the freight.

As regards the imports from India, we do not find any major change in the commodity-composition in this brief period of the revival of French trade. Monneron, while describing the exports from India, categorized the items into three parts—the first comprised general commodities such as red-wood, rattans, the *cauries*, indigo, saltpetre, cotton inflock or waste-stuff and threads: the second included cloths under the name of 'prohibited' goods destined for slave regions; and the third was composed of the white cloths.[82] It was the second and third *genre* which constituted the bulk of the Coromandel exports to Europe.

The exports from the Coromandel region consisted primarily of piece goods of different varieties.[83] Whereas the English continued to use political means to strengthen their control over the centres of production, the French were content with procuring their cargo even by means of second-hand purchases. The French Company soon after its formation attempted to purchase from all possible sources. One of the prime reasons for the re-establishment of the French Company was to tap the Indian goods to the fullest extent. The directors of the French East India Company, while replying to the memorials from the principal commercial towns, clearly brought out:[84]

> . . . among the advantages of an exclusive company must be reckoned that of a superior credit with the natives of India; that of their agents treating with the manufacturers themselves, and preparing the several cargoes before the arrival of the vessels. . . .

The French Company was investing a major share in silver specie in order to import Indian goods in sufficient quantities. They expected the returns to be in plenty and profitable. For this, the French Company, like its English counterpart, emphasized the role of contracts by making cash advances.[85] Moracin mentions three types of contracts—that of *guineas* of the north, handkerchiefs of Masulipatam, and the merchandise of the coast proper. The last covered the vast territory of Mysore, Tanjore, Marava, Arcot, Madura and north of Condavir. In the case of the first region, the active revival of the English created problems for the French in making contracts or in making direct purchases. As regards the four Northern Circars of Ellore, Rajahmundry, Chicacol and Mustafanagar, there were about 4,000 weavers but they were unable to produce the quantity required by both the companies. The combined annual demand required each weaver to manufacture 28 pieces of cloth of 28 to 30 *aunes* (1.188 m. to an *aune*) per year. Here again, the English enjoyed a distinct political advantage whereas the French themselves had to arrange funds. The French began to face serious competition in their purchase of handkerchiefs from the English and the Armenian merchants and the factors of the Philippines Company at Condavir, south of the Krishna river, a domain of the Nizam. Mons Cambemalle remarked that the French found the contracts at Masulipatam very costly and as a consequence they began to show preference for Narpelly products. The competition had made the situation difficult for the French even at their own settlement of Karikal, which was the home of numerous weavers, painters and bleachers. Here the presence of private traders and the great demand for handkerchiefs and *Ginghams* in the neighbourhood and its trade to Ceylon and Java had reduced the share of the French. The Company made such contracts with the local merchants with its financial interest protected and guarded by Mons. de Gourlade at Pondicherry. At Yanaon, contract was made with three local merchants, Mourgaya, Bouta Vincana and Comerappa.[86] In Pondicherry, Ramesh Naig and Cooruvinty provided the bulk of textile goods.[87] According to Feldbaek, the coming of French ships on the Coromandel Coast created problems for the companies of other nations because the French brought silver and got best returns. In 1787 and 1788 the French were said to have invested 8,00,000 *pagodas* of Anglo-Indian remittance capital in north coasts cloths. Most of the bills were issued by the French Company's agent at Pondicherry—Jean François Moracin and 'punctiliously honoured' in London by Sir Robert Herries & Co.[88] The French ships—*Le comte de Vergennes, Le compte d'Artois* and *Le Marechal de Duras* left Pondicherry in 1787. Together these vessels carried different varieties of textiles and cotton piece goods valued at Rs. 2,04,490.7.59½. The total value of cargo stood at Rs. 12,56,286.2.59.[89] The remaining portion of the cargo included small quantities of red wood, cauries, saltpetre procured from Bengal and some pepper from Malabar. The general picture of the French imports from the Coromandel Coast can be ascertained from Table 4.7.

There is no doubt that the French had shown a great revival of their trading activities in the 1780s, particularly after the re-establishment of their Company. It also appears, as Arnould points out, that the consumption of Asian goods in France had increased in the last few years. Before the American War the total returns from Asia had not been more than 22 million *livres*, while after the peace treaty it had increased to 33 million annually from the different purchases.[90] By 1790 the new Company was facing problems—the political upheaval

TABLE 4.7: FRENCH RETURNS FROM PONDICHERRY TO L'ORIENT (1787-9)

Name of the ship	Date of departure	Value of cargo in *rupees, anas, gandas*	Value in *livres*
Le Comte de Vergennes	31 December 1787	2,40,518.25	7,21,555
Le Comte d'Artois	31 December 1787	4,28,174.1.43	12,84,522
Le Marechal de Castries	31 December 1787	5,87,594.0.59	17,62,783
Le Duc de Normandie	30 June 1788	8,08,714.3.42	24,26,142
Le Vicomtesse de Besse	20 February 1788	5,36,807.7.17	16,10,421
La Louis Julie	30 October 1788	53,722.44	1,61,167
Le Duc de Penthiévre	28 October 1788	6,98,507.45	20,95,521
Le Marechal de Segur	15 March 1789	5,31,759.2.55	15,95,277
Le Comte d'Artois	15 June 1789	6,79,576.4	20,38,728
Le Comte d'Éstaing	31 July 1789	4,46,379.1	13,39,137
Le Necker	30 October 1789	5,02,992.1.34	15,08,976

Source: Compagnie des Indes, Bureau des Achats, 8 AQ 303, AN.

in the form of revolution at home and the Anglo-Mysore war in southern India. The English Company had reduced its purchases from the French because its energies and resources were diverted to the military expedition against Tipu. The purchases carried out in 1790 had been raised to a total of Rs. 42,29,000, besides paying the agents and cost of transportation.[91] There is no denying the fact that the French had done reasonably well in their trade. They had remitted Rs. 30,57,446 in rupees and *piastres* and Rs. 1,48,000 in trade with Madras making a total of Rs. 32,05,446.[92] In fact, the demand of the Company had exceeded the remittances.

The successful phase of the French commerce in India was brought to a sudden end soon after the outbreak of the French Revolution. On 20 March 1790 a committee of the National Assembly gave its opinion that the Compagnie des Indes should be abolished, and the commerce with India be opened free to the individuals. The Company remained in possession of its privileges till January 1792. On 3 April 1790 the French subjects were permitted to navigate freely in the seas beyond the Cape of Good Hope by the orders of the National Assembly.[93] As late as 1792, the French had purchased Indian goods worth 6,49,88,000 *livres tournois* and sent to India goods and silver valued at 71,91,000 *livres tournois*.[94]

The financial condition of the French Company was reasonably sound. During the years 1785-90, it kept up its credit assiduously, and successfully defended itself against criticism from the Chambers of Commerce as well as trading towns. It managed to borrow and pay off regularly for the outward-bound cargoes, which were mostly paid in silver and metals. It did face difficulties in marketing its products in both India and Europe but it was not an unusual feature of its commercial activities.[95] Even the English Company faced a similar situation. The noteworthy point about the French Company was its creditworthiness in its financial dealings when the other state-run departments and institutions were fast moving towards bankruptcy. The economic climate in France did not enthuse a spirit of enterprise owing to political turmoil and uncertainty. Even in this atmosphere the French Company reflected a reasonable degree of prosperity. The first dividend paid in 1788 was as high as 18 per cent and insiders were still buying its shares in 1791 and even later.[96] One of its administrators described it as the 'only safe established investment of one's property in France, because [it was] independent of government though not of robbers'.[97]

The English imports from India revealed a more balanced composition because of their powerful position in Bengal. This region provided a great variety of products ranging from raw to manufactured items. In contrast to this, the Coromandel offered limited products—primarily textile goods.[98] Hence the English efforts remained confined to the textile trade in the Coromandel, which was losing its earlier place in Europe and was increasingly being utilized in the 'country' trade. The French position was safe only in the Coromandel and hence we notice an extra drive in their efforts to find a variety of goods besides textile products in their commercial operations whereas in Bengal the English dictated to them.

NOTES

1. Letter from Court of Directors (hereafter COD.) 24 September 1783, *Fort William-India House Correspondence*, Vol. XV, pp. 47-9, NAI.
2. Letter from Court to Governor-General and Council, 27 March 1787 (Secret), *Fort William-India House Correspondence*, Vol. XV, p. 41 and pp. 703-8, xviii-dx.
3. This duty was not something new as is evident from the fact the French agents had made a similar request to the English prior to the Convention of 1783. Letter to the Court, 26 February 1786, *Fort William-India House Correspondence*, Vol. XV.
4. Strict control over European trade did not mean placing restrictions on it. The British Trade Policy under Cornwallis seems to have been, at least in theory, to increase the volume of trade instead of enhancing the duties for more revenue. The tariff on the French trade goods was not too high. Cornwallis to Campbell, 22 February 1783, *Melville Papers*, MS 3386 (microfilm), NAI.
5. Secret letters to the Court, 10 Jan. 1783, paras 24-5, *India House-Fort William Correspondence, Foreign Secret and Political*, Vol. XVI, *1787-1791*, NAI.
6. Ibid., paras 15-16.
7. Ibid., 6 Nov. 1788, paras B2-3.
8. Bourdieu to Aiquillon, 24 November 1772, *Correspondence—Political, Angletrre*, Vol. 499, Official Mémoire of 16 June 1773 (unsigned), Vol. 502, Arch. Aff. Étr. Cited by Frederick L. Nussbaum, 'The Formation of the New East India Company of Calonne', *The American Historical Review*, Vol. 38, No. 3, 1933, pp. 475-97.
9. Godieu, De Montigny de Monplailir and J.L. Borne Bonet, Political Angleterre, Vol. 550, Arch. Aff. Étr.
10. Memorial from the Deputies of the Principal Commercial Towns, published at Paris, 1787, *Manuscripts on British India*, CPL.
11. Nussbaum, op. cit.
12. But according to Milburn, no profit appeared to have arisen from it worth dividing among the proprietors. William Milburn, *Oriental Commerce*, Vol. I, London, 1813, p. 401.

13. Montaran to Vergennes, 19 June 1780, *Correspondence Political, Angleterre*, Vol. 533, Arch. Aff. Étr.; also cited by Nussbaum, op. cit.
14. Rayneval's memoir, January 1786, Mémoire et Documents (hereafter Mém. et Doc.), Asie, Vol. V, Arch. Aff. Étr.
15. Dupont to Vergennes, 28 October 1784, *Asie*, Vol. IV, Arch. Aff. Étr.
16. Hints on the Commercial Treaty with France (undated), *Auckland Papers*, Vol. XII, *Add. Ms*. 34423, Br. Mus.
17. Conan suggests that the principal role in the formation of the Company was that of Calonne, but it was Castries who attempted the first moves to the Court of London. J. Conan, *La Derniére Compagine Française des Indes, 1785-1875*, Paris, 1942, p. 38. The origin of the Nouvelle Compagnie des Indes is also discussed briefly by Jean Terrade, *Le Commerce Colonial de la France à la fin de l'ancien régime*, Tome II, Paris, 1972, p. 676.
18. Nussbaum, op. cit., also Herbert Lüthy, op. cit., p. 75.
19. Adhemar to Vergennes, 15 August 1784, *Correspondence Political, Angleterre*, Vol. 549, Arch. Aff. Étr.
20. Memorial of 6 October 1791, T-38, 1.2, AN, cited by Nussbaum, op. cit.
21. Extract of memorial presented to Mons. de Calonne by Bourdieu at Paris, May 1784, *Manuscripts on British India*, No. 11, CPL.
22. Bourdieu, Chollet and Bourdieu to COD, 13 August 1783, *Manuscripts on British India*, No. 10, CPL.
23. S. Pollard and C. Holmes, *Documents of European Economic History: The Process of Industrialization 1750-1870*, London, 1968, pp. 113-15. Also Arrêt du Conseil d'État du Roi, portant Ètablissement d'une nouvelle Compagnie des Indes, 14 April 1785, F^{12} 1403, 8 AQ 323-4 and Série AD XI-41, AN.
24. Nussbaum, op. cit.
25. David Macpherson, *The History of the European Commerce with India*, London, 1812, p. 282.
26. Ibid., p. 283.
27. Ibid.
28. Statement of the Secret Committee of the COD, *Add. Ms*. 34466, *Auckland Papers*, Vol. LV (1763-92), p. 19, Br. Mus.
29. Proposals for the Draft Treaty between the English and the French East India Company, *Manuscripts on British India, CPL.*
30. Secret Minutes of the Court of Directors, 17 August 1784, *Manuscripts on British India*, CPL.
31. W. Devaynes to Henry Dundas, September 1785, letter No. 2, *Manuscripts on British India*, CPL.
32. Ibid.
33. Ibid., 5 September 1785, 20/B, CPL.
34. Ibid.
35. Devaynes' argument was based on the following estimate:

The French Company to deposit	£ 1,50,000
Their outward investment of	£ 30,000
To be paid into the Treasury at Bengal probably amounted to	£ 45,000
To pay in London in Bills at 1 and 3 months sight	£ 1,77,500

To pay in 2 cargoes of tea, which would be in Europe before the Bengal ships	£ 70,000
To pay in 6 and 9 months sight balance	£ 1,07,500
	£ 5,80,000

That in 3 months after the receipt of the
Bills the Company would be more than paid
for the investments and in 9 months after the receipt of the Bills the whole of the Deposits would be completed.

The proposals of the English Company to liquidate the debt was to take the Rupee at 20 and to give Bills at 1 year sight without interest and delay the payment 3 years longer at 5%.

The French proposal was to take the Rupee at 2 sh. to pay in 4½ months sight, which would be an advantage to the English Company of 20 per cent difference in the exchange and 7½ months' interest at 5 per cent making it 3 per cent more. Added to that, 10 per cent was to be charged on the goods, which brought a profit to the English Company of 33 per cent on the whole of transactions without adding anything.

36. Devaynes, 5 September 1785, No. 21(B), CPL.
37. Proposals for negotiation between the English and the French East India Company, presented to the English government and to the Directors of the Company by Messrs Bourdieu and Chollet, *Manuscripts on British India*, No. 60, CPL.
38. Ibid.
39. Ibid.
40. John Manship to Court of Directors, 9 November 1785, *French in India Series*, Vol. 17, IOR.
41. Nathanial Smith and John Manship to the Secret Court of Directors, 7 December 1785, *French in India Series*, Vol. 17, IOR.
42. Warren Hastings to Laurence Sulivan, 30 November 1785, *French in India Series*, Vol. 17, IOR.
43. Francis Baring refuted the beliefs of Hastings that the Treaty was of a political as well as commercial nature. To Baring it was purely commercial. He also rejected Hastings' view about the English Company becoming a tributary in India. He thought that the whole transactions between the merchants and the governments of both the countries were not to commit themselves by their interference further than by approval of the terms to their respective companies.
44. Secret Minutes of COD, 15 August 1785, *French in India Series*, Vol. 17, IOR.
45. Secret Meeting of the COD, 26 October 1785, *French in India Series*, Vol. 17, IOR. At the same time, the Court decided to insert the following in the agreement: 'that this transaction shall be considered solely as mercantile, and that whatever disputes may arise between the two Nations or the companies, the accounts relative to it shall be liquidated with the same good faith as if the transactions were between Individuals of the respective Nations'. Secret Meeting of the COD, 26 October 1785, *French in India Series*, Vol. 17, IOR.
46. Fredrick L. Nussbaum, op. cit.
47. Mémoire of Rayneval, *Mémoire et Doc.*, Asie, Suppl. Vol. V, Arch. Aff. Étr.

48. Ibid.
49. Du Pont to M. Le Comte de Vergennes, 29 December 1784, *Mém. et Doc.*, Asia, Vol. 5, *Indes Orientales*, Arch. Aff. Étr.
50. Du Pont to M. Le Comte de Vergennes, 9 January 1785, *Mém. et Doc.*, Vol. 11, No. 2, Arch. Aff. Étr..
51. Louis Pierre Lacretalle et Blond, Mémoire á Consulter at Consultation pour les négociants faisant le commerce des marchandises des Indes contre la nouvelle Compagnie des Indes, Paris, 1786, BN.
52. Ole Feldbaek, *India Trade under the Danish Flag, 1772-1808*, Copenhagen, 1969, p. 84.
53. Ibid.
54. Among the few richest free merchants of the late eighteenth century, John Fergusson had amassed a fortune before returning to England. He was described as 'the only merchant' in Calcutta and a man 'of great integrity and unblemished reputation, generous and humane . . . '. G. Smith to H. Dundas, 7 December 1785 and 30 November 1789, MS 434 (microfilm), *Home Misc. Series*, IOR.
55. Brouillards du bureau des achats, comptoirs, de l'Inde 1786-90, 8 AQ 247, AN.
56. État somnaire des fonds disponsible par les capitalistes, Pondichéry Comptabilité, 1786-96, 8 AQ 344, AN. There is also frequent mention of messrs Lambert Rolp and Co. purchasing substantial quantity of cloths for L'Orient. Bills, March 1792, Folder No. 365, NAI, Pondicherry.
57. Moracin to Messieurs des Administrateurs de la Compagnie des Indes at Paris, 18 September 1789, Edmond Gaudart (ed.), *Correspondance des Agents à Pondichéry de la Nouvelle Compagnie des Indes avec les Administrateurs à Paris*, Pondicherry, Paris, 1931, p. 61.
58. Ibid., p. 149.
59. Orders of the Court of Directors, 17 June 1786, *Public Dept. Consultations*, Fort St. George, TSA.
60. On the orders COD, 1 September 1786, the Board consisted of James Henry Casamajor, William Hamilton Sir Edward John Holland and John Balfour. Robert Mannsell was appointed the Export Warehouse Keeper.
61. *Madras Despatches*, 27 March 1787, Vol. 13, p. 547, IOR.
62. *Report of the Select Committee on Export Trade*, 11 September 1791 in Early Parliamentary Papers relating to India, 1793, No. 28, IOR.
63. *Madras Despatches*, 31 July 1787, Vol. 13, IOR.
64. *Madras Despatches*, 27 March 1787, Vol. 13, IOR.
65. General Letter from England to Board of Trade, 12 April 1786, *Masulipatam District Correspondence*—Commercial, Vol. 2900, APA.
66. Sale of Imported Goods and Store, No. XI, MS 401 (microfilm), *Home Misc. Series*, IOR.
67. General Letter from Madras, 9 July 1787, *Military Sundries*, Vol. 86, p. 12, TSA.
68. Appendix 6, *Report of the Select Committee on Export Trade*, 7 September 1791, MS 400, IOR.
69. Propositions que la Compagnie pour le commerce de France aux Indes Orientales Soument á l'Empereur Tipou Sultan, 4 October 1788, No.1089 *Feuilles Volantes*, Série-B, Archives of Aix-en Provance, France.
70. Notes sur Le commerce du Mayssour avec Pondichéry, *Nouv. Acq.* F.R. 8935, p. 384, BN.

71. Ibid.
72. Ibid., p. 138.
73. See also the table provided in a memoir, which differs slightly from the above-mentioned table. However, the difference in amount of exports is marginal for the year 1785-6, Tableau général des expéditions, Mémoire, No. 27, p. 180, *Mém. et Doc.*, Asie, Vol., Arch, Aff. Étr.
74. J. Conan, *La Derniére Compagnie Française des Indes*, Paris, 1942, p. 95.
75. Ibid.
76. Moracin to Messrs les Administrateurs de la Compagnie, 18 September 1789, op. cit., p. 90.
77. The sale of the cargo of Boullougne in 1786 represented a profit of over 60 per cent, even after separating the unsold goods. Ibid., p. 105.
78. Ibid., p. 105.
79. Plan d'une augmentation de fonds pour la Compagnie des Indes, 7 July 1786, *Mém. et Doc.*, Vol. 5, No. 28, Arch. Aff. Étr.
80. In order to overcome the shortage of funds and to remove the defects of circulation of money—the principal cause of difficulty in India—there was a proposal to establish a bank at Calcutta. The objective was to encourage the inhabitants of the region to join this establishment for the advantage of European trade. The first part of the plan provided for the formation of a society of 100 subscribers for the sum of Rs. 20,000 each, making a capital of Rs. 2,00,000. It was to be open for all, irrespective of the country of religion. The plan provided for the introduction of money and paper currency, and was to be managed by the 'Bureau de Directors' deciding the amount of paper currency to be circulated. However, it appears, the proposal did not come through. Proposition pour L'Établissement d'une Banque á Calcutta sous la dénomination de Banque Générale de L'Inde (1786) (Mémoire), 8 AQ. 346, AN.
81. Moracin to Messrs les Administrateurs at Paris, op. cit., p. 201.
82. Mémoire lu á l'Assemblée Nationale en faveur des Colonies Française aux Indes par M. Louis Monneron, AD-VII-23, AN.
83. The textile trade is discussed in Chapter 6.
84. The observations of the directors of the Company upon the memorials (1787), Letter item I, *Manuscripts on British India*, CPL.
85. Moracin to Messrs les Administrateurs at Paris, 18 September 1789, op. cit., pp. 92-7.
86. Lagrenée to Administrators in Paris, 20 October 1791, Edmond Gaudart (ed.), *Correspondance des Agents à Pondichérry de la Nouvelle Compagnie des Indes avec les Administrateurs à Paris*, Pondicherry, 1931, p. 324.
87. Charles Floyer to Chief-in-Council, Fort St. George, 15 August 1786, *Masulipatam Consultation*, Vol. 2837, APA.
88. Ole Feldbaek, op. cit., p. 92.
89. Extracted from the trade figures—Compagnie des Indes, Cargaisons d'Importation en retour des Indes-A, 8 AQ 303, AN.
90. Ambroise Marie Arnould, *De la Balance Du Commerce et Des Relations Commerciales Extrériurs De la France*, Paris, 1983, p. 283.
91. Moracin to the Administrators of Pairs, 28 January 1790, Letter No. 63, Édmond Gaudart, op. cit., pp. 152-9.
92. Ibid., p. 157.

93. William Milburn, op. cit., Vol. 1, p. 404.
94. 1792, F [12] 252, Nos. 24 and 25 (microfilm), AN.
95. According to Furber, the book value of the unsold Indian goods on hand amounted to nearly 16 million *livres*. Of this about 7 million *livres* represented goods left over from the first purchases in Europe. There was an additional item of *gruff* goods chiefly saltpetre and redwood worth about 4½ million *livres*, which remained unsold. Besides, there was a large-scale import of illicit goods from India through the Isle de France and Bourbon. Holden Furber, op. cit., pp. 58-9.
96. Nussbaum, op. cit., p. 495.
97. Huber to Auckland, 4 October 1792, Journal and Correspondence of Lord Auckland, II, p. 451 cited by Nussbaum, op. cit.
98. See Appendix III.

Chapter 5

Weavers and Merchants in the Vortex of Trade Politics

Indian textile production was the most commercialized sector of the Coromandel economy. It played an important part in Coromandel's trade with Asia and Europe. The class of weavers constituted its backbone. The competition for trade between the English and the French made the weavers their focal point of confrontation by exploiting and subjecting them. Hameeda Hossain in a very able analysis in the context of Bengal, describes the communities of weavers becoming increasingly vulnerable with the change in the country's trade and power.[1] Though the process of change was different in the Coromandel, yet we find the weavers being placed under a complex and harsh set of economic relationship as a consequence of the Anglo-French rivalry.

The seventeenth and eighteenth centuries were a period of fluctuating fortunes for the weavers. We notice a lot of professional and regional migrations of weavers. At the earliest stage of European penetration into the Indian textile zone, there was a partial shift from temple premises to company settlements on the coast.[2] There was also a trend towards the breaking-up of the weavers' guilds. Later the regional mobility of weavers seems to have been caused as much by unstable political, economic and natural conditions as by the means systematically employed by these two rival companies to attract them to their own settlements. The idea was to make the procurement of cloth easy and cheap and to exclude the intermediaries. According to the contemporary sources, both the French and the English provided sufficient space to the immigrant weavers under the shade of trees because the preparation of the warp needed more space, the length of the Coromandel cloth being generally much longer than those from other regions.

There were certain indications of change and mobility in the weavers' caste. Yet the major traditional groups maintained their place in the social structure. In the Tamil region, Kaikolar or Kaiklava caste was regarded as an important community of weavers.[3] Their chief was called *Peridanakarance* or *attakkarane*. They dominated the big weaving centre of Montalpeth in Pondicherry. They manufactured cloths not only for local consumption but also for exports to Singapore, Malaya, etc. There were frequent migrations from this caste to the military profession. Explicit orders were issued by the English Company to place a ban on such mobility to protect their trade interests. During the days of the wars many weavers, particularly from the central districts of Carnatic, were enlisted into the Company's military service. Most of them were averse to going back to the manufacturing profession. On the other hand, there was always a risk of other family members joining them in periods of distress or instability. On the specific orders of the government the Board of Trade ordered that 'no man by profession of a weaver be henceforth enlisted into the Company's military service'.[4]

Another major group of weavers called Devangas, who usually made very dark blue cloths and silk borders, lived in the region of Andhra and Carnatic and were solely preoccupied with the weaving profession. Buchanan observed that they often obtained advances from merchants or borrowed money from bankers. They sold their goods to the merchants or to private customers but never carried them to public markets.[5] There were some other communities of weavers who prepared cloth for the European companies. The 'Salewars' were the inhabitants of the Tamil region with whom the English Company made a direct contract for the supply of coarse and fine unbleached neckcloths.[6] The Janrawar community seems to have migrated from Andhra to the Tamil region towards the close of the seventeenth century. 'Mooree Weavers' produced superfine cotton used as a base for chintz manufacture. 'Saurashtrans' or the Pattunulkaras, primarily settled in Madura, had a long tradition of migration. They probably migrated from the Somnath temple in Gujarat.[7] 'Puttuegars' were silk weavers but sometimes made thin white muslin with silk borders. They dyed much of their own silk but gave their yellow silk to *Niligaru*—the indigo dyers. The latter specialized in several shades of blue dyes. Buchanan also mentions the groups of Shynagaru and Canara weavers.[8] The former were the richest weavers, who employed servants for their work. The presence of numerous immigrant groups indicate the migratory tendencies of the weavers of the Coromandel.

According to Braudel, the Indian weaver was undoubtedly given a certain amount of leeway.[9] He received his advance in money (in Europe he was supplied materials) and he could always resort directly to the market (something not possible under the *verlags* system). He could always default, change place of work, go on strike or give up loom to return to the land or join the army.

Even Arasaratnam suggests that the weavers had greater flexibility and a larger freedom of operation when the European companies were competing in the open market and placing large orders. This mobility was supplemented by the existence of European private and Indian trade. The interchangeability of goods ordered by these various customs aiming at broadly the same export market made it possible for the weavers to play one against the other.[10] This was true on some occasions but the intense rivalry among the European powers subjected the local weavers to undue pressures and robbed them of their freedom. One alternative available to the weavers was to protest against the Company's imposition by mass migration. Many scholars have highlighted this form of protest by the weavers. However, it must be noticed that migration of weavers was a well-established phenomenon even in the pre-colonial period. Most of the weavers' migration prior to the colonial period was governed by wider market opportunities and prospects of textile export, away from the regions that were experiencing economic and political decline. The migration of Devangas and Saurashtrans is one such example. While in the seventeenth century there was a net migration of weavers out of temple towns to the European settlements, in the second half of the eighteenth century the weavers migrated to escape the unreasonable dictates of the Company. As Haynes and Roy write, in the pre-eighteenth century a large number of weavers 'movements were associated with the shifting regional pattern of state formation and declining export opportunities during the eighteenth century'.[11] The development of regional kingdoms, the strengthening of mercantile capitalism, the growing significance of external trade and the rise of European companies—all these factors stimulated this migration. However, towards the close of the century, the weavers migration were intended to avoid the servitude of the Europeans as the companies made desperate attempts to control the entire process of textile production.

The large-scale migration of weavers to the European settlements had one distinct result. The traditional social structure reflected a correlation between the caste and the production of specific varieties of cloth. As rightly pointed out by Swarnalatha and Sudhir, the system of registration of weavers by the Company authorities may have contributed to the blurring of finer nuances of caste distinction.[12] As the weavers were required to produce cloth according to the direction of the Company, the caste based specialization of production at times broke down. Increasing demand for the Coromandel textile must have provided an opportunity to the non-weaving communities to enter the profession. Although we do not get abundant evidence of this, Ravi Ahuja mentions the entry of agriculturist communities, e.g. Paraiyars, who started weaving the coarser varieties of cloth. In a survey of 396 households in 1771 in Arnee it was found that 58 Paraiyar families were engaged in cotton spinning. Similarly, the village washermen (Vanniyars) began to specialize in bleaching and dyeing the export fabric. Besides, frequent wars and drought in the Coromandel region may have caused professional migration. The East India Company's growing military force must have created greater employment opportunities and we have some evidence to suggest that weavers in large numbers joined the forces. This was not a new trend because at places the head weaver was also called *senapati* because of the traditional connection between soldiering and weaving. What was new was the phenomenal expansion of the English army.[14] It was accompanied by fluctuations in the fortunes of the weaving community. However, the economic interest of the Company led to imposition of restrictions on weavers entering the profession of soldiers. The Board of Trade wrote to the Governor of Madras to check this trend and to keep the weavers under 'strict control'.[15] This was an obvious attempt to prevent the weavers moving away so that the Company's export supply did not suffer.

Theoretically, liberties placed the Indian weaver above his European counterpart. In reality, however, the hard economic necessities placed severe restrictions on him and tied him down to his work. As Jacques Dupuis rightly points out, all this independence was mostly as precarious, as illusory as that of the small cultivator. The cultivator was dependent on the moneylender, the weaver on the master-weaver or the merchant financier for his advances.[16] Without these advances the looms could not be operated. Furthermore, unlike his European counterpart, the Indian weaver had to work under a hierarchy of functionaries—the intermediary *dalals* and merchants, the *gomastahs*, the Company or private traders, the political agents in the form of amildars, *canicoplies*, etc. He was also subject to fluctuating demands.

Apart from all these factors, cotton textile production in India was based on money advances to the weavers instead of the putting out system of Europe. The weaver's position and strength depended on market forces. His living was greatly influenced by the price of thread, colours, dyes and rice. Since the wars of the 1780s a *pagoda* could fetch only 7 *viss* of thread and 5 *cunchams* of paddy which earlier fetched 11 *viss* of thread and 20 *cunchams* of paddy.[17] The latter article was so scarce that it could not be easily procured even at that price. The weavers were equally influenced by the political and natural factors such as the supply of cotton, security of transportation, taxation and the problems relating to the entire process of production. Any abnormal situation for the weavers resulted in either their impoverishment or large-scale migration.

Thread was one of the basic requirements of a weaver, which in turn depended on the abundant supply of cotton. From the available sources it is evident that cotton production on the eastern coast was not sufficient to make all the looms work and to provide regular supply. Our knowledge of the regions of cotton production and of its marketing is very scanty. The Lombadies must have provided the bulk of cotton to the north Coromandel region from western Deccan and Berar.[18] Arasaratnam suggests, on the basis of a contemporary source, that the Krishna Tungabhadra *doab* must have produced the cotton which suited the coarser variety.[19] Legoux de Flaix mentions '*roui*' cultivated in the Telengana region, used for making Guineas.[20] He also mentions cotton being produced in the region between the Koleram and Caveri (Cauvery-Coleroon) rivers[21] for the country of Seilom (Salem). These regions must have supplied cotton to the weavers' families of south Coromandel, which was probably sold at the famous cotton markets of Ulundurpettai (35 miles west of Cuddalore), Walajanagar in north Arcot, Jingi in Madurantakam and Ariyalur near Porto Novo.[22]

It is evident that the wars disrupted communications and transportation and adversely affected the market conditions on which the weavers depended. The political wars in the south resulted in the scarcity of thread. Writing of the impact of troop movements in Ganjam district during the war, when the price of cotton had gone up by almost 100 per cent and that of grain by nearly 50 per cent, Wynch complains that the weaver was not left with any money to purchase raw materials of standard laid down by the Company.[23] This made it difficult for the weavers to survive. After the conclusion of the American War, which had revived the Anglo-French military contest, Dent wrote, 'The War being happily at end and the price of rice has fallen from 200 to 100 *pagodas* per *garce* and is daily lowering.'[24] Likewise, the Report of 1794, while discussing the impact of Hyder's wars, mentions that in 1767, Kanchipuram, Arnee and many of the principal weaving towns were destroyed. Before they had recovered in any great degree from their losses, the dreadful wars of 1780 broke out. It nearly annihilated the manufactures, both in the Carnatic and Tanjore country.[25] The Report brought out that 'in the great weaving towns of Sheally, Bonagnerry, Porto Novo, etc., scarcely a loom is now to be seen, and in the company's village of Chinnamanaickpollam, where there were seldom less than 1200 looms constantly employed, the number at present does not exceed 150'. The competition had raised the price of piece goods whereas weavers' income had remained stagnant. The Company officials were aware of the plight of weavers, on which Alexander Davidson wrote, 'It is to be particularly observed that the weaver's gain is variable and is regulated by the price of Rice and Cotton.'[26]

The increasing price of the thread and the inflexible rate of payment of the Company compelled the weavers to lower the quality of cotton fabric. A piece of good standard 14 *punjam* was usually made of 25 or 26 *seers* of thread. The price paid to the weaver was Rs. 7½. If the threads were bought at 3¼ *seers* a rupee, it would cost about Rs. 8 to purchase them. Consequently the weaver was obliged to reduce the quantity of thread in order to save at least Rs. 1½ out of the total of Rs. 7½ to enable him to sustain his family. So if the piece of cloth which ought to have contained 25 or 26 *seers* of thread had only 20 or 21 *seers*, it was evident that the texture was defective.[27] A tense situation arose when the English Company made advances, rejected the cloths as substandard and the French, through their ready money, made large purchases without advances. In the process they avoided the risk of outstanding balances. The superiority of the fabric insisted upon and the diminishing wages were the principal deterrents, which dissuaded the weavers from working for the Company (though economic compulsions reduced their options and forced them to be tied down to the Company's contracts). If the weaver had to manufacture for individuals, he could have debased the textile and delivered 3 or 4 pieces per month at a price nearly equal to what the Company allowed, while of the Company's assortments, the weaver could not possibly manufacture more than 2 pieces per month. As Richard Dillon noted, the Company's prices were inadequate to afford a subsistence to the weavers, owing to the extreme scarcity and great advance in price of cotton. . . .[28] To accommodate a weaver and his family and to set up his business, Roger Darval advocated an immediate advance of about 31 *pagodas*. A migrant weaver needed about 30 *pagodas* for the houseroom, necessary for his loom and another 5-6 *pagodas* to purchase looms and other domestic goods.[29]

While some of the junior officials blamed the weavers themselves for their deteriorating condition, the two rival companies had been adopting all possible means to entice the weavers to work for them in as many numbers as possible. Each Company tried to bring them under its political sway or make them economically dependent on it in numerous ways.[30]

The two rival companies usually refrained from direct dealings with the weavers. They depended on Company merchants for their requirements. At the same time, the two powers adopted measures to attract the weavers to settle in their respective *comptoirs*. The French had been pursuing this policy since the time of François Martin. He and, later, Dupleix encouraged the immigrants to settle there with the intention of starting the manufacture of dyes and painted cloths. Some sheds were constructed and trees planted for this purpose. Karikal gained importance for its quality *Ginghams*. These were brought to Pondicherry to be exported to Manila. Yanaon was known for its *Guineas du Nord, Jamedanies, Organdis*, etc. Cartloads of unbleached cloths were brought to Pondicherry to be bleached at Moutalpet (Muttiyahepattai), long considered the home of the reputed bleachers of India.[31] Pondicherry also earned its name for the dyeing industry. Cloth was brought from places like Kanchipuram, Vandavasi, Tiruvanamalai, Salem, Tarangambadi and Cuddalore.[32] Piece goods were also brought from distant places like Bengal or Orissa. Moracin made a serious effort to help through money advances about two to three hundred families of weavers from the famous temple in the Carnatic to settle in Pondicherry.[33] He believed that by encouraging and attracting the workers, the French would procure sufficient cargo for their ships that would relieve them of their English dependence. It is also to be noted that the concentration of weaving looms in the Guntur Circar was primarily due to the efforts of the French agents, after the migration of weavers from Nizampatam.[34] The English cloth investments had ceased owing to the disastrous wars in 1780, and it was the French demand for *chay* goods that kept the weavers occupied.[35]

The English Company was equally conscious of the importance of the weavers of the Coromandel, as on them depended the bulk of their exports. As early as 1733 the directors had forbidden the levying of duties on tobacco and betel by tax farmers in the outlying villages of Egmore and Trevitore. The Court hoped that the measure would induce the weavers, spinners and textile workers to come and settle in big numbers.[36] It was argued that if the Company could receive a sufficient quantity of cloth from within its settlements, the prime cost would fall. In the post-1763 period, we notice the English employing political means in the form of concessions and coercions to achieve this end.

The English were aware that the head weavers held considerable sway on their community. This is reflected in the Company's endeavours to ascertain the precise number of looms employed and the quantity of cloth manufactured at each centre. Their aim was clearly stated thus, '. . . they may be induced to enter into engagements for appropriating as many weavers and looms to be employed solely in manufacturing cloth for the company as may be thought necessary and we should be able to afford the resident such support by means of the zamindars as would effectively secure the performance of their engagements'.[37]

The official policy of the directors of the Company was to create conditions conducive to unhindered supply of material and to keep the weavers attracted to the Company investments. The junior officials in their zeal to fulfil the orders of their superiors or to participate in the private trade created conditions most oppressive for the weavers. The most notable illustration of this was the policy pursued by Anthony Sadlier, the chief at Ingeram. The French chief at Yanaon, Drudgeon charged, on the basis of a written complaint of weavers who were employed by the French, that the English agents went to their houses and seized cloth for which the French had made a cash advance.[38] They also accused Sadlier of publishing certain prohibitions for the weavers through the beat of tom tom, forbidding them under the threat of severe penalties, to manufacture cloths for the French. They could only manufacture cloths for the English Company.[39] The offenders were to be punished by 20 blows of *rattan* and a fine of 112 *pagodas*.[40] Sadlier denied having ordered such a prohibition and wrote that it was done without his knowledge. He stated that 'my transactions with them (weavers) were public, their engagements were voluntary'.[41] There were numerous allegations and counter-allegations on this subject. The French complained that the weavers, who were indebted to them and were producing cloths for them, were sometimes tempted not to fulfil the orders of the French or were prevented by the execution of threats of *chabouc,* fines and other punishments.[42] The Dutch made similar complaints against the English.[43]

One common method adopted by the English and occasionally by the French was to constantly place orders with the weavers through an advance even before the first piece was woven. The French lodged protests against this practice, as all the best weavers were kept employed by the English by physical compulsions. Drudgeon mentions another crafty method that the English adopted to employ good weavers. Gotavala Tommyah, one of the able weavers working for the French, had thrice refused the offer of an English *gomastah*. On his refusal his young son was obliged by wily devices to take 8 *pagodas* with an order to make cloth. This forced engagement fell on the father.[44] Another weaver Gantee Vencatram was enticed in the same way to sign a written contract. There were numerous cases of this kind. Such exploitation must have been common in the period of Anglo-French rivalry to control more and more cotton producing centres.

Sadlier had introduced a scheme of enlisting weavers.[45] This proved to be prejudicial to the French interests. The scheme was later withdrawn when the superior authority feared that the entire weaver community would be antagonized by its implementation. His own colleagues and subordinates voiced resentment against Sadlier's policy. It was alleged that Sadlier had regularly deducted 2.5 per cent from the sums advanced to the weavers under the pretext of making an additional allowance for the Canicoplys.[46] Mathew Yeats wrote,

> he (Sadlier) forced men naturally of the most fearful and timid dispositions to such acts as the most desperate and resolute never embrace but with reluctance, he occasioned a loss of some thousand to the company . . . and drove about 500 weavers to the cruel necessity of leaving their homes and connections, of flying to Foreigners for protection . . . that were either the French as capable as they are willing or Dutch as willing as they are capable to employ them, you would not have a single weaver in the course of the month.[47]

In the same context, Mathew described the plight of the weaver in the following way:

> To such a degree of wretched dependence are those weavers in particular reduced, who formerly wove fine cloth but were forced contrary to their inclination to receive the company's money, as to be obliged to bribe those very peons, etc. to allow them to weave few fine pieces for the support of themselves and families.[48]

Any shift in the Company's investment made to further its own commercial interest usually adversely affected the weavers. One such instance was the Company's decision to control the sale of thread, on which the price of cotton depended, in order to control the price of cotton goods. The English Company introduced a new scheme in 1772, which it described as the 'double advance' system of thread and money.[49] The method of forcing thread on the weavers proved very unpopular. The idea behind this was to control the price of cotton goods and to maintain its standard; to preclude the possibility of coarse thread being used that rendered the manufactures uneven; by providing an investment in the form of materials so that the time of delivery could be ascertained; and to prevent the weavers from providing flimsy excuses for not finding the thread in times of scarcity or disturbance. The weavers as a community resisted this measure. The framers of the policy, on the contrary, maintained that it was opposed not by the weavers but by members of vested interest groups who supplied thread. These included thread merchants, shopkeepers and some of the *gomastahs*.

The weavers in the English settlements were distinctly unhappy with this double advance scheme. They registered their protest by migrating to the neighbouring regions. Some of them went to the French settlements. This practice of advancing thread caused weavers' migrations and a few officials of the English Company also brought this out. In one of the letters to the Governor of Fort St. George, it was mentioned, 'Having severally informed ourselves of the causes which induce the weavers, still to continue refractory and to reside in the French bounds, we are of the opinion that it is on account of their reluctance to receive the thread for the provision of the investment.'[50] They also mention the extraordinary encouragement held out by the French at Pondicherry, which induced a large number of weavers to desert English settlements. At Chinnamanaickpollam, there was a rumour that the Company had brought thread to be distributed as a part of their advance. The whole community of weavers deserted and sought shelter in the districts of Trevidy Warriarpollam, Bonagery and Vencatampettah.[51] Skarton was sent to enquire into the state of manufactures of that region and to encourage the manufacturers to return.[52] The amildars were asked to compel the weavers to return to their original settlements.[53] Similar directives were issued for the inhabitants of Cuddalore, with the threat of confiscation of property if they did not return.[54] Even the lucrative offer of raising their labour payment by as much as 20 per cent could not induce the migrants to return.[55] The English decided to discontinue the system on Balfour's recommendation to the Board of Trade. However, the method of 'double advance' proved beneficial to the French.

As an incentive to attract the weavers the English Company made a major concession in the form of abolition of the loom tax in the *jaghire* lands. The Board of Trade recommended abolition of taxes on the profession of weavers in the *jaghire* and *havelly* lands and if possible in the zamindari lands.[56] This was done to meet the prevalent difficulty in procuring cloth of the Company's standard and at old prices. It was based on the argument that in India, 'an exemption from taxes is at the same time an exemption from grievances and vexations . . .'.[57]

Those who favoured the abolition of looms tax hoped that the exemption would draw the manufacturers away from the Nawab's country and zamindari lands into the Company's settlements. It would check the interference of foreigners and private traders, and would provide exclusive advantages to the manufacturers and thus to the Company's trade. They also maintained that the increase of population in the Company's land would probably more than compensate for the sums given up by the abolition of the tax.[58] They assumed that this would be an ideal measure to counter the French move of attracting the best weavers. Holland in his important minute regarded this concession as a measure of indulgence.[59] He opposed this idea as he believed that the cloth required for the Company's investment was too inconsiderable to bear any proportion to the loss of revenue due to the remission of loom tax. He argued that the tax was not detrimental to the weavers as it fell only on the purchasers, who were mostly Europeans. He therefore preferred to collect the tax in his '*jaghire*' However, Haliburton and Montray held opposite views.[60] They firmly believed that the remission of tax was not considerable and that its abolition was bound to have a salutary effect by encouraging manufacture. Ultimately it was the latter view that prevailed. But the measure did not elevate the status and position of the weaver in any tangible way. As mentioned earlier, it was the Company, rather than the weaver, which was to have immediately gained. Another suggestion of suspending inland duties on cotton imported for the use of the Company's investment was made with a similar motive.[61]

The intense Anglo-French competition for the procurement of the best textiles had thus driven the Indian weaver into the vortex of this rivalry from which retreat was not easy. The ordinary weaver was placed in an increasingly complex situation in which he was losing his independence and mobility. He had to function under the oppression and exaction of several agencies. The situation for him became worse because of the interplay of economic forces generated by European rivalry and political disarray. The commercial requirement of the two companies had placed the class of weavers on a different footing from the rest of the inhabitants. From the Anglo-French agreement made in Bengal, it is evident that the weavers had virtually become slaves of either of the two companies.[62] The English Company clearly stated, that if a weaver failed to deliver at the stipulated period, the cloth engaged, the Company's agent or representative was at a liberty to attach peon upon him in order to quicken his delivery. If a Company weaver sold his goods independently prior to his completion of orders, he was to be prosecuted and was liable to forfeit to the Company all the produce of the cloth so sold in bazaar value. The weavers were to be registered by the commercial agents in the *cutchery* of each region and were to be verified weekly or monthly. This left little scope for the weaver to exercise his options. The weavers were subjected to a system of coercion, which was institutionalized through official regulations. In order to maintain their profits and in view of the growing threat of competition, the European companies tried to squeeze the weavers.

POLICY TOWARDS THE INDIAN MERCHANTS

This period of trade revival was also significant from the point of view of the future of Indian merchants' participation in foreign trade. The intense Anglo-French rivalry throughout the second half of the eighteenth century to control the weaving centres on the eastern coast seems to have influenced the market relationship of this region. It is difficult to determine its impact in precise terms. There is an absence of systematic information on Indian merchants in local sources, which makes our reliance on European sources unavoidable. Even the available European sources left behind by the companies do not throw sufficient light on the plight of local merchants. It is highly probable that the Coromandel merchants, who were drawn to the European trading system, were losing their independence and many of them were ruined through the stringent system of contracts. The last quarter of the eighteenth century witnessed a deliberate policy of the Europeans to exclude Indian merchants in order to directly control the weavers and other producers. The various plans of Sadlier, Cochrane and Dick reflect this trend.[63]

During the period of our study the English Company tried to do away with the institution of Indian merchants. A similar kind of attempt in Bengal by the French was probably resisted by the English, as is evident from the letter of Chevalier to Warren Hastings. He wrote:

> Before the war and even two years after our establishment in Bengal, it is true we carried on our commerce in the aurungs in the neighbourhood of Chandernagar, by the means of a Body of merchants composed of the Natives of the country; but since that time their Insolubility and roguery, having laid us under the necessity of giving up that method, we were obliged to follow another plan and it was then we took the method of sending company's servants into the aurungs instead of Block gomastahs whom we formerly kept there. Our commerce benefited thereby. . . . Why would you at this time deprive us of a mode in which we have been successful?[64]

The English also tried to set aside the 'Company merchants' in their investment of coarse goods by 'means of *gomastahs*'. It proved successful in the short run when the Board of Examination made favourable recommendation and found the new mode vastly superior to that of the previous year, which was based on contract with the Indian merchants. Yet they adopted a pragmatic approach by retaining the institution of 'Company merchants'.[66] More significant, however, was the experiment made on the insistence of Basil Cochrane in 1786. This attempt may be described as the 'mode of direct investment' or 'investment through English contractors'.

Basil Cochrane was made the contractor of the English Company on the Coromandel Coast. He sought all political assistance to make his plan a success. His plan was based on the assumption that the employment of local merchants was not necessary. On the contrary, it was detrimental to the Company's interests in certain ways. He argued that the Company obtained no additional security by employing such intermediate agents against whom large outstanding balances were pending. Furthermore, the Company ran an additional risk if the merchants as well as the original manufacturers failed in their obligations, causing a 'double risk'. The Company's attitude towards Indian merchants can be inferred from the letter of the Board of Trade which stated, 'we wished to show the merchants we could do without them, we gave a preference to Mr. Cochrane's proposal as being the best'.[67] The plan also attempted to prevent the foreigners or British private traders from getting their supplies through the native servants, who usually received advances from the English and delivered goods to outsiders.

Cochrane's contract plan was introduced on 18 December 1786 and stipulated that he would deliver to the Company 30,530 pieces of cloth valued at current 88,676.22.76 *pagodas*—one half in six months and the whole in twelve months. In case of failure to deliver the stipulated goods, he was to be fined 25 per cent of the contracted amount. He was to receive an advance of 25 per cent and receive the rest when three-fourths of the stipulated material was delivered. However, when his annual contract expired on 18 December 1787, he was deficient in supplies up to 26,169 pieces valued at 74,790.2.53 *pagodas*.[68]

Cochrane had tried to use political influence through Anthony Sadlier, the chief of Masulipatam. He also suggested to the Board that directives be issued to zamindars for controlling the manufacture of cloth. The zamindars of Peddanore, Muglatore, Ramachandraporam and Pettapore were given written instructions to assist Cochrane in his endeavour to procure quality goods at the minimum cost by constantly examining the looms, and to bring all manufactured cloth of their region to some central point or *cutcheries* to be stamped after proper examination.[69] The zamindars were to permit such contracts as were entered into by the weavers with Cochrane and were to give positive orders so that they could be fulfilled by the weavers. For this purpose an agent was to be appointed by the zamindars to carry out these transactions. The Board also obliged Cochrane by providing all assistance in fulfilling the contract.[70] Raja Juggapelli Rauze obliged the Board by complying with its wishes. Cochrane issued orders to the weavers, merchants and other agents in his district, stating that 'in future all the combs made use of in manufacturing the Company's cloth must be chopped' and the cloth and comb together must be delivered to Cochrane's peon on a receipt being granted.[71]

Cochrane was confident that these orders would be able to break the link between the native merchants and *copdars*,[72] who were so formidably combined against him and the English interests.[73] The orders also asked the weavers to deliver two pieces of cloth per month to Cochrane, though he had made advances for only one piece. Cochrane's Plan of Investment also provided for the registration of the weavers who were working for the Company's supplies.[74] This method, along with some other measures, Cochrane believed, would bring to an end all cabal and intrigue. The Company would be sure of enjoying the labour of those weavers employed for the investment and would know the exact quantity of goods manufactured and supplied. He was optimistic that even the agents of the French Company would accede to these regulations.

As against this note of optimism, certain officials of the English Company were pointing out the disadvantages of this plan. The chief of Masulipatam pointed out that as the plan implied the exclusion of other merchants, it would render the recovery of balances already due from the merchants, more precarious.[75] The plan, it was assumed, would benefit the individual contractors, not the Company. It was also believed that it would afford grounds to the foreign merchants for complaint, which ought to be avoided. The chief of Masulipatam maintained that it was a plan similar to that of Sadlier and its experience would show that the expenses of the investment would considerably increase beyond the previous period.

Cochrane charged Yeats with hindering his reforms with the support of the black [Indian]merchants, although the plan enjoyed the support of foreigners. In fact, one can say that Cochrane's plan was destined to be a failure, not for want of exertion on his part, but from the competition that was likely to arise and the want of authority in him as a contractor. It was neither the want of manufacturers nor any decay in the production that prevented the Company investments from being procured. This failure, therefore, seems to have been caused by the anomalous nature of the post created for the new mode of investment. Since the resident as well as Cochrane were empowered to purchase cloth of the Company it must have created a competition for the cloth. As such, the merchants, who had been set aside by the latter, were still employed by the former; it was but natural for these people to purchase the cloth for which Cochrane had made an advance.

The Board of Trade gave a similar explanation while suggesting the withdrawal of Cochrane's contract system.[76] It wrote,

> Experience has, however, proved that the Residents at the Factories have not the authority or influence that is necessary over the zamindars, for enabling them to carry their plans for the provision of the Investment into effect, and if their influence were to be by any means increased, it could scarcely fail to clash—where different authorities independent of each other are to be exercised within the same District, where responsibility of being thus divided becomes weakened.

With the failure of Basil Cochrane's plan, the Company reverted to the familiar plan of investment through 'Company's Merchants'.

But the severity of implementation of this policy was apparent. This unnecessary severity and ruthlessness must have brought about the ruin of numerous Company merchants who had incurred debts for some reason or another.

Though the two rival companies were depended on the class of native merchants through annual contracts, the English, after the failure of Cochrane's plan, tried new modes to reach the producers directly, thus eliminating the Indian merchants. They had amply revealed their distrust of this class but were compelled to utilize their services in the absence of any other mode of investment. Dicks proposed a new plan of investment and the Court of Directors made a provisional approval of this plan.[77] It was in fact a modification of the 'Agency System' and was considered to be advantageous to the weavers and individual traders.

The plan was based on the belief that it was better to employ agents to make investments than to give contracts to the natives. The experiment made at Vizagapatnam proved successful but it required the British agents to know the local language and customs. Efforts were to be made to keep the weavers engaged to the Company alone, to obviate the problems for the Company caused either by price fluctuations or debasement of fabrics through competition. Free competition would have resulted in unsettling the weavers and traders through indiscriminate advances. The plan suggested that individual merchants, instead of shipping their goods under their own responsibility, were to hand them over to the Company and receive their share in the net profits.

The new plan provided for annual supply to each factory in the Presidency, the total value being 24 lakh *pagodas* worth of goods. Of this the Company's indents were to be of 16 lakh and the remaining 8 lakh were to be indented for the subscribers, each contributing not less than 1,000 *pagodas*. The object of admitting subscribers was to deter them from opening up trade with foreigners. After meeting the charges for washing, baling and freight, subscribers were to pay an additional 12.5 per cent, out of which commissions were to be paid to the Company's servants. The residents were also to get commission on the sales of rejected cloth.

It is evident that the plan evolved out of the pressure exerted by the free traders, which wanted to participate in the cotton trade. It was also the avowed policy of the Company to do away with contracts with Indian merchants to maximize profits. The question of shortage of funds for investment was also answered to an extent in this plan, and thus it received the approval of the directors.

Since the Peace Treaty of 1783 and the revival of French trade, it can be noticed that the Company merchants were unable to provide cloth at the price demanded by the Company at Vizagapatnam. The rate fixed by the Company was Rs. 7½ per piece. The merchants wanted Rs. 8 and the Chief and Council recommended the same rate. The Board took a serious note of this increased demand and recommended that the engagements be annulled and ordered withdrawal of the Company protection from those merchants as a 'punishment for their contumacious behaviour'.[78] Together with the official policy, the political disturbances, the Anglo-French competition and the natural calamities constantly played a major part in the fortunes of the Company merchants.

In the Masulipatam region, the *chay* goods were supplied by the Company merchants—Annum Lingiah, Nareadhamilly Veeranah, Cotohgoond Budriah, Narcadamilly Veerastalingam, Povada Soobiah, Manjetty Venkiaty, Cotah Goondah Ramiah, Mamady Lingiah, etc.[79] They had superintended the *chay* merchandise for the English, the French and the Dutch companies. As the English Company did not have sufficient investment, these merchants contracted with the French private merchants such as Messrs Farcy, Le Coute & Co., Mons. Moracin, etc.[80] The French chief had also sent the French Company's investments to Manapakum Ramanah, who in turn, transacted through the relations or sons of the Company merchants and through his *gomastahs*.[81] They were accused by the English Company of supplying goods to the French. They had made advances of a large sum to the weavers to carry out the Company's investment. But soon hostilities commenced. The zamindars of Murtazanagar quarrelled with one another. This resulted in the total destruction of the dwellings of the weavers. Later, Meer Sahib, an officer of Hyder's army, invaded the region with seven to eight thousand cavalry and completed the ruin.[82] It created such a scarcity of provisions that *jannalloo* was sold at 25 *pagodas* per candy. This ruined the weavers, most of whom absconded, thus putting the merchants in arrears to the Company, which they had been serving since 1766.

Charles Floyer recommended fresh contracts with the same set of merchants.[83] He believed that it was necessary to employ them for the obvious reason, that many of the weavers resided in the Guntoor Circar, where a great part of the dye was produced. Since the English had no influence or authority at this place, the direct mode would have ruined their interest through political rivalries and jealousies. He suggested that the liquidation of the whole property of the merchants would go a very little way towards the discharge of their debts whereas their continuing employment might help in the recovery of debts in a short time. He also argued that the Company's debts were decreasing gradually.[84] The Board, while rejecting these suggestions, stated, 'If the merchants are indeed as unable to discharge their debts to the company as they would make it appear, it seems highly ineligible to continue making advances to persons of so little responsibility.'[85]

The intense competition existing between the English and the French must have worsened the plight of the Indian merchants. In the normal interaction of market forces this kind of competition would have favourable results for the local merchants. But the political might of the Europeans created an unfavourable situation for these merchants. This can be inferred from several sources. Ramah Naig and Coortuvinty Chellimiah were providing *chay* goods to Mons. Moracin, the French chief at Pondicherry. The former also served as a Dubash to Darvall in his private capacity. It appears that Ramah Naig had written authority from Moracin to supply *chay* goods, which he had been doing for the last eighteen years.[86] When questioned, he told the English officials that in his opinion the Company's orders and parliamentary directives disallowing trade with foreigners were applicable to Europeans and not to the Indian merchants. He had advanced 30,000 *pagodas* for the goods to be supplied to the French, and was planning to invest another 20,000 *pagodas*.[87] His investments included the Nizam's territories as well as the Company's *jaghire* lands. Similarly, Coortuvinty Chellimiah had also invested about 15,000 *pagodas*, but made no advance to the Company's weavers. It was for this flimsy reason that Cottagondoo Ramiah lost his huge property. The Company decided to value his two houses and assign them to the administration. [88]

It is evident from the Company's records that the French had sought engagements with some of the relations of English 'Company merchants'. By this means, the French fared reasonably well in their trade endeavours. They succeeded in procuring substantial amounts of *chay* goods. In Masulipatam, foreigners or individuals purchased through Indian merchants or directly the amount of goods in 1786 given in Table 5.1.

There were occasions when the Indian merchants showed unwillingness to enter into a contract without ascertaining its stipulations. Some 'company merchants' such as Chocapah Chetti, Nagapah Chetti,

Table 5.1: GOODS PURCHASED BY FOREIGNERS IN MASULIPATAM (in 1786)[89]

	In Madras *pagodas*
Mons Bomcauss in the Guntoor Circar had a remittance from Pondicherry to advance to the weavers a sum of	50,000
Mons Monzam, at the same place employed the Danish merchants at Tranquebar, a sum of	5,000
A Dubash agent employed by the Portuguese and Armenians settled at Madras, a sum of	35,000
The Dutch sent advance from Palicut	5,000
Ramah Naig, a French Dubash, advanced a sum of	70,000
Coortuvinty Chellimiah, a Danish Dubash at Masulipatam, advanced	15,000
Armenian Merchants advanced	3,000
French chief at Masulipatam advanced to Elendrapilley	5,000
The French advanced to weavers, sundry merchants and brokers, a sum of	3,000

Panlatta Chetti, Curry Ratna Chetti, Murogapah Chetti and Andenarrain Chetti wished to know in 1784 the form of contract, its period and its related conditions, whether it would be made with a set of merchants or with individuals, the sum to be advanced and the mode of payment. They declined to enter into a contract when they did not receive a satisfactory answer.[90] This concern was expressed by Warren Hamilton also. During the period of war between the English and the French, the price of cotton had risen exorbitantly (the growing competition was caused by the presence of French agents) and the scanty and uncertain supply of ready money created problems for the English as well. 'It was with difficulty' wrote Hamilton, 'that the merchants could be induced to accept advances, they refused to enter into written contracts. . . .' He was forced to discontinue the deduction of 5 per cent from the advances for their earlier arrears.[91] The harsh treatment of the Indian merchants was accepted by Calland as early as 1763. In course of his enquiry to know why the Cuddalore merchants did not perform their contracts, he accepted that the merchants were most severely treated and, in fact, some of their[92] cloth was found to be superior to the earlier one.

At Vizagapatnam the merchants who had contracted for the provision of the investment were to be called before the Board and strictly warned against making any other engagement. In case of any deficiency, they were to pay a fine of 15 per cent, not upon the quantity found deficient but upon the whole amount of their contracts.[93] Such rigid rules were applied at other places as well, at the time of sorting.

The French had also terminated the contract with Naynatte Modelier, who had not been able to provide cloths at the Company's price. The market forces did not permit him to supply goods at the price offered by the French Company.[94] Similarly Mons. Panon, the chief at Yanaon, kept aside the traditional services of the Company merchant—Tirvidy Balchetty in the consignment of handkerchiefs and other articles, and instead decided to have direct dealings with the weavers. Bovelleau, likewise rejected all the proposals of the merchants who had contracted in the previous years. He was trying a new scheme of speculation by buying from the merchants of the English Company a considerable portion of goods, which had been rejected at the Madras inspection. We find a new set of merchants the following year, with which contract was signed. It included the names of Vallat Chetti, Decou Begnian and Trivangadom as brokers.[95] During war periods both the European powers faced shortage of funds to maintain the troops and their investments. It was a common practice in such situations to extort funds from the Indian mercantile class. In 1760, at the time of the English attack on Pondicherry, financial and military pressure was exerted on the merchants when Vellalas, Agammudaiyans, Komattis, Chettis and Elavaniyans were sent for and told that they must bear to pay for 1,300 sepoys at the rate of Rs. 353 per 50 sepoys each month.[96] Bapu Rao, Ramchandra Rao and Rangappa Mudali's son and some other Company merchants were imprisoned for not being able to pay the amount.[97] Similarly, the English convened the principal shroffs and other merchants and asked them to lend on bonds bearing 8 per cent interest on a sum of 3 lakh *pagodas*. The principal merchants were sent to higher authorities for not sparing the amount demanded.[98] Only the agents of Buccanjee, the famous banker of Madras, offered to pay 1 lakh *pagodas*. Thus, we find the declining profitability of overseas trade, the political turmoil in the southern states, hazards caused by the Anglo-French rivalry and the use of political means by European agencies to control the market and production created adverse conditions for the Indian merchants. Their profit avenues were getting increasingly reduced with the extension of European influence. This must have seriously affected the local merchants and converted a large number of them into debtors.

NOTES

1. Hameeda Hossain, 'The Alienation of Weavers: Impact of the Conflict between the Revenue and Commercial Interest of the East India Company 1750-1800', *IESHR*, Vol. XVI, No. III, 1979, pp. 323-46.
2. Vijaya Ramaswamy, *Textiles and Weavers in Medieval South India*, Delhi, 1985, p. 121.
3. Henry de Closets d'Errey, *L'Histoire de L'Inde Française, 1666-1814*, Paris, 1940, p. 108.
4. Board of Trade to Governor and Council, 9 November 1786, *Public Consultations*, 140A, Fort St. George, TSA.
5. Francis Buchanan, *Journey from Madras through the Countries of Mysore, Canara and Malabar*, Vol. I, London, 1807, p. 216.
6. Vijaya Ramaswamy, op. cit., p. 151.
7. Ibid., p. 152; Richard A. Frasca, 'Weavers in Pre-Modern South India', *Economic and Political Weekly*, Vol. 10, 26 July 1975, pp. 119-23.
8. F. Buchanan, op. cit., p. 216.
9. Fernand Braudel, *Civilization and Capitalism, 15th to 18th Centuries*, Vol. III: *The Perspective of the World*, London, 1984, p. 508.
10. S. Arasaratnam, 'Weavers, Merchants and Company: The Handloom Industry in South-eastern India 1750-1790', in Sanjay Subrahmanyan, (ed.), *Merchants, Markets and the State in Early Modern India*, Delhi, 1990, pp. 190-214.
11. Doglas E. Haynes and Tirthankar Roy, 'Conceiving Mobility: Weavers' Migration in Pre-colonial and Colonial India', *IESHR*, 36,1,1999, pp. 35-67.
12. P. Swarnalatha and P. Sudhir, 'The Company and the Coromandel Weaver: Structural Change in the Short Term 1790-1820', *Indian History Congress Proceedings*, 48th Session, 1987, pp. 461-6.
13. Ravi Ahuja, 'Labour unsettled: Mobility and protest in the Madras region, 1750-1800', *IESHR*, 35, 4, 1998, pp. 381-404.
14. Ibid.
15. Board of Trade to Governor and Council, 9 November 1786, *Public Consultations*, No. 140A, TSA.
16. Jacques Dupuis, *Madras et Le Nord du Coromandel*, Paris, 1960, p. 204.
17. John Rowley to the Board of Trade, 8 December 1792, Godavari District Factory Record, Vol. 830 (1792-96), APA.
18. J. Revell to Anthony Sadlier,15December1789, *Public Consultations*, Fort St. George, No. 160B, p. 129, TSA.
    He mentions that in the last 3 or 4 years, the lambardars bought cotton at 8 to 11 Madras *pagoda* a bullock load containing 10 maunds or 80 *viss* retaining nearly 22 per cent.
19. S. Arasaratnam, *Merchants, Companies and Commerce*, op. cit., pp. 61-3.
20. Flaix, op. cit., Tome II, p. 11.
21. Ibid., p. 30. He mentions that the fur of the wool (duvet) gave very long and fine thread, though it was not too strong. It was difficult to spin and was mainly used in the manufacture of Salempore.
22. According to Flaix, cotton cultivation in India suffered from one important limitation. The cultivators continued the traditional practice of pulling out plants

each year and sowing new ones. This did not give sufficient time to the plants to grow fully. Otherwise Indians could have produced greater quantity of cotton. Flaix, op. cit., Tome II, pp. 165-6.

23. George Wynch to John Holland Governor and Council, 12 February 1790, *Public Consultations*, 161B, TSA.
24. Minute of Dent, 30 April 1784, *Public Consultations*, Fort St. George, No. 133A, TSA.
25. Henry Dodwell, 'The Madras Weavers under the Company', *Proceedings of Indian Historical Records Commission*, Vol. IV, 1922, p. 44.
26. Alexander Davidson to the President of Board of Trade, 15 December 1789, *Vizagapatnam District Commercial Consultation*, p. 396, APA.
27. Letter from the Commercial Resident at Vizagapatnam to the Board of Revenues (Extract), 26 June 1796, *Godavari District Records*, APA.
28. Richard Dillon to Board of Trade, 18 January 1794, *Godavari District Records*, Vol. 830, APA.
29. Roger Darvell to David Haliburton, President Board of Revenue, 18 May 1793, *Chingleput District Records*, Vol. 445, TSA.
30. While complaining that the weavers received payment from foreigner individuals and did not confer themselves to their engagements, the Board of Trade described them thus: 'neither are they all equally industrious being naturally of so knavish and indolent disposition, that few of them will devote a longer time to labour than will barely suffice to earn the common necessities of life'.
    Board of Trade to Governor and Council, 25 January 1790, *Public Consultations*, Fort St. George, TSA.
    At another place, the Board of Trade observed: 'They [weavers] appear in effect to destroy their own credit [by caste ceremonies], evincing themselves not worthy to be trusted with advances of money. . . .'
    Proceedings of the Board of Trade, 14 August 1786, *Public Consultations*, Fort St. George, TSA.
31. *Gazetteer of Pondicherry*, Vol. I, Pondicherry, 1982, p. 546.
32. Ibid.
33. Conway to le ministre de la marine, 6 February 1788, C^2 184, microfilm, No. 9, AN.
34. Samuel Statham to Charles Floyers, 26 July 1786, *Masulipatam District Consultation—Commercial*, Vol. 2900, APA.
35. However, the French did not succeed in the long run owing to the vacillating political fortunes of the French settlements in the war periods compelling the weavers to flee to safer places.
36. K.N. Chaudhuri, *The Trading World of Asia and the English East India Company 1660-1760*, London, 1978, p. 250.
37. General Letters (Extract), Fort St. George, 12 July 1774, *French in India Series*, No. 5, IOR.
38. Drudgeon to Anthony Sadlier, 30 December 1774, *French in India Series*, 5, IOR. Mons. Law to Robert Harland, 1 May 1774, *French in India Series*, 5, IOR.
39. General Consultations (Extract) of Fort St. George, 1 July 1774, *French in India Series*, 5, IOR.
40. Vencataramiah to John Whitehall, Chief at Masulipatam General Consultations of Fort St. George (Extract), *French in India Series*, 5, IOR.

41. Sadlier to De Mars 12 November 1775, *Public Consultations*, Fort St. George, TSA.
42. De Mars to Sadlier, 27 October 1775, *Public Consultations*, Fort St. George, TSA.
43. Johannes Occama, Dutch Chief at Palicat to Anthony Sadlier, 31 May 1775, *Public Consultations*, Fort St. George, TSA.
44. Durdgeon to Sadlier, 6 June 1775, *Public Consultations*, Fort St. George, TSA.
45. Under this scheme, all the reputed weavers, without exception, were ordered to receive 3 or 4 *pagodas* in advance and made to sign *muchilka* forbidding them from making cloths for the foreigners. He had divided the *circars* of Ellore and Rajamundry into thirty districts or *mootahs* and appointed in each *mootah* four head weavers, two peons, who were overseen by two *gomastahs* and a *paigasidaronloo*. These nine took constant care of the English cloth and kept the weavers perpetually indebted to the English through their advances. De Mars to Sadlier, 27 October 1775, *Public Consultations*, Fort St. George, TSA.
46. Canicoply was a local official concerned with collecting the Company's investments.
47. Mathew Yeats to Alexander Wynch, 26 September 1775, *Public Consultations*, Fort St. George, TSA.
48. Ibid.
49. Board of Trade to Archibald Campbell and Council, 20 July 1786, *Public Consultations*, Fort St. George, TSA.
50. General Letter to A. Campbell and Council, 4 July 1786, *Public Consultations*, Fort St. George, TSA.
51. J.H. Skardon to Alexander Davidson, 25 June 1785, *Public Consultations*, Fort St. George, TSA.
52. Charles Truman to John Humphrey Skardon, 20 February 1785, *Public Consultations*, Fort St. George, TSA.
53. J.H. Skardon to Alexander Davidson, op. cit.
54. A. Cambell and Council to C.B. Dent, 21 June 1786, *Public Consultations*, Fort St. George, TSA.
55. Proceedings of the Board of Trade (Extract), 14 August 1786, *Public Consultations*, Fort St. George, TSA.
56. Governor and Council to Charles Floyer, 11 November 1786, *Masulipatam Correspondence—Commercial*, Vol. 2900, p. 88, APA.
57. Ibid.
58. Balfour to Cambell and Board of Trade, 6 October 1786, *Public Consultations*, Fort St. George, TSA.
59. *Guide to the Record of the Chingleput District Madras*, 1934, Vol. 444, Correspondence regarding *jaghire* Lands, 1786-8, pp. 597-9.
60. Ibid.
61. Dick to Goddard, 15 January 1790, *General Letters to England*—Commercial Department, TSA.
62. Regulation on the weavers between Calcutta Council and Le Comite á Chandernagar, 1786, 8 AQ 346, AN.

    The French and the Dutch had made proposals to the English Company through their letters of 6 and 15 May 1767 respectively, to divide the weavers of the Bengal region among the three European nations. The English Council at Calcutta rejected these proposals through its letter of 20 May 1767 expressing its annoyance with such schemes. Yet, almost twenty years later a similar scheme was carried out in Bengal based on the French proposals. This kind of scheme could not be introduced in the Coromandel because the French Revolution broke out soon after, affecting the Anglo-French relations yet another time. Letters Nos. 2423, 2424, 2431, *Inde-Série-B*, Feuilles Volantes, Archives D'Outre-mer, Aix-en-Provence.

63. These were not plans of individuals in isolation but had the full support of the Company government at Madras.
64. Mons. Chevalier and Council to Warren Hastings, 21 June 1773 (1), *Foreign Secret*, NAI.
65. Board of Examinations of Recommendations, 25 January 1772, *Public Consultations*, TSA.
66. A similar kind of attempt was earlier made through Sadlier. The President and Council of Masulipatam described it as a new mode of 'recourse to the weavers and discontinuing the merchants. . . .' Anthony Sadlier to John Whitehall and Council, Masulipatam, 28 June 1774, *French in India Series*, No. 5, IOR.
67. Board of Trade to Campbell and Council, 23 November 1786, *Public Consultations*, Fort St. George, TSA.
68. Mathew Yeats, Resident at Ingeram to the Board of Trade, 7 April 1788, *Masulipatam Consultation—Commercial*, Vol. 2839, APA.
69. Campbell and Council to Charles Floyer, 12 May 1787, *Masulipatam Consultation—Commercial*, Vol. 2838, APA.
70. A. Scott, Secretary of Board to Basil Cochrane, 16 July 1787, *Masulipatam Consultation—Commercial*, Vol. 2838, APA.
71. Basil Cochrane to A. Sadlier, 15 November 1787l, *Masulipatam Consultation—Commercial*, Vol. 2838, APA.
72. *Copdar*, or the broker of Telugu villages, was an important functionary. Though a part of the weaving community, he acted as a broker and assisted the Company in keeping control over the quality of product and helped at the time of sorting or assortment. The English Company tried to ignore them but were compelled to re-employ them on practical grounds on a brokerage free of 1.5 per cent. Minutes of Fort St. George Council, 16 January 1775, *Public Consultations*, TSA.
73. Basil Cochrane to Anthony Sadlier, 15 November 1787, *Masulipatam Consultation—Commercial*, Vol. 2838, APA.
74. B. Cochrane to Board of Trade, 9 June 1788, *Masulipatam Correspondence—Commercial*, Vol. 2839, APA.
75. Chief and Council of Masulipatam to the Board, 4 December 1787, *Masulipatam Correspondence*, Vol. 2839, APA.
76. Board of Trade to Chief and Council, Masulipatam, 4 December 1787, *Masulipatam Correspondence—Commercial*, Vol. 2838, APA.
77. Extract from Commercial Letter from Court of Directors, 23 June 1802, Godavari District Factory Records, Vol. 882, in *Guide to Godavari District Records*, Vol. I.
78. Board of Trade to John Holland and Council, 31 December 1789, *Public Consultations*, Fort St. George, TSA.
79. When the French became the political masters of the region, they contracted their business along with the Dutch through the same set of merchants. Later, the English did the same.
80. Company Merchants to Charles Floyer, 6 August 1786, *Masulipatam Correspondence—Commercial*, Vol. 2900, APA.

81. Ibid.
82. Ibid., 19 August 1786.
83. Charles Floyer to Chief-in Council, Fort St. George, 31 May 1787, *Masulipatam Correspondence—Commercial*, Vol. 2838, APA.
84. In 1786, the Company owed current 16,156.9.3 *pagodas* and by March 1787, it owed 14,446.31.31 *pagodas*, a reduction of 1,707.13.43 *pagodas*.
85. Board of Trade to Chief and Council, Masulipatam, 12 June 1787, *Masulipatam Correspondence—Commercial*, Vol. 2838, APA.
86. Charles Floyer and Company's Orders, 15 August 1786, *Masulipatam, Correspondence—Commercial*, Vol. 2838, APA.
87. Ramah Naig procured goods from Narecadamillu Baupiah, son of Narecadamillu Veeranah, Narecadamillu Chillimiah, son of Narecadamillu Lingaum, Majetty Vencatarama, brother of Majetty Venkiah, Annum Sooriah, son of Annum Lingia, Poovada Reddy, brother of Poovada Soobiah, etc.
88. Charles Floyer and Company's Order, 15 August 1786, *Masulipatam Correspondence—Commercial*, Vol. 2838, APA.
89. Table mentioned in Masulipatam Correspondence—letters received—Commercial, 1786-8, Vol. 2900, APA. There seems to be an error in the total of Madras *pagodas*, which states 2,10,000 instead of the calculated amount of 2,01,000.
90. Alexander Davidson's Minute on Investments, 31 March 1784, *Public Consultations*, Fort St. George, TSA.
91. Warren Hamilton to Board of Trade, 23 January 1789, *Public Consultations*, Fort St. George, TSA.
92. General Letter from Pigot to COD. 7 November 1763, *Add. Ms* 34688, Br. Mus.
93. General Letter to England, 16 January 1792, Commercial Department Despatches, Fort St. George, TSA.
94. Moracin to the Administrators at Paris, op. cit., p. 315. The copy of contract with Mouniapa Chetti, for the goods valued at 29,884 star *pagodas* clearly mentions the payment of 20 per cent as damages for not supplying goods on time. Copie du Contract, dated 20 May 1785, No. 361, NAI, Pondicherry.
95. Mémoire presented to Mons. de Boynes, 7 August 1771, C^2 107 (microfilm), AN.
96. *The Diary of Ananda Ranga Pillai*, Vol. 12, Delhi, 1985, p. 20.
97. Ibid., pp. 51 and 56.
98. Edward Hughes and Hector Munro to Lord Macartney, 2 December 1781, *Add. Ms* 22417, Br. Mus.

Chapter 6

The Role of Indian Textiles in Anglo-French Relations

THE TRADE between the western world and India often changed hands. It turned into different channels and enriched those who carried it on. A passion for Indian manufactures and textile products induced the people of every age and region to procure the delicate and fine, as well as the coarser cotton fabrics from India. It is interesting to note that while the cotton industry was virtually unknown in Europe, in India it was in a flourishing state.

Several sources refer to the trade between south India and Rome from time immemorial. The weaving industry of the south prospered throughout the medieval period, except for brief intervals during calamities. It reached its zenith in the time of the Vijayanagar Empire when the weavers and the cloth traders seemed to have received incentives and various facilities. The entry of European traders into the Coromandel economy brought about a gradual change in the structure of textile production and its market organization. The European companies began to participate in the Asian trade and carried the Indian textiles to the far-flung regions. The profit margin was sufficient to attract ready cash. By the mid-eighteenth century, an intense rivalry ensued between the English and the French to establish control over important textile producing centres. It was carried on through financial and, whenever possible, political means.

The role of Indian products in the French trade with Africa has been well brought out by Jean Terrade. The Indian cloths constituted 54 per cent of the total value of goods (10.5 million *livres tournois* in 1775) and 57 per cent (14.7 million *livres tournois*) in 1788 and gave sufficient profits from which slaves were purchased.[1] The bulk of these textiles were of the coarse variety from Coromandel. A similar picture was presented by the British trade, where the Indian goods constituted a very high proportion of the total trade. During the eighteenth century, textiles accounted for 68 per cent of all goods to Africa, of which the Indian textile constituted 40 per cent and formed the single largest item. This position existed till the end of the century.

THE INDIAN TEXTILE VARIETY

The eastern coast of India produced an immense variety of textiles for local consumption or for inter-regional trade as is shown in Map 6.1. Some genres of cloths occupied an important place in the export market. The English and the French companies and their agents showed their preference for those products which rendered them profits in the markets of Europe, Asia, Africa or the New World.

The Indian textiles consisted of numerous varieties of cloths such as long cloth, muslin, *Doorea, Mooree, Betteela*, thick Cambric, Chintz (striped, red and blue), *Salempore, Bafta*, and various types of handkerchief. The Indian textiles may be divided into two major categories—plain and patterned. The patterned ones may further be classified into two main types: (a) textiles in which artistic treatment was carried out after the weaving, and (b) those in which the artistic treatment was given while they were still on the loom.

Among the plain textiles the long cloth was extremely popular with the foreign traders. Long cloth was the largest single variety exported by the European companies. It was not an important item in the inter-regional trade but it adequately met the European requirement. It was classified into four categories on the basis of its texture—ordinary, middling, fine and superfine. The long cloth was mostly 37 yards in length and 1 yard in breadth. For the fine variety the thread was bought from Ginji and the surrounding villages, while for the middling type it was procured from Woolandoo petah. It took 8 days to prepare the thread and 12 days to weave the cloth on a loom by two men. The labour cost was about 1 *pagoda*, 10 *fanams* and 40 *cash*.[2] It was made of staple cotton. This cloth was produced primarily in the villages of Salem, Warrangal and Udayapatnam and sent out from Madras, Vizagapatnam, Ingeram, Madapollam and Cuddalore factories. It was in great demand till as late as 1792. Even its inferior quality was sold at considerable profit. This can be judged from the fact that the Court of Directors regretted its decision of not ordering double the quantity of the indent.[3]

The Indian muslin consisted of several assortments and was sorted into numbers. The highest price paid by the Company was usually

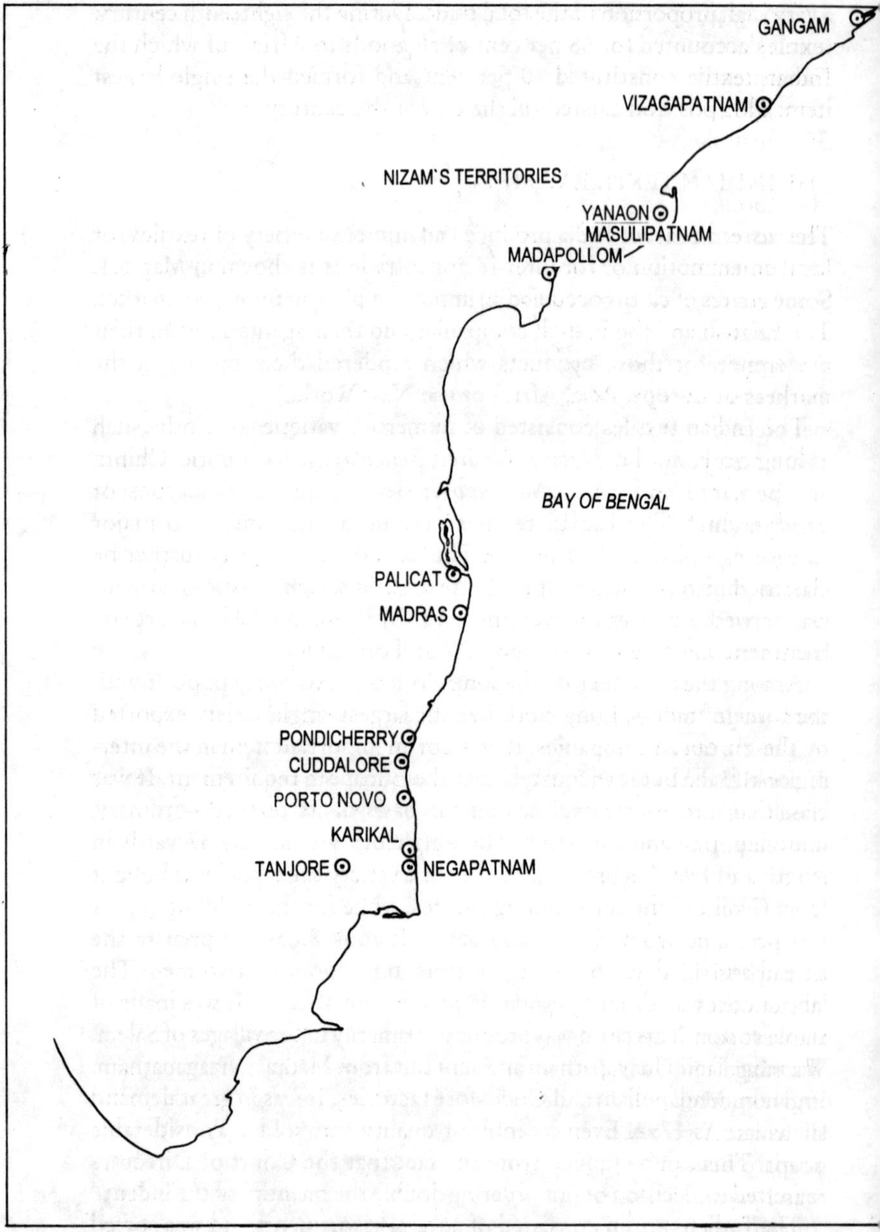

MAP 6.1: TEXTILE WEAVING AREAS IN COROMANDEL

7 *pagodas* per piece. For each advance, the weavers purchased thread in small skeins not at any fixed rate but according to the market price.[4] Each piece of muslin required an elaborate method of preparation. To make a piece of muslin 34 *covid* long and 3 *covid* broad, it required 320 small skeins of thread.[5] To prepare it for the loom it was necessary to keep it moist for 4 days. It was then placed on the reel, which needed the labour of eight persons every day. It was then run upon another reel to examine the texture of the thread and then placed on an instrument called *ansoormany.* It then required three men to work for 4 days to comb and rub the thread thrice daily. It was constantly washed before it was put on the loom. Three men worked on the loom to prepare a piece of muslin, which required 8 days to complete. The cost of thread was about 4 *pagodas* and the *coolie* hire was around 3 *pagodas* per piece of number one. The inferior qualities showed proportionate abatement of ¼ *pagoda* per quality.[6] Muslin *Doorea* were manufactured in the same manner. The process of washing muslin was very cumbersome and difficult. The washing alone required several days of uninterrupted labour.[7] On completion, the brokers who delivered them to the *gomastahs* or *canicoplys* first sorted the muslins. These were transported on bullock carts to Madras and Pondicherry. The cloths were carefully sorted by the warehouse-keeper. The differences between the advance and the amount due were settled with the brokers who in turn settled accounts with the weavers.

The thread for superfine *Mooree* was brought from different places. It took 15 days for two men, 10 days for three men and 8 days for four men to manufacture a piece of superfine *Mooree.* The process of washing was elaborate and time-consuming. It required, on an average, over 20 days of labour to complete the washing, before it was delivered to the brokers.[8]

Betteela or *Bethile* was striped or flowered muslin greatly in demand in Europe till the first half of the nineteenth century. It was used for neckclothes and ladies' dresses (shown in Plates 4 and 5), and the clearest sort was used for bonnets and veilings. It was procured from Warrangal and Khammamet districts of Andhra and was also produced and exported from Cuddalore, Nagore, Arnee and Madrapakan districts. A piece of cloth required two men to weave for 8 days to prepare *Betteela* 32 *covid* long and 3 *covid* broad. The cost of thread was 1 *pagoda* 20 *fanam* and the coolie charges amounted to 27 *fanams* 20 *cash* per piece.[9] *Betteela* was an article of some importance in the European trade from the Coromandel. Before its abolition in 1769, the French Company carried this article as an item of export. It constituted a twelfth of the total exports of the Company and was always wholly purchased at the annual sales at L'Orient.[10]

Since the suppression of the Company's monopoly the private traders speculated very little on this article. As a result, the Swiss muslin, through an imitation, made rapid advance in different markets of Europe. It was in the Levant, Syria, Persia, Arabia and their neighbouring countries where this textile from the Coromandel was consumed in bulk. Flaix blamed the private traders of France for neglecting this article, which could have assured a definite profit.[11] According to him, this lapse produced a progressive decline in their exchanges with the Levant. This article could have been used in the expansion of their 'country' trade as well. As regards England, the manufacturers of England, toward the close of the century, successfully imitated this item. Hence the sale of this Indian variety experienced a rapid decline.[12]

The principal manufacturing centres of *Betteela* were in the region of Carnatic, at Chetour, Attur and in the market town of Ettour. But the quality was not so good as the one found near Tirupati. There was another muslin called *Doorea*. It was a light fabric and usually contained two stripes. It was locally called *Karasari*.[13] The *Doorea* and the *Betteela* were so similar to each other that they were interchangeable in their sale. Only those with special knowledge could distinguish between the two. According to Flaix, besides *Karasaris*, there were two other types of *Betteela*—the *Parchari* and the *Dimdisse*. The first was distinguished by its two broad stripes with thin stripes of 5-6 threads at the middle. Chintz or *Chites* were the painted cloths which were also known by the name of *Perses*.[14] They constituted only about a twentieth part of the total exports from the Coromandel.[15] The best variety of chintz came from Nellore, Masulipatam (see Plate 3), Madras and St. Thome. The water of these regions was considered most suitable for dyeing. This cloth had beautiful *Finesse*. In Europe there was a special craze for this variety. In the wardrobe of the aristocratic women and of rich families at least one or two robes of chintz were considered a status symbol.[16] There was a special variety of chintz by the name of *Chite Metabi*.[17] It was a precious article, greatly sought after but forming a very small proportion of the cargo. Chintz was considered an oriental luxury. Even if we consider Flaix's description of the Indian chintz an exaggeration,[18] the clamour against its import in France and England suggests its real importance. The export of this article progressively declined because of the prohibitory regulations that the European nations placed on the painted and printed cloths from India.

Organdi was not a major article of export, yet there was fascination for it in the upper classes of Europe. It was also a type of muslin, but it had its own distinctive features such as equal spacing and beautiful netting of threads and the arrangement of ply in the texture. The main centres of its production were at Kanchipuram, Madras and in the neighbouring villages of Arcot. At the time of its abolition in 1769, the French Company imported from India *Organdis* worth Rs. 54,000, while the English bought *Organdi* worth Rs. 52,000, the Dutch spent Rs. 63,000 and the Danish Company spent Rs. 20,000 on it.[19]

Among the loom—decorated fabrics of Coromandel, the flowered and figured weaves called *Jamedani* enjoyed a worldwide reputation. *Jamedani* did not differ much from *Organdi* except that the former was brocaded and stitched. While the muslin was woven on the looms, the *Jamedanis* were different in their patterns based on flower and figure motifs and also in their treatment and in the technique employed. Each pattern required a different mode of treatment. This article constituted a minor proportion of the total exports. The English Company was the primary purchaser, buying annually about Rs. 45,000 worth of *Jamedani*.[20] This was exported only to the region around the Red Sea and Persia at double the profit. The French Company before its abolition sought this article worth up to Rs. 30,000 for Cochin China (Vietnam) and for the countries of that region in return for bullion, tea, porcelains and spices.[21]

Gingham was a pure cotton fabric woven with dyed yarn and patterned either striped or checkered. It was usually in red or blue shade. This fabric was well known in European markets, though the cities of Rouen in France and Birmingham in England were full of manufactories producing a similar variety. They imitated *Gingham* of the Coromandel but could not match its excellence of paints and texture, especially the four-thread tissue.[22] The red *Gingham* needed 80 days to prepare and dye the thread for a single piece, and 6 days to weave [the cost of thread was 36 *fanams* 60 *cash* while the labour cost was 20 *fanams*] while the blue *Gingham* required 10 days to prepare the thread and 6 days to weave it (the cost of thread was 36 *fanam* 60 *cash* and the labour cost 20 *fanams*).[23] This variety was usually exported to Manila and Batavia as a commodity of exchange in the 'country' trade.[24]

Guinea and the semi-*Guinea* formed an important proportion of the European cargo from India. It was of the same texture and weave as the long cloth but was woven from cotton thread and dyed in bright shades. It was manufactured in the Andhra lowlands up to Bimilapatam,[25] Cuddalore and Cheynoor districts as well as in Tanjore and Ramnad states. The price of *Guinea* varied considerably according to its type and the nature of demand. It was almost 20 to 22 per cent cheaper a century before 1786.[26] The *Guinea* of 23 and 19 *conjons* was dyed in blue and exported to Africa and Antilles. It was used for table covers, bed sheets and for furnishings. *Guinea* of 50 *conjons* was consumed for shirtings.[27]

It was the colonial establishment and the ever-expanding slave traffic, which established the importance of semi-*Guinea* as an object of commerce. The Arabs were the first carriers of this traffic who made it popular on the eastern coast of Africa. The English Company became the leading exporter of this article from the Coromandel, but the French also carried away about Rs. 5 million worth of *Guineas* during the period of free trade.[28]

Salempore belonged to the staple variety of cotton cloth manufactured throughout the Coromandel Coast ranging from coarse to very fine in plain white, blue or brown colour. Even the length varied from 16 to 22 yards. The best variety was to found near Masulipatam, Nellore, Cuddalore and Tanjore. It was one of the popular items of export, both to South-East Asia and Europe. Another staple textile was *Mori* but it was finer and of superior variety. The length was much shorter and sold as painted chintz in South-East Asian countries.

To prepare a piece of *Salempore*, cotton was purchased at Rs. 5½ per Ganjam maund in 1789.[29] The detailed cost of manufacturing can be seen in Table 6.1.

Generally a woman with three children dressed cotton and prepared the thread for a piece of cloth, ready for the weaver's loom, in 15 days. An ordinary weaver could weave no more than 3 pieces of cloth in 2 months, provided the thread was available without interruption.[30]

Palempores were basically painted fabric depicting scenes from the ancient epics, mythological themes and religious patterns (as can be seen in Plate 2), which created a pleasant cavalcade of motifs and designs, harmonizing block printing and hand painting. *Palempores* were prepared by the Uriya weavers known as Dera, Tonti and Rongoni, and Telugu weavers consisting of Devangulu, Salelu and Pottusalelu castes. This variety of cloth was probably first shipped from Ganjam to Europe in 1771 and later, in 1779, the Court of Directors wrote, 'As those [*palempores*] from Ganjam are much approved, you must endeavour to send a larger portion of that.' The resident expressed

TABLE 6.1: THE COST OF MANUFACTURE, *SALEMPORE* (1789)

		Rs.	A.	P.
The price of thread was Rs. 3.5 per *seer*		Rs.	A.	P.
11 *seers* of thread was needed		3	2	3
Payment to *gomastahs* was		-	2	-
Cost of labour		-	8	-
Total cost		3	12	3
Time needed for cordoning cotton	30 days			
Spinning thread and setting the loom	2 days			
Weaving *Salempore*	8 days			
Total	40 days			
For the preparation of cloths of 14 *punjams*,[31]				
26 *seers* of cotton was needed at		Rs.	A.	P.
6 *seers* per rupee		4	5	4
Cost of spinning		1	14	1
Weavers labour and contingent charges		1	8	0
Total cost		7	11	5
For the preparation of cotton piece of 18 *punjams*,				
21½ *seers* of cotton were needed at		Rs.	A.	P.
6 *seers* per rupee		3	9	4
Cost of spinning		2	13	11
Weavers labour and contingent charges		2	2	0
Total cost		8	9	3
For the preparation of cotton of 20 *punjams*,				
19½ *seers* of cotton was needed at		Rs.	A.	P.
6 *seers* per rupee		3	4	0
Cost of spinning		3	13	9
Weavers labour and contingent charges		2	12	0
Total cost		9	13	9

some apprehension of making contracts with the merchants for European investments because he feared the merchants of Berhampore (chief town of Ganjam district) under the control of refractory zamindars, were insolvent and could not be depended upon.[32] Otherwise also these merchants preferred dealing with private merchants rather than supplying *Palempores* to the English Company. Berhampore merchants had dealings with the French, especially in the time of Mons. Bussy.

In June 1779, Fanin succeeded in making a contract to supply *Palempore* to the English Company.[33] He had planned to implement the investment work in a systematic manner by dividing the weaving villages into six units in order to superintend the weavers and supply them cotton and thread according to their need. The acting Resident

PLATE 1: TEXTILE PATTERNS OF LATE EIGHTEENTH CENTURY

Sources: Selected from John Irwin and Margaret Hall, *Indian Painted and Printed Fabrics*; Brij Bhushan Jamila, *The Costumes and Textiles of India*; and Edgar Thurston, *Monograph on the Cotton Fabric Industry of the Madras Presidency.*

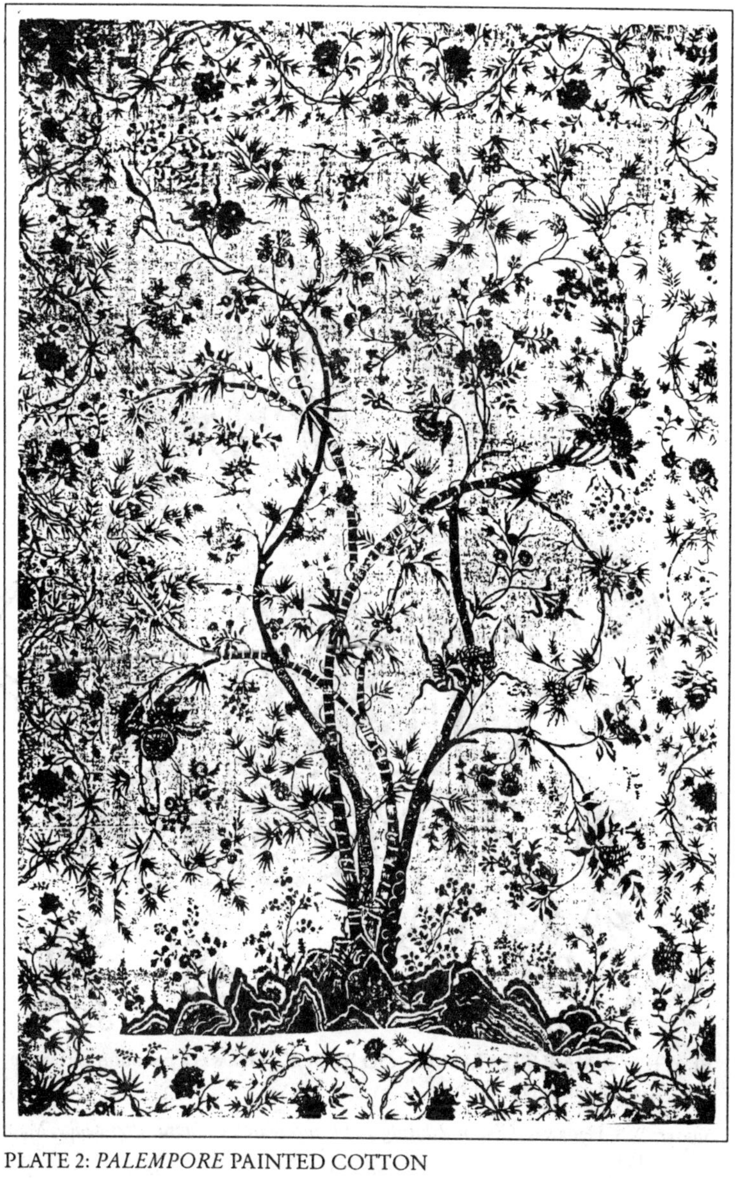

PLATE 2: *PALEMPORE* PAINTED COTTON

Source: The Chnitz, The Calico Museum of Textile, India, Ahmedabad, 1983.

PLATE 3: A MASULIPATAM WOOD BLOCK (This was a common pattern in Masulipatam cloth.)

Source: W.S. Hadaway, *Cotton Painting and Printing in the Madras Presidency*, Madras, 1917.

PLATE 4: EUROPEAN DRESSES MADE FROM INDIAN TEXTILES

Source: Brij Bhushan Jamila, *The Costumes and Textiles of India*, Bombay, 1958.

PLATE 5: SKIRT MADE FROM INDIAN TEXTILES

Source: Brij Bhushan Jamila, *The Costumes and Textiles of India*, Bombay, 1958.

PLATE 6: WEAVER AT WORK

Courtesy: National Archives of India, New Delhi.

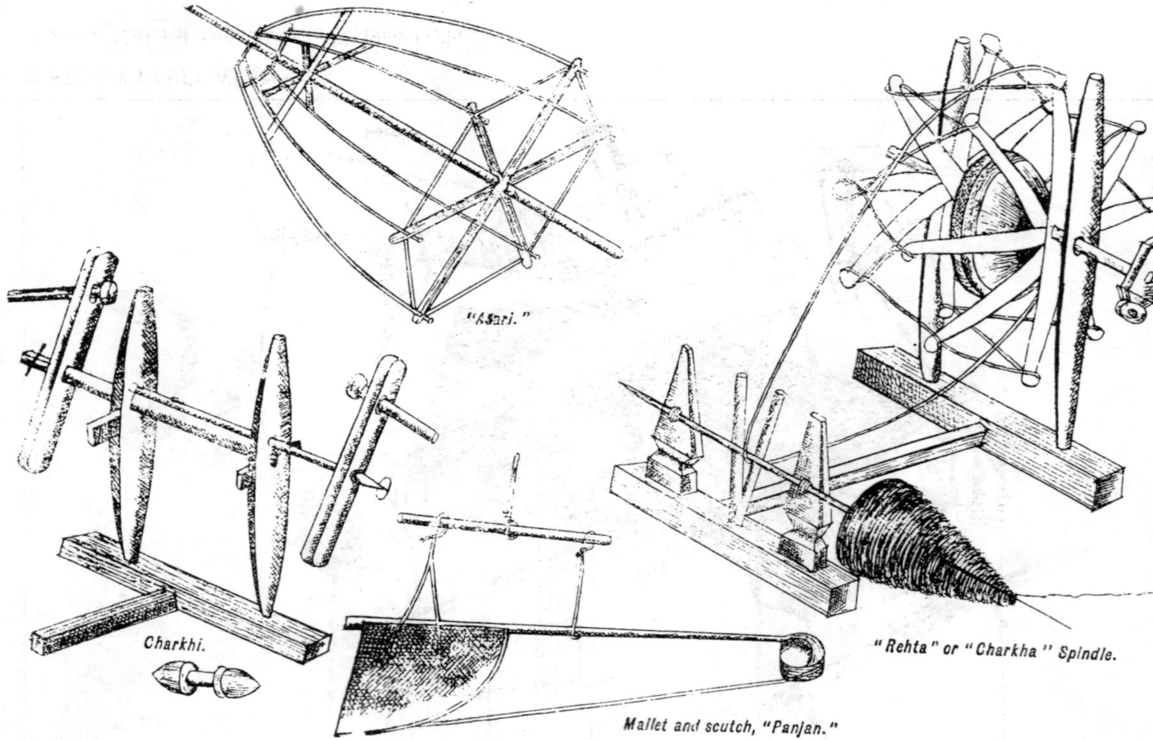

PLATE 7: TOOLS OF INDIAN WEAVERS (These instruments were in use all over India.)

Source: H.F. Samman, *Monograph on the Cotton Fabric of Assam*, Calcutta, 1897.

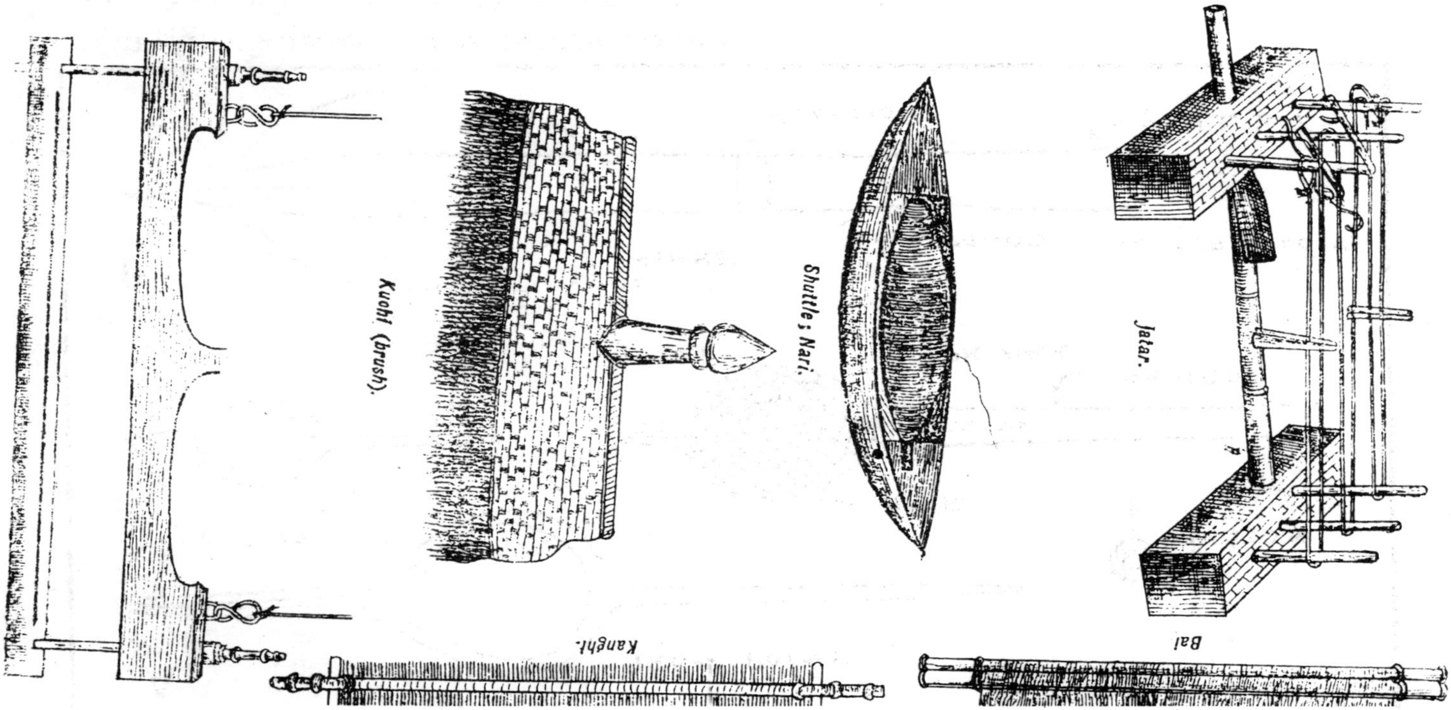

PLATE 8: TOOLS OF INDIAN WEAVERS

Source: H.F. Samman, *Monograph on the Cotton Fabric of Assam*, Calcutta, 1897.

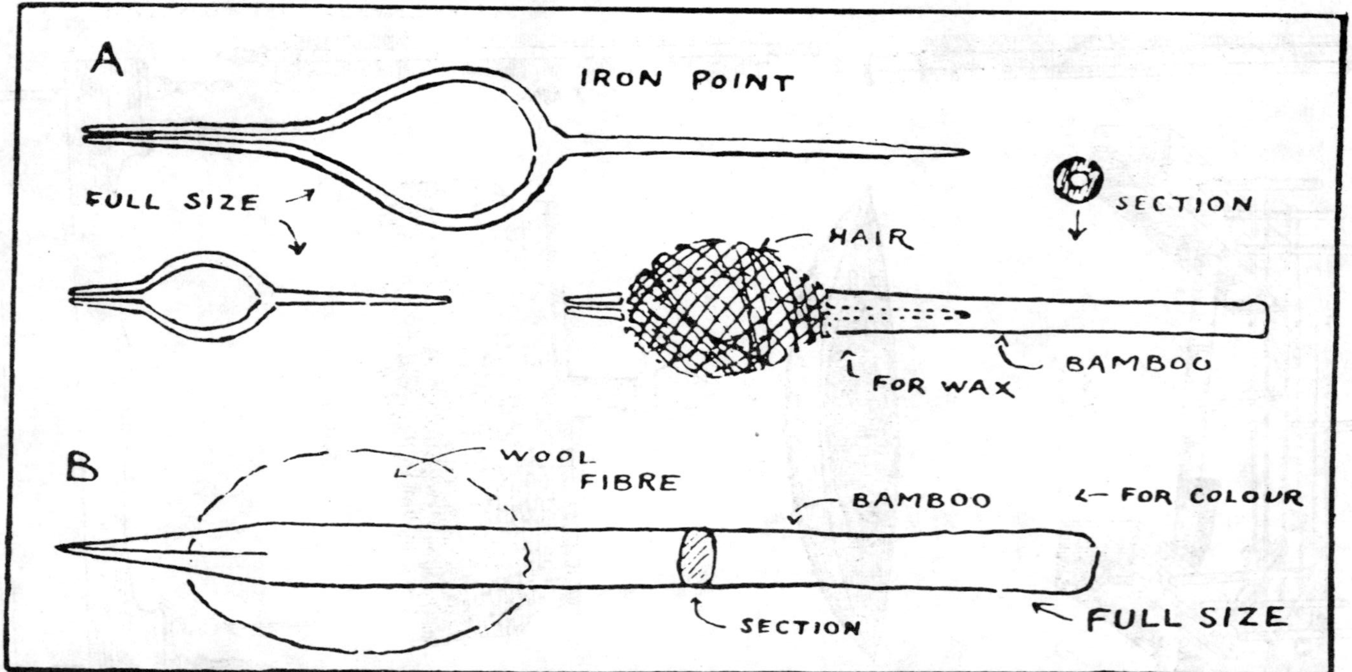

PLATE 9: PENS USED FOR HANDWORK IN COTTON PAINTING

Source: W.S. Hadaway, *Cotton Painting and Printing in the Madras Presidency*, Madras, 1917.

Morgan Williams viewed the entire scheme with skepticism and hence the scheme did not succeed. The scheme was also opposed by Balakrishna Naidu, the renter of Haveli lands.[34] The political condition in and around Ganjam also adversely affected the trade and manufacture in this region and the export of *Palempore* remained erratic and insignificant.

Perkales was a superfine cloth of the Tamil region and was considered an important item of commerce. It was regarded as a beautiful white cloth, made with cotton called *Maipangi* grown in the fertile plains near the rivers. According to Flaix, the fine *Chite* or *Perses* that were painted or coloured at the coast of the Coromandel, were made from this cloth.[35]

The handkerchiefs of Masulipatam constituted a very important item in the European exports from the Coromandel Coast. Probably it was for its technique of dyeing that these handkerchiefs could never be imitated in Europe. They were always made in very bright and glowing colours. In the region of Condavir[36] two varieties of handkerchiefs were produced—*Sawargaon* and *Vetapalem* (according to Flaix, the two varieties were *Vetepaleom* and *Sacurgaon*).[37] The first variety contained fine squares and coloured threads, and each piece consisted of 12 handkerchiefs of a yard and a half square. However, the dimensions varied on the order and requirements of the various companies. The English showed preference for smaller squares than those bought by the French and Dutch companies.[38] The main centres of manufacture spread along the banks of the Krishna river. Despite the absence of new spinning machines in India, the cotton spun on the simple wheels was strong and uniform. The price of *Romals* had risen ever since the Europeans started this trade. From the beginning of the eighteenth century till the 1780s, the price of this commodity had increased by 30 to 40 per cent.[39] This could have been for several other reasons, apart from the demand factor.

Another major commodity of export were the handkerchiefs of Palicat, known by the name of Madras handkerchiefs. This variety was sought in the 'new world', in Peru, Mexico and in the various islands of the West Indies. It was appreciated for its quality but more for its variety and extraordinary colours. There were seven types of handkerchiefs—those of 23, 26, 28, 32, 36, 40 and 48 *conjons*—all sold in pieces of ten. The first two varieties had a good market on the African coast.[40] The blue handkerchiefs of Palicat (Pullicad) took 20 days to prepare thread and 3 days to weave a piece. The cost of thread was

29 *fanams* and the labour cost of the weaver was 25 *fanam* 48 *cash*.[41] The French Company prior to 1769 had a flourishing trade in this item. However, in the absence of the Company, the private traders could not maintain their stronghold over it.

Basin was another export article and was mostly manufactured in the northern and southern coasts of the Coromandel, including Kondavid, Rajamundry and the environs of Cuddalore. There were two main types of *Basin—Demiti Telingana* and *Demito Tamoulana*. The first was considered better on account of its quality. Flaix suggests that the French Company exported *Basins* of the value of 57,00,000 *livres*, of which only 30 per cent was consumed in France while the rest was re-exported.[42] Its share was only one-eighth of the total value of imports from India. During the period of free trade the annual import never exceeded 12,00,000 *livres*. At this time several manufacturing centres had emerged at Rouen, Troies, and some other towns in France and in England. They captured the local market although their products were of inferior quality and were less durable. The special type of Indian *Basin* was the four-thread texture—two horizontal and two vertical. This particular kind was extremely suited for men's vests, waistcoats, cullots and trousers.[43]

There were various other omnifarious textiles such as *Dungari* (a coarse cotton fabric for the poor people, consumed in the country trade for the common folk of South-East Asia and Persia), *Sastracundi* (cloth made out of coloured threads in Masulipatam and exported mainly to West Asia). Thus it can be said that the Indian textiles and white cloths suited the inhabitants of all climates—from the temperate regions to the hot zones of Africa. The cost, despite long transportation and re-export charges, was reasonable and within the reach of every class of buyer. The Indian textiles had certain distinct advantages over their European counterparts before Europe adopted the mechanized mode of production. The period of the late eighteenth century reflected this changing trend.

Throughout the eighteenth century, the governments of Britain and France placed increasing restrictions on the consumption and sale of Indian textile products within their respective kingdoms. Yet through re-export trade Indian goods reached distant places and markets. A large number of merchants and shipping interests began to depend on this trade. This process continued till we find a sudden rise of Chinese trade on the one hand (diverting the energies of the European mercantile class in that direction) and the progress of industrialization, changing the entire pattern of export trade, on the other. This, however, did not happen till the last few years of the eighteenth century.

TEXTILE IMPORT POLICY OF THE RIVAL POWERS

Throughout the latter half of the eighteenth century, certain important developments outside India had tremendous bearing on the textile industry of India, and consequently on the lives of the textile producers. Profound economic changes, particularly in Britain, resulted in the ascent of new commercial interests in the field of cotton manufacture which influenced the cotton policy of the two companies and brought about a shift in the trade structure.

Clamour against the import of Indian fine cotton goods and calicoes (commonly termed as piece goods) was not a new phenomenon of the late eighteenth century. It had started almost a century earlier. There was widespread impression that the sale of Indian textiles was achieved at the expense of local industries, which caused displacement of their own weavers. The Spitsfield riot in 1697 reflected this sentiment. Moreover, a group of mercantilists believed that the import of Indian calicoes meant a drain of bullion from England. Thus, in 1700 a law was passed by which all wrought silks, mixed stuffs and figured calicoes, the manufactures of Persia, China or of the East Indies were forbidden to be worn or used otherwise in Great Britain.[44] It was particularly designed for the protection of the Spitsfield silk manufacture but proved of little or no avail against 'the prodigious importation and tempting cheapness of Indian piece-goods at that time'.[45] As to why the government acted in support of local pressure, K.N. Chaudhuri lists various reasons. According to him, the government had a deep rooted fear of social disorders caused by economic depressions; it wished to protect the domestic industry; the European approach towards prohibition also influenced the policy; and there was a shift in government's tariff policy to provide sufficient revenue to finance a costly foreign policy of William III.[46] Nevertheless, the Company resisted those prohibitions by changing the variety, from one type of textile which was banned, to another type. It re-exported the Indian piece goods to the eastern Mediterranean, Africa and the American settlements.

The East India Company at first imported Indian fabrics only as novelties or curiosities and used them mainly for exchange in the spice trade with Malaya. But by 1643 the directors of the Company quickly grasped the trends of potential home market. So they started providing designs, which suited the taste of Londoners.[47] They sent patterns to be copied. The technique of printing fustians with bright coloured designs was perfected before it developed into the calico-printing industry. Most dyes available in the seventeenth century were weak and the basic technique was copied from the Indian craftsmen—that of applying mordants to fix the dye in the cloth. It could be washed without losing its character.[48] Calico printing of London began to achieve success by imitating the popular oriental designs. The English fustian was becoming increasingly difficult to distinguish from Indian calico. The English manufacturers took advantage of this similarity, not only in the domestic market but also in the markets of the continent. *The Report on the Cotton Manufacture* explicitly mentioned this trend. The Report revealed:

> The Home Manufacture has increased to an immense extent whilst the internal consumption of Indian calicoes and muslins has been reduced almost to nothing. Every shop offers British muslins for sale, equal in appearance, of more elegant patterns, than those of India, for one-fourth or perhaps more than one-third less in price . . . there is the strongest reason to believe that not one-tenth of the whole of the calicoes and muslins imported from India are consumed in Great Britain.[49]

Indian textiles survived the prohibitory legislation of British Parliament till the end of the eighteenth century. This was primarily due to its vast market outside Europe. The Parliamentary Acts of 1700 and 1704 had already placed a heavy duty of about 15 per cent on cotton stuffs from the East Indies.[50] Since then the English commercial policy was constantly influenced by manufacturing interests and protectionist ideas. During the second half of the century the concept of colonial empire and its utilization through trade or political means was taking a definite shape. With the beginning of the Industrial Revolution the cotton policy of England came to be dictated by the economic interest of the English manufacturers. A duty of 5 per cent was levied in 1765 upon the wrought silks and printed calicoes from the East Indies. These could only be imported for the purpose of re-export. In 1779, an additional 5 per cent import duty was placed upon all previous duties and in 1782 a further 5 per cent was imposed. The Act of 1781 prohibited the export of machines, tools and labour employed in the cotton or silk industry of England. In 1783, Parliament passed another act of considerable importance. It repealed all previous duties upon plain muslins, unrated muslins and calicoes, and nankeen cloths. Instead, a single import duty of 18 per cent *ad valorem* was levied subject to drawback of 10 per cent upon re-export. By another Act of 1787, the duty upon rated calicoes was fixed at 5s. 27/10 d. for every piece of 10-11 yards, together with an *ad valorem* duty of £ 16 10s. per cent. These two levies together were broadly equivalent to a duty of 40 per cent.[51]

France witnessed a similar situation. There was growing pressure on the government of France by silk and cotton manufacturers against the imports of Compagnie des Indes. In fact, there always existed a pressure group against the import of Indian textiles in France.[52]

In 1701, the workers of Paris, the silk, gold and silver-thread workers of the city of Lyon and Tours and some other manufacturing centres (which made silk cloth for domestic and foreign markets) made a strong representation to the governments on this issue.[53] They pointed out that not far back they had supplied silk, gold and silver thread cloths within the kingdom of France and to Spain, Portugal, Germany and some other states of Europe. But of late their commerce had declined sharply. The number of workers in Lyon had come down from about 8,000 or 9,000 to only about 600. The writers of this mémoire blamed the Compagnie des Indes for this decline, as it received permission to bring and sell silk cloths with gold or silver within the kingdom of the value of 5,00,000 *livres* annually. This opened all the gates of France to the foreigners. Satin and several other types of cloth entered France by fraudulent means. They disclosed that in the last one year 19 Dutch and 4 English ships reached the French coast. The value of the cargo of the last 4 ships was estimated at 6 million *livres*. The signatories suggested a total ban on these imports and on the use of Indian textiles. They also pleaded for a total ban on grounds of trade balance. The manufacturers argued that the Compagnie des Indes was established with the object of trading only in drugs and spices. The Company, however, earned enormous profit in the textile trade of India, and since then it had neglected all that commerce for which it was established. It was felt that the Indian silk and cotton textiles destroyed the French manufacturers, took away bullion from the kingdom, created trade imbalances and was the real cause for the ruin of the manufactures of France. They suggested to the Company directors that they trade in paints, plain muslins, cotton threads and cotton wool for the benefit of the kingdom.

In the second half of the eighteenth century the government of the *ancien régime* pursued the earlier policy of maintaining strict restrictions on textile imports. Some orders, such as those of 5 September 1759,

4 March 1760 and 29 October 1763, laid down regulations for the production of imitated cotton from India. These included all types of white cotton, making the mention of name and place of manufacture obligatory.[54] There is a reference to the increasing popularity and greater consumption of Indian muslins in France in a mémoire of 1764. This was because of the *finesse* and visual beauty of Indian textiles. The writer of the memoir felt that despite systematic attempts to replace Indian muslins by the batiste (French Cambric) and the French linens, success could not be achieved. He felt that by such prohibitions and restrictions, the craze could not be checked for the painted and fine cloths, but the Swiss could gain at the expense of national industry.[55]

French policy towards Indian cotton textiles was not influenced by industrial development alone. The growing imbalance in foreign trade, the general unrest among the working class and the protectionist policy to pacify the mounting criticism were factors, that shaped the French policy. The French silk and cotton textile industry was facing growing competition from its neighbours, particularly from British products. France was also undergoing rapid transformation in the textile sector, though not as briskly as England. At Rouen the number of workers shot up by 337 per cent between 1730 and 1789, and in the 1780s, there were about 25,000 workers in Alsace alone in the trade of linen, silk and woollen items.[56] The French government was at the brink of economic and political crisis. It had remained largely unresponsive to the national needs, unlike the English Parliament. The French were not in a position to adopt a policy similar to the British, i.e. of shift from manufactured goods to semi-manufactured or raw material as items of import. In India, the French, unlike the English, lacked political means needed for the purpose. So we do not find any major shift in the French policy towards Indian cotton goods. The earlier prohibitions continued. The trade of Indian textiles was maintained primarily for the purpose of re-export.

France faced an interesting situation after 1785. The Compagnie des Indes de Calonne was established to revive French commercial activity in India. But the state prohibition against the import of Indian textiles created a contradictory situation. The orders of 10 July 1786 banned the entry of muslins, checked cloths, tapestry, brocaded stuff and other Indian commodities.[57] A temporary solution was found when the Company shipowners were exempted from this order till January 1788. They were permitted to bring 8,000 pieces of such material if their voyage had commenced prior to the first order. The production of printed and painted cloth in France was already regulated and controlled by various regulations, e.g. the orders of 18 April 1782, by which each piece of manufactured cloth was to be inscribed with the name, surname and place of the manufacturer by the registrar of the province (*Greassier de la Jurisdiction*) and checked at the Bureau de Visit.[58]

On the basis of the available material on French import of textile products from the Coromandel, it can be said that one does not find any sharp decline in French purchase of cotton textiles for re-exports. This was so in spite of oft-repeated prohibitions and constraints. The data on this aspect of trade are scanty. Yet the figures of three different years do provide some idea of cotton exports to France from the Coromandel Coast. This is evident from the following figures.

The French Company purchased merchandise valued at *livres* 26,84,896.18.4 in 1768 (this included *Salempores*—white and blue, *Guineas*—white and blue, *Percale*, *Betteela*, *Organdi*, *Taznatanne*, *Limenea*, *Neganepaus*, chintz, *Gingham* of Pondicherry, Madras and Masulipatam, *Basin*, *Nankin* and handkerchiefs of all varieties). These were sold for *livres* 40,71,960.15 at a profit of *livres* 13,87,003.16.8 (i.e. approximately £ 57,794).[59] *Salempore*, *Guinea*, *Betteela*, *Mouchoirs* (handkerchiefs) and *Nankins* constituted the bulk of the items as can be seen in Table 6.2. The entire exports consisted of textile variety except an insignificant quantity of red-wool.

The place of Coromandel in the total volume of sales made by the French Company can be ascertained from Table 6.3.

The margin of profit in the case of the Coromandel goods picked up from Pondicherry was not so high as we notice in the case of China goods or Bengal goods. This was probably because the latter regions included several luxury items, whereas the piece goods from the Coromandel were based on a regular inflexible demand and more or less steady supply.

We also have the figures of textile exports from Pondicherry for the year 1789. That was a good year from the point of view of the French Company when its ships—*Le Marechal de Segur, Le Comte d Artois, Le Compte d'Estaing, Le compte. d'Artois and Le Necker* carried cotton goods worth Rs. 20,07,021.14.28 (approximately £ 2,25,761.7.5) out of a total cargo valued at Rs. 22,20,706.9.9 (i.e. approximately £ 2,49,798.2).[60] In other words, over 90 per cent of the shipment to France from the Coromandel Coast consisted of cotton items. Compared to this the English exports from the Madras Presidency

TABLE 6.2: PURCHASES FROM PONDICHERRY BY THE FRENCH COMPANY IN 1768

(*in livres tournois*)

Item	Pieces	Cost price	Sale price
Salempore (white)	7,532	80,190	13,771.0
Guineas (white)	54,020	10,86,797.5.0	14,42,448.17.0
Perkales (i)	800	8,887.0.0	34,745.15.0
Perkales (ii)	342	6,897.0.0	16,452.16.0
Dimities	90	684	1,239.6.0
Betteela	3,770	57,403	1,44,272.4
Tarnatanes	840	12,465	41,926.10
Organdis (fine thread)	832	23,974.10.0	51,723.10
Organdies	915	32,400.16.0	34,318.4
Handkerchiefs (Masulipatam)	13,177	1,65,932.5	5,48,872.13
Handkerchiefs (Tranquebar)	3,000	31,861	59,184.19
Handkerchiefs (Pulicat)	3,320	93,093	2,49,646
Handkerchiefs (Pondicherry)	3,231	32,372	31,500
Salempores (blue)	1,680	25,855	47,114
Guineas (blue)	37,970	5,24,624	6,15,062.2
Limeneas	6,320	59,697	23,085
Negapaut	1,840	21,919	36,704
Bejutapaut	2,000	20,872	50,136
Chaselas (Chachellas) blue & red	4,560	52,148	49,06,2.10
Chelas	4,912	31,911	35,267.12
Nekanias	8,480	1,01,524	1,43,792
Chintz	480	6,542	7,211.18
Korotes	3,290	29,172	18,080.3
Bolkas	10,225	10,383.2.4	8,734.2
Fottes	360	3,712	4,320
Ginghams (Pondicherry)	13,126	7,33,42.5	90,417.4
Ginghams (Madras)	2,240	13,381	28,905
Ginghams (Masulipatam)	380	5,106.15	31,449.8
Basin	1,260	32,604	48,587.13
Redwood	6,84,100	39,119	40,893.17
Total		26,84,896.18.4	40,71,900.15

Source: Compagnie des Indes, C^2 256, p. 129, AN, Paris.

amounted to *pagodas* 6,79,833.26.8 (i.e. about £ 2,71,933.2) in 1788.[61] In the sale at Port L'Orient in 1791 the article of cotton goods formed the most prominent part of the French imports from India. Out of a total of 7,17,042 pieces valued at £ 12,27,887, the Coromandel Coast provided 1,34,673 pieces of white calicoes valued at £ 4,85,137, besides 37,383 pieces of muslins worth £ 44,261 and 85,478 pieces of prohibited goods worth £ 1,01,266.[62] However, after this Indian exports to France

TABLE 6.3: SALE OF INDIAN GOODS BY THE FRENCH COMPANY (1768)

Goods obtained from	Cost price in *livres*	Sale price	Profits
China	28,80,572.7.10	58,13,755.0.7	29,33,182.12.9
Pondicherry	26,84,896.18.4	40,71,960.15.0	13,87,003.16.8
Bengal	43,27,909.4.0	81,62,468.19.0	38,34,559.15.0
Mahé	5,73,032.18.0	12,45,346.8.7	6,72,313.10.7
Isles	6,29,599.0.0	18,65,741.1.8	12,361,42.1.8
	1,10,96,010.8.2	2,11,59,212.4.10	1,00,68,201.16.8

Source: Compagnie des Indes, C^2 256, p. 129, AN, Paris.

rapidly diminished because the National Assembly withdrew the privilege of the Compagnie des Indes in April 1790, and France was increasingly getting involved in the Revolutionary War.

These figures indicate that the export of cotton items from the Coromandel Coast was not as insignificant as is generally believed. Despite numerous shackles—lack of political means, stiff competition with the English, shortage of capital, limited interest of the French in this region compared to the more lucrative channels of trade in the Western hemisphere and the disturbed political climate both in India and Europe, the French Company and traders managed to do reasonably well. It was only when the actual impact of the French Revolution began to be felt on their settlements that their trade diminished abruptly. Henceforth, the French could never revive it to the pre-1791 level.

On the other hand we notice a shift in English attitude towards the import of Indian goods for quite different reasons. In the second half of the eighteenth century, the cotton industry of England played a role in the international trade 'which was out of all proportion to its share'.[63] The fourth decade of the century was a turning point in the English textile trade. The acceleration in its growth rate brought about a revolution in cotton textile production. This resulted in a marked expansion of trade. An important feature of this transformation was the emergence and rapid expansion of the Lancashire cotton industry.

The sprouting of the new factory industry in England was of quite a different order from what the old domestic industry had witnessed in the first seventy years of the century. In the 1740s production quickened and in the next quarter of a century, new cotton imports more than doubled and registered a further eight-fold increase in the last 20 years.[64]

The introduction of mechanized carding and spinning augmented the output in a spectacular way. The use of power for spinning set in motion a sequence of technical and organizational changes in some related branches of the industry. The mechanized produce placed the manual labour-based cotton manufactures of India at a disadvantage. It is very difficult to make any fair comparison between the labour productivity of an Indian and a European producer. The nature, the quality and the ornamentation of products differed greatly. Yet historians generally agree on the point that the British industry in the mid-eighteenth century had a higher level of productivity than the Indian industry. The mechanized form reduced the cost of production and increased productivity. Catling demonstrated this by his labour productivity data in cotton spinning.[65]

Despite this limitation of unequal competition with a mechanized mode of production, Indian cotton products continued to vie with cotton textile products of the English and the French industries. This was possible so long as there was a relatively free interplay of market forces. However, once the European groups began to exercise economic pressures through political means to shut the Indian goods from the European markets and the East India Company was pushed back by these very interest groups, Indian cotton manufactures were bound to suffer.

It appears from Table 6.4 that the European wars seriously affected the export market of Indian piece goods. During the period of the American War, Coromandel was the most affected region in India. This must have retarded the growth of cotton production. In the late 1780s we notice another steady revival of coastal export, but this seems to have lasted only for a short while. The rise of the cotton interest of England, the glut in the European market, the beginning of another long European war and the gradual shift in the Company's export policy from manufactured textiles to raw cotton were some of the significant factors which seem to have adversely affected the Indian cotton manufacturer. Nevertheless so long as the competition in the industrial products was principally focused on quantity, the Indian producers could still compete by virtue of the quality of their products.

In the 1780s the fast rising cotton industry of England was facing temporary but serious crisis. The local production suffered because of a shrinking market. The leading calico printers in the trade—Livesey Hargreaves & Co. of Blackburn became bankrupt in 1787-8.[66] Once again there was clamour against the import of Indian manufactures. The British manufacturers blamed the Company for their plight. The Company, on the other hand, tried to show that its sales had not been

TABLE 6.4: PIECE GOODS IMPORTED FROM MADRAS PRESIDENCY (1771-92)

Year	Madras Presidency		Total sale in Indian piece goods including Bengal, Madras & Surat	
	Pieces	Value in £	Pieces	Value in £
1771	1,14,710	2,61,893	8,50,665	1,27,034
1772	2,73,766	52,309	10,46,955	16,45,956
1773	1,34,789	5,23,094	10,46,955	16,45,956
1774	2,07,086	6,44,563	8,61,678	18,04,591
1775	1,81,950	5,83,765	7,47,116	16,06,364
1776	2,09,538	5,15,557	8,36,238	16,19,609
1777	2,24,183	4,92,926	9,62,539	16,56,128
1778	2,96,182	4,22,213	11,62,477	16,49,033
1779	74,676	2,03,186	4,44,666	4,71,052
1780	1,07,130	2,57,626	6,00,438	12,53,738
1781	95,868	2,33,643	4,30,629	8,38,888
1782	72,188	2,04,163	5,55,273	12,67,123
1783	—	—	5,20,768	1,29,168
1784	44,810	1,16,883	5,92,028	10,47,860
1785	45,352	1,15,632	8,40,347	15,60,847
1786	43,240	97,511	8,07,413	15,55,927
1787	38,641	84,598	8,25,972	14,31,092
1788	96,455	1,91,826	7,32,989	12,00,270
1789	1,12,216	2,25,169	7,71,770	12,01,622
1790	1,262	2,53,625	10,25,634	17,48,344
1791	1,44,996	4,75,590	9,11,616	16,51,678
1792	2,40,108	5,77,400	8,73,347	17,93,325

Source: Milburn, *Oriental Commerce*, Vol. II, p. 234.

prejudicial to the improvement and extension of the manufactures of Great Britain.[67]

In England the rapid increase in production along with huge imports of muslin from India lowered its price. Already not less than 5,00,000 pieces of muslins were annually manufactured by 1787.[68] On the other hand, there was an unexpected increase in the quantity of import of Indian cotton goods as evident from Table 6.5. These two factors resulted in a sudden reduction of the price of Indian cloths. The overall volume of exports from India rose sharply. This had a great bearing on the future textile policy of the Company as is seen in the following statistics.[69]

As a result of this enhanced import into England and over-

TABLE 6.5: COTTON IMPORTS IN ENGLAND (1780-7)

	Cotton imports in 1787	Average imports and sale for preceding 6 years (1780-6)
Pieces of muslins	3,04,762	1,85,964
Pieces of calicoes	4,03,875	2,53,450
Pieces of nankeens	83,009	27,380
Total	7,91,646	4,64,794

production within England, fine cassock muslin was sold at 50 per cent of the previous market price, inferior cassock muslin at 60 per cent, the coarsest muslin at 50 per cent and *Mulmuls* at 33 per cent below the price of the previous season.[70] Such a situation must have applied brakes on the future productivity of Indian cotton manufacturers, besides affecting it in more than one way. Despite this setback, the import of Indian cotton goods continued for some more time because it was estimated that 17/20 of the calicoes and 3/5 of the muslins brought into England were re-exported.[71] By 1799, the entire volume of calicoes imported was sent out from England.[72]

Another crucial but related development of the same period was the shift in the Company's cotton policy. From the various plans and correspondence mentioned in the contemporary records, it is evident that India was to increase its export of raw cotton instead of cotton textiles. The following figures of Table 6.6 reflect this changing trend.

Though the ratio of Indian raw cotton in Britain's total imports was still very small, it steadily increased in the next few years. This shift in

TABLE 6.6: COTTON EXPORTS FROM INDIA

(*in lbs*)

1783	78,16,645
1784	1,14,82,083
1785	1,84,00,384
1786	1,94,75,020
1787	2,32,50,268
1788	2,04,67,436
1789	3,25,76,023
1790	3,14,47,605

Source: Fifth Report of the Select Committee, 1 February 1795, MS 400, *Home Misc. Series*, IOR.

the export policy of the English Company was a significant feature of its commercial activities during the period. For this, political means were exercised unhesitatingly. The increase in the export of raw cotton from India was expected to provide great advantage and benefit not only to the Company but also the British nation, where 3,50,000 persons were employed in spinning and manufacturing, with 143 water mills and upwards of 20,500 engines that did the work of 19,41,100 spindles.[73] From the import of Indian cotton, it was expected that the nation would save a sum of about a million and half that would become the national capital, 'which will no doubt', as George Smith pointed out, 'be employed in other branches of industry, commerce or agriculture'.[74]

From this period we notice that systematic efforts were made to encourage cotton cultivation in the coastal region. The commercial resident of Godavari district wrote an important note to the Board of Revenue on the cotton cultivation in that region.[75] In order to give it sufficient importance, he suggested measures to promote its extension in other regions. He argued for the introduction of Mauritius cotton in that region as it required little care. It had a high yield and once planted could stand for several years without additional labour. He was in favour of renting the land on longer leases to promote cotton cultivation. He stated, 'to render the culture of cotton more general if proper encouragement were given to the Ryots, it is but reasonable to suppose, he would give it the preference to a more precious crop of dry grain which certainly cannot yield him an equal profit or advantage. . . .'[76]

A similar sentiment was expressed about Popham's efforts to cultivate cotton on the eastern coast. It was observed that 'its culture appears likely to be attended with essential advantages to our Hon'ble Employers as well as a staple of commerce that may be expected to yield a considerable profit'.[77]

However, from the available evidence it appears that the efforts to develop cotton plantation on the Coromandel Coast did not succeed. But small tracts of land lying along the Krishna and Godavari rivers including Northern Circars did augment the supply of cotton wool, which was meant for local consumption rather than for export.[78] Despite the Company's efforts, these areas could not develop as major producers of raw cotton for export. Gujarat and Berar remained the main suppliers of Indian cotton, which was regarded as the best for English textile industries. This shift in the import policy of England in favour of raw cotton must have led to a rise in the price of Indian cotton and reduced its supply for the Indian manufacturers, thereby increasing the production costs for the artisans.

Thus, we find the English reverses in America and the loss of American colonies seem to have brought about shifts in their colonial perspective. The rapid spread of industrialization was giving rise to some friction between the oligarchy of the East India Company and the emerging industrial bourgeoisie. The Company was compelled to switch investment to the export of agricultural products like cotton, indigo, raw silk and tobacco, while retaining control of the export of handmade Indian textiles—more than half of which was re-exported. Hence, we find some distinct English attempts to introduce the cultivation of such plants and crops which served the interest of the manufacturing sector and possessed commercial value. Priority was given to cotton cultivation in the southern region. There were probably two motives for this—

(a) to compensate for the American loss in the British economy; and
(b) to meet the Company's demand for cotton piece goods.

In 1788 the Court of Directors clearly advised the Company authorities that India should take part in the supply of cotton.[79] Dr. Anderson was engaged at Madras in 1790 to distribute a variety of foreign cotton seeds obtained from Malta and Mauritius and to popularize its cultivation. Sudat cotton was cultivated under the direction of the Board of Revenue and sold at Madras for 22 to 25 *pagodas* per *pootty*.[80]

Another item which drew the attention of the Company authorities was indigo. The low price of Coromandel indigo attracted the official interest because with the loss of American colonies, which were the chief supplier of indigo, and because of its immense demand as a dye stuff in the woollen industry of Britain, there was an urgent need to augment its supply. The officials were asked to provide every possible encouragement to promote its cultivation. It was described as a very valuable article of commerce which stated that 'no effort should be spared in the collection and improvement of indigo culture'.[81] Mr. Roxburg was appointed for this purpose.

Similar efforts are to be seen in promoting mulberry cultivation in Andhra and Tamil region.[82] But the most interesting attempt was to introduce cochineal culture in southern India to break the Spanish monopoly created in Central America, and for this purpose an experienced botanist—Dr. Anderson was appointed. Cochineal was used as a colouring matter and as a medical drug and was regarded next to gold and silver for its commercial value. However, although the experiment succeeded to a great extent, the invention of chemical dyes during the period of experiment made the entire effort futile.[83]

As regards the failure of the Indian textiles to compete with the industrial products, the primitive state of technology for cotton production in India is generally held responsible for the ultimate decline of Indian textile exports. As Pavlov argues, India's conversion from a supplier of cloth for the whole of Europe into a consumer of British fabrics was due above all to the technical superiority of the British mill over the Indian hand weaver. He contends that in India no basic premise had taken shape for transition to factory production, i.e. a developed capitalist workshop with a detailed division of labour.[84] In other words, petty commodity production in India did not, after all, mature to the extent of providing an extensive basis for the emergence of capitalist relations. Wherever pockets of such relations did take shape in industry, they were fed by rent, while merchant capital was just in the process of securing control of the existing forms of economy without modifying the process of reproduction itself or its technology. It is also argued that the very limited division of labour within the production forces reflected the limited development of Indian productive organization. It is commonly asserted that the want of capital in manufacture and agriculture prevented the division of labour.

One cannot dispute the premise that the Indian textile manufacturing technology in the eighteenth century was inferior to that of England as can be noted from Plates 6, 7 and 8. Still, the excellent quality of the Indian weaver's product and his dexterity counterbalanced this limitation to some extent. Indian cotton goods had succeeded in maintaining a vast market by their sheer quality, beauty of colours and low cost. While the quality and beauty of the product continued to be maintained, the cost factor could no longer hold good because of the cheap machine-made fabrics from Europe. Besides, the tariff policy of the British government involving imposition of prohibitive duties on Indian goods placed them at a disadvantage. Hamilton's argument that the destruction of the Indian cotton manufacture was 'not the result of the tariff policy of England'[85] can be valid so long as other factors did not become important. But it was certainly one of the important factors in the decline of Indian cotton manufactures when the European powers strengthened their grip over colonial markets. In the early nineteenth century, France was at a severe competitive disadvantage vis-à-vis Britain. France survived this challenge by adopting restrictive tariff policy. Britain had started dominating the goods of mass consumption through capital intensive production while France enjoyed good reputation in *articles de gout* due to the advantage of lower wages. Thus, *indiennages* and woollen *nouveautès* were able to withstand the competition in the first half of the nineteenth century.

It should also be noted that any radical change in the mode of production is caused, to some extent, by the pressure of expanding market. Furthermore, the accumulation of profit with the chief producers results in its productive utilization and in the long run affects the mode of production through technical innovations. In the second half of the eighteenth century the productive and market structure was frequently disturbed owing to political turmoils and instability caused by the absence of strong political authority. And the Anglo-French rivalry provided the *coup de grace.* The regular eruption of Anglo-French wars at short intervals, totally unrelated to the events within India, dislocated the entire production mechanism. This is attested by all the trade records of that period. These wars caused artificial scarcities of the articles of consumption and production. The impact was felt more in this region because the textile production of the coast had begun to depend, to some extent, on export trade. Moreover, the European companies with their rigid set of regulations for investment, purchase and pricing used political means to keep down the prices. The free play of the market forces remained checked. The Indian producers, because of their growing dependence on the companies or private traders, could not benefit from the conditions which could have been otherwise advantageous to them. The profits were siphoned off to non-productive channels and proved detrimental to local interest. In the process the petty commodity producers (weavers) were placed under a new set of regulations and control in the early 1770s, the paucity of rain effected the quality of indigo and raised its price in Cuddalore. The dyers found the quality of indigo so bad that instead of the normal practice of dyeing the Company's *Chinnamanaick pollam* cloths 6 times they had to be dyed 9 times. Instead of having a sympathetic view, the board felt that the dyers should be severely punished. Wynch, the chief of the factory wrote, 'The obstinacy and imprudence of the dyers at Cuddalore are justly deserving punishment.'[86]

In short, the operation of the market forces had considerable bearing on the development or decline of Indian textiles. We can argue that it was the overseas market carefully cultivated through political means that was one of the crucial factors determining the success of European cotton goods vis-a-vis Indian textile stuffs.

NOTES

1. Jean Terrade, *Le Commerce Colonial de La France à la fin de L'Ancien Régime*, Paris, 1972, Tome 2, p. 126, James D. Tracy (ed.), *The Rise of Merchant Empires, Long Distance Trade in the Early Modern World 1350-1750*, Cambridge, 1990, p. 292.
2. John Milford to the Board of Trade, 7 January 1790, *Public Consultations*, No. 160 B, TSA.
3. *Madras Despatches* from COD, 11 April 1792, E/4/878, Vol. 18, pp. 650-1, IOR.
4. To make a piece of muslin of 34 *covid* long and 3 *covid* broad, it required 320 small skeins of thread called *coodenool.*
5. John Milford to Board of Trade, 7 January 1799, *Public Consultations*, Fort St. George, No. 160, p. 401, TSA.
6. Ibid.
7. The washing procedure is separately described, by John Milford and Legoux de Flaix. According to Milford, *Mooree* superfine was soaked in cold water for two days, then put in water mixed with cowdung, then washed on the fourth day. On the fifth day, it was dipped in *chuna* (lime) water, dried and heated on the sixth and seventh days, laid in the air and sprinkled with water on the eighth day, washed and put into soap water and then exposed to the sun. By the twelfth day it was put into soap water and heated, exposed to the sun on the thirteenth and fourteenth days, again washed and then soaked in lime juice, put into soap water, heated and exposed to the sun. The process was repeated till the twenty-fourth day. The washing of muslin was done in sheep's dung and lime water for about eight to nine days. The bleaching of white textiles required immersion of cloth in sour milk and at the end starching with rice water.
8. Ibid.
9. John Milford to the Board of Trade, 7 January 1790, *Public Consultations*, 160b, TSA.
10. M. Legoux de Flaix, *Essai Historique, Gèographique et Politique sur L'Indoustan avec la tableau de son Commerce*, Paris, 1807, Tome I, p. 110.
11. Ibid., p. 7.
12. *Madras Despatches*, 11 April 1792, Vol. 18, IOR.
13. Flaix, op. cit., p. 108.
14. These were named *Perses* probably because they were carried to Europe through Persia in caravans and then deposited at the Levant.
15. Flaix, op. cit., p. 79.
16. Ibid.
17. Ibid., p. 9.

18. According to Flaix, the most beautiful *Chite* [chintz] made at the well-known manufactory of Lyon in France, were nothing compared to Chite Metabi, Flaix, op. cit., p. 112.
19. Flaix, op. cit., p. 113.
20. Ibid., p. 117.
21. Ibid.
22. Ibid., p. 127.
23. John Milford to Board of Trade, 7 January 1799, *Public Consultations*, Fort St. George, No. 160, TSA.
24. J.R. Racine, 'Ésquissée d'une Histoire Commerciale de Pondichéry jusqu'en 1954', *Revue Historique*, Vol. 10, 1972, p. 16.
25. S. Arasaratnam, *Merchants, Company and Commerce*, op. cit., p. 99.
26. Flaix, op. cit., Tome II, p. 11.
27. According to Flaix, when M. de Bussy went back to Europe after the French disaster in India, he presented to Mme. de Pompadour, the Queen, a dozen beautiful shirts for Women—each wrapped up in a separate box. Flaix, op. cit., Tome II, p. 12.
28. Flaix, op. cit., Tome II, p. 134.
29. Wynch to Board of Trade, 15 December 1789, Ganjam Proceedings, *Public Consultations*, 160 B, TSA.
30. Alexander Davidson to President, Board of Trade, ibid.
31. Ibid.
32. Letter of the Resident, 22 March 1771, *The Ganjam District Manual*, Madras, 1882, p. 129; ibid., p. 130.
33. Ibid., pp. 147-8.
34. Ibid.
35. Ibid., p. 28.
36. This was probably the region of Guntur, as one contemporary source clearly mentions it—Compte rendu a Mons. la ministre de la Marine despêche par M. de Conway, 6 February 1788, C^2 184 (microfilm), AN.
37. Flaix, op. cit., Tome II, p. 42.
38. Ibid., p. 43.
39. Ibid., p. 60.
40. Ibid., p. 63.
41. John Milford to the Board of Trade, op. cit.
42. Ibid., p. 124.
43. Ibid.
44. Calicoes included *Byrampants*, *Baftas*, *Doosooties*, *Dotties* white, *Durangess*, *Immarties*, *Gurrahs Gingham* white, *Izzarees*, longcloth white, *Moorees*, *Salampores*, *Percales*; while muslins included *Betteelas*, *Dooreas*, *Jamadanees*, *Mulmuls*, *Nainsooks*, *Tanjeebs*, etc.
45. Edgar Thurston, *Monograph on the Cotton Fabric Industry of the Madras Presidency*, Madras, 1897, p. 3.
46. K.N. Chaudhuri, *The Trading World of Asia and the English East India Company, 1660-1760*, London, 1978, p. 279.
47. John Irwin and Katherine Brett, 'Origins of Chintz' quoted by S.D. Chapman, *The Cotton Industry in the Industrial Revolution*, London, 1972, p. 16.
48. S.D. Chapman, op. cit.

49. Report of the Select Committee of the Court of Directors on the Cotton Manufacture in Britain, 1 February 1793, L/Parl./2/28, IOR.
50. C.J. Hamilton, *The Trade Relations between England and India, 1600-1896*, Delhi, 1919, p. 103.
51. Ibid.
52. Numerous *arrêts* placed these prohibitions as those of 6 April 1688,1 February 1689, 3 and 14 December 1697, 13 July 1700, 24 December 1701, 22 August, 18 September and 18 November 1702, 17 February and 16 May 1705, 24 August 1706, 10 May 1707, 7 February and 5 June 1708, 27 August and 10 December 1709, 7 April, 22 July 1710, 28 April 1711, 16 February, 21 May and 4 June 1715, and 20 January 1716. H. Weber, *La Compagnie Française des Indes 1604-1875*, Paris, 1904, p. 236.
53. Mémoire au Roy, 1701, Série F^{12} 1403, AN.
54. Mémoire sur toiles peintes (1785), No. 11665, F^{12} 1403, AN.
55. C. Lis and H. Soly (eds.), *Poverty & Capitalism in Pre-Industrial Europe*, Sussex, 1979, p. 145.
56. Mémoire sur le commerce des Indes Orientales et sur celuy de la Compagnie des Indes en particulier (1764), C^2 47 (microfilm), p. 260, AN.
57. *Arret du Conseil d'État du Roi*, 18 January 1787 (Extract des Registres du Conseil d'État), AD XI-41, A.N.
58. Mémoire sur les toiles peintes et imprimées 1785, F^{12} 1403, AN.
59. Table of the Compagnie des Indes, C^2 256 (microfilm), p. 129, AN.
60. Compagnie des Indes, Bureau des Achats, Cargaisons d'Importation en retour des Indes-A, 8 AQ 303, AN.
61. Commercial Department - *Despatches from England*, 9 April 1788, Fort St. George, General Letter No. 1, TSA.
62. William Milburn, op. cit., p. 405. The sudden rise in the total volume indicates that these items were not directly received from the Coromandel Coast but were procured from all possible places, including European markets.
63. Phyllis Deans and W.A. Cole, *British Economic Growth 1688-1959*, Cambridge, 1969, p. 295.
64. Ibid., pp. 50-1.
65. H. Catling tried to prove through the modern concept of OHP (the number of operative hours to process 100 lbs of cotton, by applying it to any given situation.

Indian hand spinners (eighteenth century)	50,000 + OHP
Crompton's Mule (1780)	2,000 + OHP
100 Spindle-Mule (1790)	1,000 + OHP
Power-assisted Mules (1795)	300 + OHP

H. Catling, *The Spinning Mule*, Newton Abbot, 1970, in D. Chapman, op. cit., p. 20.
66. S.D. Chapman, op. cit., p. 40.
67. Report of the Select Committee on Export Trade from Great Britain, 1788, *Home Miscellaneous Series*, MS 401 (microfilm), p. 128, NAI.
68. Milburn, *Oriental Commerce*, Vol. II, p. 232.
69. George Smith to Henry Dundas, 1 December 1790, MS 434, *Home Miscellaneous Series* (microfilm), IOR.
70. Ibid.

71. C.J. Hamilton, op. cit., p. 176.
72. Ibid., p. 177.
73. George Smith to Dundas, 1 December 1790, *Home Miscellaneous Series*, MS 434 (microfilm), IOR.
74. Ibid.
75. Charles A. White, Report on cotton cultivation, 26 June 1796, Letter to Board of Revenue, *Godavari District Records*, Vol. 885, APA.
76. Ibid.
77. Letter of Fallofield, Dent Weff and Mitchell to Governor and Council, 30 January 1973, *Miscellaneous Correspondence*, Bundle 472 D, *Chingleput District Records*, TSA.
78. India House to Board of Trade, 29 April 1818, *Godavari District Records*, Vol. 882, p. 126, APA.
79. Despatch of the Court of Directors to the Governor-General, 20 August 1788, *Reports on Cotton Wool*, 1836, p. 3, IOR.
80. *Godavari Factory Records 1795-1820*, Vol. 882, APA.
81. Letter to the Board of Revenue, 17 January 1798, *Godavari District Records*, Vol. 847, APA, Letter from Commercial Resident to Board of Trade, 20 March 1793 and 18 April 1793, *Nagore Factory Correspondence*, Vols. 3323 and 3345, *Godavari District Records*, APA.
82. Measures adopted for introducing and establishing the filature of silk in the Carnatic and Northern Circars, *Madras Despatches*, Vol. 18, E/4/878, IOR.
83. Letters to the Board of Revenue, 3 November 1795 and 26 June 1796, Vols. 884-5, *Godavari District Records*, APA.
84. V.I. Pavlov, *Historical Premises for India's Transition to Capitalism*, Moscow, 1978, pp. 157, 279.
85. C.J. Hamilton, op. cit., p. 184.
86. Petition of Pollam dyers to Chief and Council at Cuddalore, 7 June 1775 , *Public Dept. Despatches*, TSA.

Conclusion

IT IS A COMMON belief that the French gave up their political ambitions after 1763, that their trade very much receded and that their interest and activities in India virtually disappeared in the post-1763 period. Several scholars believe that after1763, French trade in India was reduced to such an extent that it was not worth the trouble of writing on it and that the English had totally routed them.[1] However, our scrutiny of evidence hardly bears this out. On the contrary, we find that the French made serious efforts to revive and increase their trade with India with the final objective of annihilating the English political might. We do notice a significant rise in the volume of French trade with India during the period of peace, i.e. after the Treaty of Paris till the abolition of the French Company, between 1771 and 1776 and then again during 1785 to 1789.

The very presence of the French on the Coromandel Coast created fear in the minds of the English. It precipitated their involvement in Indian politics. Even though the fear may not have been always real, it provided an excellent pretext for the aggressive policy of the English towards the Indian ruling class. It is a known fact that Wellesley's annexationist plans were executed and justified in the name of 'Francophobia'. The English policies towards the regional states were intended to seek more power in the Coromandel than in Bengal owing to the effective presence of the French in that area. In the Coromandel region the issue of political supremacy was yet to be resolved, whereas in Bengal the English had begun to enjoy the invidious position of the ruler-cum-merchants. The geopolitics of the Coromandel enabled the French to enjoy greater freedom at their *comptoirs* and *loges* than what was allowed to them in Bengal. This factor seems to have influenced English relations with the southern states. The English advance was systematic, and extended to those regions, which were considered the prime source of revenue and commerce. They made special efforts to control them directly or indirectly, lest these territories became French possessions. We find a link between trade and politics recurs during this period.

There is general impression that the English had forsworn the policy of aggrandizement after 1763 till the coming of Wellesley. Brian Kennedy contends '... it remains broadly true that the period 1763 to 1793 was a relatively tranquil one in which the only open struggle against the French and their Indian allies was waged to preserve and not to extend the Company's dominion'.[2] However, after examining the political and diplomatic moves of the English in southern India, it is difficult to agree with his reasoning. It was not the instinct of self-preservation but the aggressive designs of the English and the French *revanche* that had drawn the two European rivals into a direct confrontation. We cannot ignore the English policy towards the Marathas or the Mysore rulers in this context. Though the political threat from the French had nearly ceased in the 1770s, their moves to send various emissaries to the courts of local princes and the plans of Law de Lauriston and Bellecombe clearly demonstrate their designs. It is another thing that these plans remained non-operational for most of the time because of lack of active governmental support due to the worsening financial condition of the French state. Nevertheless, the very presence of the French along the Coromandel Coast and the wars between the two European powers or with local rulers had tremendous bearing on the Indian political structure. While describing the combined effects of the Anglo-French War (1778-83) and the Anglo-Mysore War, Charles Mallet wrote, 'The war has ruined all the quarters of Coromandel Coast ... a good number of them [inhabitants] perished because of starvation, some of them went away and stayed with Paleagars [poligars] chiefs who lived in the jungles and mountains, and to the lands of Tipu.'[3] Brian Davey also points out that the continued warfare and the heavy exactions of the Company and its rivals in south India led to extensive areas going out of cultivation. Physical force had to be used to compel the raiyats to cultivate their lands.[4] Commercial interests started moving from trade to the acquisition of territories or revenues. The English Company grew with every territorial annexation and became enmeshed in local politics. This is evident from its dealings with Tanjore, the Carnatic and the Nizam's territories. In his dealings with the Raja of Tanjore, the Governor of Fort St. George demanded that he should fight the French during the American War, something with which he had no concern. Thus, it appears that the political presence of the French and their inability to effectively resist the English colonial expansion, provided the latter with an excuse to interfere in local politics.

This study demonstrates the factors, which determined French commercial policy towards India and the English response to the frequent changes in that policy. The reasons for the abolition of the French Company are to be seen not in its trade performance but in the sphere of politics. The Compagnie des Indes was abolished in 1769 after a prolonged controversy raised by the physiocratic group of economic thinkers. The official view was influenced by the arguments of Abbé Morellet. The Company was abolished, in fact, not so much because of its organizational defects or its trade performance (which was showing distinct signs of revival after 1765), but rather because of the speedy political success of the English in India. This element brought about a major shift in the trade policy of the French.

During the period of free trade the official relationship between the English and the French remained strained and full of mutual recrimination, but at the private level it was complementary and friendly. The period of free trade witnessed numerous official difficulties existing between the local governments of the two rival European powers on the Coromandel Coast, but this did not have any deterrent effect on the newly-emerging relationship between the private interest groups of the two nations. A peculiar coalition of these groups arose to actively participate in Indian shipments. This cooperation of the private banking and financial houses existed in Europe as much as in India. It led to a large-scale remittance of the savings of the English individuals through French channels. The revival of French trade in India after 1771 was principally due to this alignment. The formation of the Nouvelle Compagnie des Indes was the direct outcome of the dialogue of the private banking houses on either side of the English Channel (which has been discussed in Chapters 3 and 4 of the present work). The formation of a new Company in 1785 was the last attempt by the French to capture what they could of the India trade and this they did in some form of workable cooperation with the British. This period also witnessed the emergence of an international ring of financiers to support the French trade in India. Many of them operated from outside France.

The commodity-composition and the pattern of trade of the two rival powers differed marginally from each other. They traded in almost the same goods with the commonly practised mode of contracts and advances. The main difference in their exports to India lay in the fact that the French had to bring bullion specie from Europe to pay for the Indian exports, whereas the English successfully converted the revenue surplus of Bengal into merchant capital to meet the needs of investments on the Coromandel Coast. Their export of woollens and metals was slightly more than that of the French nation. Cotton textile goods dominated the Coromandel exports. The trade figures suggest that the export of cotton goods to France was not as insignificant as is generally believed. Numerous shackles notwithstanding, the French Company and its traders fared reasonably well.

The re-export trade of cotton textiles began to serve the interest of a large number of merchants and shippers of France and England. More significantly, a substantial portion of the textile trade was invested in the slave trade, thereby linking India with the New World.

As to the impact of Anglo-French commerce on the life of the Coromandel region, it is difficult to assess it precisely in the absence of sufficient data. Still, by drawing inferences from the contemporary travelogues, tracts and memoirs, a tentative picture can be presented. First, we notice that there was an increasing participation of European traders in the field of 'country' trade. Their growing control (later complete English domination) meant the virtual replacement of Indian agency by foreign *armateurs*. It had been one of the most profitable sources of gain for the commercially active Indian traders and shippers. The role of credit, insurance and banking instruments in this sphere of trade by European agency reduced the traditional Indian merchants to the status of mere credit suppliers. They were pushed down as intermediaries with inadequate remuneration in the most risky field of credit advance. As regards the Anglo-French participation in the 'country' trade, it can be said that despite their valiant attempt during our period of study, the French had to remain satisfied with a subordinate role. Their ultimate failure was not only due to lack of capital but also due to their failure to find profitable trade items, something like opium or cotton, which the English had discovered to their advantage. The examination of 'country' and coastal trade in the Indian Ocean suggests that the French concentrated on the western Indian Ocean, leaving the East almost free for the British during the period of this study. This was not the situation earlier.

Secondly, the disorganized state of affairs in southern India caused by frequent Anglo-French wars and English wars with the local rulers seem to have given incentive to the Bengal shipping industry for a brief period. These wars were accompanied by regular famines in the Carnatic territories, creating shortage of food grains and resulting in the unusual and pressing demand for their shipments along with the transportation of troops and military stores on the Coromandel Coast. This seems to have increased the freight charges and drawn the attention of the private traders in this direction, thus raising demand for the tonnage. This was probably the reason for the rise of the Bengal shipping industry during the 1770s and 1780s.

Thirdly, one cannot deny the fact that the Anglo-French commercial relationship had a negative impact on the economy of the Coromandel. It caused frequent fluctuations and dislocation of trade during the period of military activities. It caused the scarcity of food grains, raised the price of thread and indigo and dislocated transportation activity. During these disturbances we find large-scale migration of weavers and other artisans away from the main centres of production. Their migration towards the coastal towns and European ports had commenced with the earliest stage of European penetration into the Indian textile zone. The subsequent regional mobility of this class of producers—the most sought after by the Europeans—was caused as much by unstable political, economic and natural forces as by the systematic means pursued by these two rival companies to allure them to their respective settlements. The Indian weavers seemed to be enjoying greater leeway than their counterparts in Europe in the marketability of manufactured cloth. But this description is more apt for the pre-European days, when cotton production was dependent on money advances to the weavers. In such a situation their independence and strength were dependent on market forces, i.e. the price of thread and rice. But we see the prices of these items rising steadily. This rise was exceptional during the time of war. The constant wars and droughts and the increasing political influence of the Europeans adversely affected the market forces and made conditions difficult for the weavers to survive. Added to this, the insistence of the European companies on the old rates of purchase and the physical compulsions imposed on the weavers made their condition all the more unbearable. Professional migration from the weaving community was discouraged through official regulations. All the contemporary evidence testifies to the miserable plight of the Indian weavers and indicates the existence of a feeling of resentment and protest among some of them. This was further aggravated by the arbitrary schemes, such as the 'double advance' scheme or the schemes of Sadlier or Cochrane. The Agency system had a crucial role to play in the process of the squeeze from above.

The presence of the two rival European powers could have furnished advantageous alternatives to the class of manufacturers in the Coromandel. In reality, however, this rivalry created a difficult situation for them and hastened the pace of their enslavement. The division of the weavers between the rival companies and their registration brought them directly under the Europeans. The commercial requirements of the two companies had placed the class of weavers on a different footing from the rest of the inhabitants. Political pressures were exerted on the local authorities to bring this class of producers under English control to sustain their trade. Towards the last decade of the eighteenth century, we notice a shift of emphasis in the Company's textile policy—from manufactured cloths to semi-manufactured and raw-products. This was accompanied by the total rout of the French trading centres and the rapid decline of the proportion of Coromandel textiles in the 'country' trade. All these factors brought about devastating effects on the traditional weaving class, in addition to obliterating those merchants who were dependent on this sector of the economy.

Thus, we notice that the Anglo-French penetration in the southern region of India was guided by the objective of bringing the weaving villages under their political control. But the powers aimed at seizing the main centres of cloth production. Numerous schemes were devised to achieve this goal. In the process the weaving community was nearly enslaved and brought into the vortex of power politics.

Although the Indian weavers produced a multitudinous variety of textiles ranging from longcloth and muslin to *Gingham*, *Guineas* and *Romals* (handkerchiefs), the documentation of evidence suggest that coarse cloth rather than the finer varieties formed the staple of Coromandel exports. However, this does not imply that the trade in finer varieties of textile was insignificant. Each variety was excellent in its quality and durability. These textiles were still sought for all over the world including the most distant regions. It held a special place in the re-export trade of the French and the English. These omnifarious textile products suited the inhabitants of all climates from the point of view of quality and cost. Their prices remained reasonable despite transportation and re-export charges. It is rather unfortunate that though the textile industry of India with all its limitations enjoyed a vast market outside India, but its transformation into a modern industry was not possible as it had to function within the framework of imperial exploitation. Although Indian cotton textiles were barred from the

European markets by political means, yet its craze continued. In spite of this limitation of competing against a mechanized mode of production, Indian cotton textile products held their ground. This was possible so long as market forces operated freely. But the European groups exercised economic pressure through political means to push out Indian goods from their markets. The English Company had to heed to its critics by altering its export policy after 1788. It was the unrestricted imitation of Indian textiles and its overproduction accompanied by unplanned export of Indian muslin, which created an unfavourable condition for them. This situation gave rise to powerful interest groups, which compelled the Company to change its textile policy. Also in the case of France, there was a growing pressure on the government by silk and cotton manufacturers against the imports of Compagnie des Indes. But the French were not in a position to bring about any structural shift in the policy towards Coromandel textiles, i.e. a shift from manufactured to semi-manufactured or raw material items from India, because of their lack of political base. In the case of the English, the first shift from the early form of colonialism to colonial status can be seen in this region once the French were completely ousted. There is plenty of evidence referring to the English Company's fresh interest during the 1790s in commercialized agricultural products such as cotton, indigo, cochineal, pepper, filature of silk and tobacco, as well as in new items that not only assist their shipping industry but also promoted the Company's exports to Europe or elsewhere. Throughout this period we notice that the operation of market forces had a considerable bearing on the development of Indian textile production. The transition from commercial expansion to industrial production is normally feasible under a free interplay of market forces, not under strict mercantilist control and stringent regulations imposed through political domination. Moreover, in the initial stages of economic development an important pre-condition for sustained economic growth and capital formation is political. The State can either play a positive role in creating conditions, as in Japan in the Meiji period, or it may itself hinder development, as early British rule demonstrates. The political control of the English Company was not conducive to capital accumulations within the class of merchants and master craftsmen of the Coromandel region owing to its strict market control.

Thus, we find that in the post-1763 period, despite official confrontations, the English and the French cooperated in establishing European dominance over the market forces to share the profits. But they chose to differ in their approach. It appears that the English success during this period was primarily because they used political means to further their trade interests, whereas the French were probably interested in Indian trade to achieve their political ambitions.

NOTES

1. R.C. Mitra, 'Political and Commercial Relations of the French in India before 1777', *Proceedings of Indian Historical Records Commission*, Vol. 28, No. 2, pp. 67-70.
2. Brian Ernest Kennedy, 'Anglo-French Rivalry in India and the Eastern Seas 1763-1793: A Study of Anglo-French Tensions and of their Impact on the Consolidation of British Power in the Region', p. 3, unpublished thesis, Australian National University, Canberra, 1969 (microfilm).
3. Charles Mallet, 'Mémoire sur le moyen d'augmenter la produit du revenu territorials de Française à la côte de Coromandel', AD VII-23, AN.
4. Brian Davey, *The Economic Development of India*, Bristol, 1975, p. 41.

Appendices

APPENDIX I: TABLE OF EXPORTS FROM FRANCE TO THE EAST INDIES (1749-50 TO 1769-70)

Year	No. of ships	Shipments in goods in *livres*	Shipments in *specie* in marcs
1749-50	16	30,54,030	3,00,321
1750-51	20	40,25,988	2,85,713
1751-52	15	54,58,387	2,74,173
1752-53	24	66,18,484	1,35,202
1753-54	19	59,47,128	1,91,654
1954-55	24	59,78,324	3,03,135
1955-56	10	21,70,092	60,000
1956-57	8	39,97,678	1,21,152
1957-58	13	19,62,535	1,07,871
1958-59	15	27,42,110	—
1959-60	8	18,46,553	—
1760-61	11	30,64,264	2,400
1761-62	8	18,86,603	13,640
1762-63	6	13,48,201	12,848
1763-64	5	6,11,565	82,762
1764-65	7	23,22,133	1,88,804
1765-66	10	34,81,279	2,13,138
1766-67	13	36,42,003	1,13,331
1767-68	10	43,96,053	1,09,578
1768-69	15	77,93,372	1,09,578
1769-70	3	1,51,269	—

Source: *Encylopéd Méthodique*, article-France, Dictionnaire du Commerce.

APPENDIX II: AVERAGE ANNUAL TRADE OF FRANCE WITH INDIA (1763-88)

(in livres tournois)

Year	Importation of Indian goods in France	French Exports to India
1763	64,15,987	52,85,030
1764	1,28,79,147	99,64,000
1765	1,31,49,518	1,07,42,800
1766	1,39,87,518	1,21,39,200
1767	1,48,17,159	1,10,47,152
1768	1,64,73,817	1,42,90,145
1769	1,71,28,916	1,39,17,137
1770	1,79,90,000	1,48,99,120
1771	1,98,97,132	1,40,80,000
1772	2,16,59,210	1,31,00,310
1773	2,34,39,117	1,22,15,409
1774	2,49,87,200	1,38,43,209
1775	2,58,39,505	1,39,00,000
1776	2,60,38,761	1,35,35,508
1777	10,04,252	84,90,000
1778	9,94,298	98,17,562
1779	8,20,050	94,12,917
1780	7,17,173	1,13,98,811
1781	7,00,000	1,04,00,000
1782	6,25,000	1,25,23,929
1783	10,62,227	1,14,49,781
1784	2,80,49,117	2,48,42,215
1785	3,12,17,614	2,73,99,958
1786	3,43,17,911	2,29,84,000
1787	3,73,46,815	2,83,68,951
1788	3,80,53,543	3,05,49,876

Source: Tableau de commerce-Indes (microfilm), C^{256}, AN.

APPENDIX III: STATEMENT OF THE ENGLISH INVESTMENTS FROM MADRAS COAST

	1776		*1,777*		*1,778*	
Prime Cost	1,91,598		1,84,884		2,04,885	
Customs	1,73,545		2,30,308		1,94,140	
Freight	30,203		45,190		37,122	
Merchandise at 5%	27,531		36,269		28,896	
	4,22,877		5,96,651		4,65,043	
Profit (%)	91,956	(40%)	81,580	(28%)	75,323	
Total	£ 5,14,833		£ 6,78,231		5,40,366	

	1779		*1,780*		*1,781*	
Prime Cost	79,397		—		80,087	
Customs	64,515		—		72,466	
Freight	14,002		—		17,529	
Merchandise at 5%	11,077		—		12,361	
	1,68,991		—		1,82,443	
Profit (%)	38,167	(48%)	—		48,711	(61%)
Total	£ 2,07,158		—		£ 2,31,154	

	1782		*1,783*		*1,784*	
Prime Cost	60,328		—		49,585	
Customs	68,153		—		49,585	
Freight	16,604		—		16,072	
Merchandise at 5%	10,206		—		7,024	
	1,55,291		—		1,22,266	
Profit (%)	35,575	(59%)	—		9,086	(18%)
Total	£ 1,90,866		—		£ 1,31,352	

	1,785		*1,786*	
Prime Cost	36,667		35,671	
Customs	36,664		35,671	
Freight	11,334		5,628	
Merchandise at 5%	5,248		4,875	
	89,916		81,845	
Profit (%)	15,042	(59%)	15,666	(44%)
Total	£ 1,04,958		£ 97,511	

Source: *Madras Despatches*, 27 March 1787 E/4/873(13) IOR, pp. 515-20 (the calculation is made at 8 sh. = 1 *pagoda*).

APPENDIX IV: A COMPARISON OF TEXTILE PRICES PAID BY THE FRENCH AT PONDICHERRY IN 1784 AND 1788

Name of the Textile	Quality	Length	Width	Price of Corge in star *pagodas*	
				1784	1788
Organdis	Premir ...	12 to 12A¾	1A1/3	102	105
"	Premie no. 2	"	"	93	95
"	Second	"	"	84	85
"	Premier	"	1 *aune*	93	95
"	Premier no. 2	"	"	83	85
"	Second	"	"	72	75
"	Premier no. 2	"	5/6	78	80
"	Second	"	"	72	75
"	Premier	"	3/4	72	75
"	Premier no. 2	"	"	68	70
"	Second	"	"	63	65
Tarnatanes	Premier	"	1A 7/8	48	48
"	Premier no. 2	"	"	42	43
"	Second	"	"	38	38
"	Premier no. 2	"	1 *aune*	43	42
"	Second	"	"	35	33
"	Premier	"	7/8	35	35
"	Second	"	"	31	31
"	Third	"	"	28	28
Betteela	Premier	16 *aune*	1A 7/8	46	48
"	Premier no. 2	"	"	42	44
"	"	"	1 *aune*	35	35
"	"	"	7/8	29	30
"	"	"	5/6	55	50
"	"	"	"	50	45
Doreas	Premier	"	"	55	58
"	Second	"	"	50	52
Perkales	Premier	8	23/25	100	92
"	Second	"	"	84	80
Basins	Premier	9 to 9½	5/6	70	72
of Coddalore)	Second	"	"	60	62
Guineas (blue)	18 conjons	14	7/8	28	32
"	16 conjons	"	"	26	27
" (white)	"	7	"	11½	13
Gingham	4 thread	6A ½	5/8	11	12
Bejuta Pauts		14	5/6	22	24
Negapauts		"	"	25	26
Lemanees		7	7/8	18	18
Canvates (blue & red)		14	5/6	25	26

(*contd.*)

APPENDIX IV (contd.)

Name of the Textile	Quality	Length	Width	Price of Corge in star *pagodas*	
				1784	1788
Chiavony		$6^2/_3$		$8^3/_4$	9
	Organdis Premier	16 to a piece	3/4	73	75
	Second	"	"	68	70
	Third	"	"	62	65
Handkerchiefs	Coast Premeir	20 to a piece	"	38	34
	Second	"	"	30	30
	Madras very good	8 to a piece	3/4	110	110
	Madras no. 2	"	"	95	95
	Madras no. 3	"	"	80	80

Source: Pierre Blancard, pp. 255-9.

Glossary

amildar	Land revenue collector of a group of villages but by eighteenth century became like a subedar enjoying administrative powers
bar	A unit of weight of about 8 maunds
cash or *casu*	Smallest monetary unit in a *pagoda*
chay	Cotton cloth of deep red shade obtained from the roots of *chaya* plants, mainly found in Nizam's territory
banjara	A hereditary group of travellers who usually moves in caravans, buying and selling consumer goods in bulk in the course of their journey
canicoply	A local official concerned with collecting company's investments
caurie or *cowry*	The small white shell popular as money unit mostly in Bengal but also used in other parts of the country. It was used as a trade item
chetti	Merchant
coolie	Hired labour
copdar	A broker in the weaving community who also assisted the European companies in the assortment of cloth.
covid	From *covade*, Portuguese word for cubit. It was a unit of measurement for cloth, consisting of 15, 27 or 36 inches
dalal	Broker
dastak	A permit, chiefly for the transit of goods
fanans	A small monetary unit, also called *panans*. Each *fanan* consisted of 60 to 80 *cash* depending on the region and time. Similarly 24 to 45 *fanans* made a *pagoda*

firman — An imperial decree or edict in the times of the Mughals

gomastah — A person who acted as a merchant's agent. His services were usually utilized by the Europeans

hundi — A bill of exchange

Jaghire or jagir — An administrative unit given to an official for a specific period of time along with the right to collect revenue in lieu of salary

livre — A pre-revolutionary French monetary unit, approximately 10½ to 11 pence of English currency or one rupee equivalent to about 2 *livres*, 12 *sous* or *sols*. Each *livre* was further divided into *sols* and *derniers*, 12 *derniers* making one *sol* and 20 *sols* forming 1 *livre*

maund — A unit of weight which consisted of about 40 *seers* but it varied from one region to another. Each *seer* consisted of about 20 *palons*

muchalka — A written obligation or bond

pagoda — A major currency of the Coromandel, subdivided into *fanons* and *cashs*. Each *pagoda* consisted of 24 to 45 *fanons*, and was equivalent of about Rs. 3.35 to Rs. 3.60 or 8 shillings to 8 shillings 9 pence. There were two types of *pagodas*–star *pagoda* and 3 swami *pagoda*. The golden *pagoda* was made of 22 carats gold, the Madras *pagoda* of 21 carats and the Porto Novo of 19 carats. The exchange value depended on their gold content

parwanas — A letter of authority from an official, usually to his subordinate

paykat or *payakatt* — Territorial unit consisting of a cluster of weaving villages

pettai — The traditonal internal market that developed into a permanent market near rural production centre.

poligar — Head of a territory enjoying enormous powers

romal — Handkerchief

rupee — A major monetary unit but more popular in northern and eastern India. In Pondicherry it was equal to about 2 *livres* 12 *sols* of the French currency or about 2 shillings 2 pence

saraf	A money changer who occasionally acted as a banker and charged commission on lendings
Spanish *piastre*	Changed by *Sarafs* at 12½ to 17¾ *fanons*
vara sante	Weekly markets
viss	A unit of weight. The number of *viss* in a maund varied abnormally according to local customs and the type of items. Usually 6 *viss* made a *tulam* and 8 *tulams* made maund

Bibliography

MANUSCRIPT SOURCES

1. Archives Nationales, Paris, Série 8 AQ - *Compagnie des Indes*, Vol. Nos. 192-6, 247, 249, 270, 302, 303, 304, 377. These registers of Compagnie des Indes provide detailed information on sales and purchases made between 1785 and 1792 by the new French Company.
   Sèrie F^3 48 - *Colonies, Indes Orientales*, XVIIIe Siècle
   Sèrie F^{12} 1403-1405 - *Commerce et industrie*
   Sèrie AD VII-23 *Marine et Colonies* and AD XI-41
   Sèrie C^2 - *Fonds des Colonies*, Inde et Compagnie des Indes (microfilms), Nos. 47, 48, 56, 105, 106, 107, 108, 113, 114, 171, 183, 184, 192, 244, 245, 256.
2. Archives des Affaires Ètrangers, Paris
   Série - *Mémoires et Documents*, Asie, Indes Orientales, Vols. 4, 5, 7, 8, 11, 12 and 16.
   Série - Correspondance Political, *Angleterre*, Vols. 550 to 556.
3. Bibliothèque Nationale, Paris, Série-*Ariel, F.R.Nouvelle Acquisition*, Nos. 8925-30, 8934-6, 9366-8, 22085, 23143, 24216. This series includes correspondence from the different French settlements in Asia.
4. Depôt des Archives, D'Outre-mer, Aix-en-Provence, France, Séries-B, Fonds de L'Inde, *Feuilles Volantes*, Correspondence General.
5. India Office Records, London, *French in India Series*, Vols. 1-10, 12, 13, 15, 17. *Madras Dispatches*, Vols. 3, 4, 8, 13, 16 and 18. *The Verlée Collection*, Folio Nos. 4, 5, 12, 23, 26, 33 and 102.
6. British Museum, London, *Add. Mss* 34466, 34467, 34468, 34469, 34686, 38223, 38341 and 38398 (including *Auckland Papers* and *North Papers*).
7. (a) National Archives of India, Delhi, *Foreign Department, Secret* (1772-86) Proceedings. *Palk Papers*, City Exter Library, London (microfilms in NAI). *Pitt Papers*, MSS 931, 932, 933, John Rylands Library, Manchester, UK (microfilms in NAI). John Hawkins on Indian Trade (1786), National Library of Wales (microfilms in NAI). *Melville Papers*, MS 3386, National Library, Scotland, Edinburgh (microfilms in NAI). *Nouvelle Acquisition Série* and *Fonds Française*, Bibliothèque Nationale,

Paris, Nos. 9932, 9949, 9365, 9366, 23331, 23345, 22085, 22134 (microfilms in NAI). *Home Miscellaneous Series* from India Office Records, MSS 106, 123, 191, 223, 399-401, 434, 454, 642(microfilms in NAI).

(b) National Archives of India, Pondicherry, *Lagrenée Correspondence*, Papiers de Bellecombe et Law (1777), *Moracin Comptes* Nos. 102, 301, 316, 355, 356, 351, 358-67.

8. Tamil Nadu State Archives, Madras, *Public Department Consultations*, Vols. 101-11, 125-41, 147-62.
Despatches from England (1786-92).
Despatches to England (1786-92).
Military Department *Sundry Books*, Nos. 86-8.
Chingleput District Records, Bundle 472.
9. Andhra Pradesh State Archives, Hyderabad—*Godavari District Records*, Vols. 830, 885, 4632. *Masulipatam District Correspondence*, Vols. 2837, 2838, 2839, 2841, 2900.
10. Cleveland Public Library, Ohio, USA, *Manuscripts on British India*.

PRINTED SOURCES

Forest, Sir George William (ed.), *Selections from the letters, despatches and other state papers preserved in the foreign department of India, 1772-1785*, Calcutta, 1890, 3 vols.

Fullarton, W., *A View of the English Interests in India: an account of the military operations in the southern parts of the Peninsula, 1782-1784*, London, 1788.

Gaudart, Edmond (ed.), *Correspondance des Agents á Pondichéry de la nouvelle Compagnie des Indes avec les Administrateurs à Paris, 1788-1803*, Paris, 1931.

Indian Record Series, New Delhi.

Fort William-India House Correspondence.

Volume IV, *Public Series, 1764-6*, Delhi, 1962.
Volume V, *Public Series, 1767-9*, Delhi, 1949.
Volume VI, *Public Select and Secret, 1770-2*, Delhi, 1960.
Volume XV, *Foreign and Secret, 1782-6*, Delhi, 1963
Volume XVI, *Foreign, Secret and Political, 1787-91*, Delhi, 1976.
Volume XVII, *Foreign, Political and Secret, 1792-5*, Delhi, 1955.

Martineau, Alfred (ed.), *Correspondence du Conseil Supérieur de Pondichéry et de la Compagnie*, Pondichery, 1920-31, 6 vols.

Pollard, S. and C. Holmes (eds.), *Documents of European Economic History: The Process of Industrialization, 1750-1870*, Vol. I, London, 1968.

Wilson, Charles and Geoffrey Parker (eds.), *An Introduction to the Sources of Economic History, 1500-1800*, Cornell, 1977.

CONTEMPORARY WRITINGS

Bartolomeo, Fra Paolinoda San, *A Voyage to the East Indies*, London, 1800.

Baudeau L'abbé (ed.), *Encyclopédie Mèthodique—Commerce*, Paris, 1783, Tome I and II.

Blancard, Pierre, *Manuel du Commerce des Indes Orientales et de la Chine*, Paris, 1806.

Buchanan, Francis, *Journey from Madras through the Countries of Mysore, Canara and Malabar*, Vol. I, London, 1807.

Duperron, Anquetil, *L'Inde en Rapport avec L'Europe*, Paris, 1798, Tome I et II.

Flaix, Legoux de, *Essai Historique, Gèographique et Politique sur L'Indoustan avec le tableau de son commerce*, Paris, 1807, Tome I et II.

Flotte, M. de la, *Essais historiques sur l'Inde precedés d'un journal de voyages et d'une description géographie de la Côte de Coromandel*, Paris, 1769.

Lacrettele, Pierre Louis and Blond, *Mémoire à consulter et consultation pour les negociants faisant le commerce des merchandises de Indes contre la nouvelle Compagnie des Indes*, Paris, 1786.

Laugragnais, Le Comte de, *Mémoire sur la Compagnie des Indes*, Paris, 1786.

Macpherson, David, *The History of the European Commerce with India*, London, 1812.

Milburn, William, *Oriental Commerce*, London, 1813, 2 vols.

Morellet, L'abbé, *Mémoire sur la situation actuelle de la Compagnie des Indes*, Paris, 1769.

Necker, Jacques, *Reponse au Mémoire de M. L'abbé Morellet sur la Compagnie des Indes*, Paris, 1769.

Orme, Robert, *A History of Military Transactions of the British Nation in Indostan*, London, 1778, 2 vols. (rpt. Delhi, 1985).

Peuchet, M., *État des Colonies et du Commerce*, Paris, 1783.

Pillai, Ananda Ranga, *The Private Diary of Ananda Ranga Pillai*, 12 vols., J. Frederick and K. Rangachari (eds.), Delhi, rpt. 1985.

Raynal, Abbé, *A Philosophical and Political History of the Settlements and Trade of the Europeans in the East and West Indies* (tr. J. Justamond), Vol. II, London, 1777.

Rennell, Major, *Memoir of a Map of the Peninsula of India*, London, 1793.

Sulivan, Richard Joseph, *An Analysis of the Political History of India*, London, 1774.

BOOKS

Antony, Francis Cyril (ed.), *Pondicherry Gazetteer*, Pondicherry, 1982, 2 vols.

Arasaratnam, Sinnappah, *Merchants, Companies and Commerce on the Coromandel Coast 1650-1740*, Delhi, 1986.

———, *Maritime India in the Seventeenth Century*, Delhi, 1994.

———, *Maritime Commerce and English Power in South East India 1750-1800*, Aldershot, 1996.

Assett, Arthur Blennerh, *Monograph on the Cotton Fabrics of the Central Provinces*, Allahabad, 1898.

Balkrishna, *Commercial Relations between India and England, 1601-1757*, London, 1924.

Banga, Indu (ed.), *The City in Indian History, Urban Demography Society and Politics*, Delhi, 1991.

Bayly, C.A., *Indian Society and the Making of the British Empire*, Bombay, 1988.

Berg, Maxine, *The Age of Manufactures, 1700-1820*, London, 1985.

Besson, Maurice, *Les Adventuriers Francais aux Indes 1775-1820*, Paris, 1932.

Bhattacharya, S., *The East India Company and the Economy of Bengal from 1704-1740*, London, 1954.

Blussé, L. and F. Gaastra (eds.), *Companies and Trade: Essays on Overseas Trading Companies during the Ancient Regime*, Leiden, 1981.

Bowry, Thomas, *A Geographical Account of Countries round the Bay of Bengal, 1669-1679*, Cambridge, 1905.

Braudel, Fernand, *Civilization and Capitalism, 15th to 18th Centuries*, Vol. II—*The Wheels of Commerce*, London, 1982.
Vol. III—*The Perspective of the World*, London, 1984.

———, *After-thoughts on Material Civilization and Capitalism*, London, 1977.

Brennig, Joseph, *The Textile Trade of Seventeenth Century Northern Coromandel*, Michigan, USA, photocopy of the thesis at ICHR, Delhi.

Chapman, S.D., *The Cotton Industry in the Industrial Revolution*, London, 1972.

Chaudhuri, K.N., *The Trading World of Asia and the English East India Company 1660-1760*, London, 1978.

———, *Trade and Civilization in the Indian Ocean: An Economic History from the Rise of Islam to 1750*, Cambridge, 1985.

Chaudhury, Sushil and Michel Morineau (eds.), *Merchants, Companies and Trade, Europe and Asia in the Early Modern Era*, Cam-bridge, 1999.

Chicherov, A.I., *India's Economic Development in the 16th-18th Centuries*, Moscow, 1971.

Cipolla, M. Carlo (ed), *The Emergence of Industrial Societies, Fontana Economic History of Europe*, Vol. 4, Pt. 1, Harvester, 1976.

Conan, J., *La Derniere Compagnie Francaise des Indes, 1785-1875*, Paris, 1942.

Crowhurst, Patrick, *The Defence of British Trade 1689-1815*, Dawson, 1977.

Dalgliesh, Wilbert Harold, *The Perpetual Company of the Indies in the days of Dupleix, 1722-1756*, Philadelphia, 1933.

Das Gupta, Ashin, *Malabar in Asian Trade 1740-1800*, Cambridge, 1967.

———, 'Trade and Politics in 18th Century India', in D.S. Richards (ed.), *Islam and the Trade of Asia,* Oxford, 1970.

Das Gupta, Ashin and M.N. Pearson (eds.), *India and the Indian Ocean 1500-1800*, Oxford, 1987.

Dutta, Rajat, *Society, Economy and the Market, Commercialization in Rural Bengal c.1760-1800*, Delhi, 2000.

Deloche, Jean, *La Circulation en Inde Avant la Revolution des Transports*, Paris, 1980, 2 vols.

———, *Transport and communications in India*, Vols. I-II, Oxford, 1994.

Dermigny, Louis, *Cargaisons Indiennes, Soliers et Cie 1781-1793*, Paris, 1960, 2 vols.

Dodwell, H.H.(ed.), *Cambridge History of India*, Vol. V, London, 1929.

———, *Dupleix and Clive, the Beginning of Empire*, London, 1920, reprinted 1962.

———, *The Nabobs of Madras*, London, 1926.

Dupuis, Jacques, *Madras et Le Nord du Coromandel*, Paris, 1960.

Ehrman, J., *The British Government and Commercial Negotiations with Europe*, Cambridge, 1962.

Feldbaek, Ole, *India Trade under the Danish Flag 1772-1808*, Copenhagen, 1969.

Francis, W. (ed.), *Madura District Gazetteer*, Madras, 1906.

———, *South Arcot District Gazetteer*, Madras, 1906.

Furber, Holden, *John Company at Work: A Study of Commercial Expansion in India in the Late 18th Century*, New York, 1970.

———, *Rival Empires of Trade in the Orient, 1600-1800*, Minneapolis, 1976.

———, *Private Fortunes and Company Profits in the Indian Trade in the 18th Century*, Hampshire, 1997.

Gaudart, Edmond (ed.), *Les Privileges du Commerce Français L'Inde*, Paris, 1931.

Habakkuk, H.J. and M. Postan (eds.), *The Cambridge Economic History of Europe*, Vol. VI, Pt. I, Cambridge, 1966.

Habib, Irfan, *Essays in Indian History, Towards a Marxist Perception*, Delhi, 1995.

Hamilton, C.J., *The Trade Relations between England and India 1600-1896*, Delhi, 1919, rpt. 1975.

Hartwell, R.M.(ed.), *The Causes of the Industrial Revolution in England*, London, 1967.

Harlow, Vincent T., *The Founding of the Second British Empire 1763-1793*, Longmans, 1964, Vol. II.

Hatalkar, V.T., *Relations between the French and the Marathas 1668-1815*, Bombay, 1958.

Haudrere, Pierre, *La Compagnie Française des Indes au XVIIIe Siècle (1719-1795)*, Paris, 1989.

Heckscher, Eli F., *Mercantilism*, London, 1955.

Herman, Louis, *Histoire de la Rivalitè des Français et des Anglais dans L'Inde*, Paris, 1847.

Hossain, Hameeda, *The Company Weavers of Bengal, The East India Company and the Organization of Textile Production in Bengal 1750-1813*, Oxford, 1988.

Irwin, John and P.R. Schwartz, *Studies in Indo-European Textile History*, Ahmedabad, 1966, Vols. 1-4, Paris, 1989.

Jamila, Brij Bhushan, *The Costumes and Textiles of India*, Bombay, 1958.

Jarrett, Derek, *The Begetters of Revolution, England's Involvement with France 1759-1789*, New Jersey, 1973.

Kaeppelin, Paul, *La Compagnie des Indes Orientales et François Martin*, Paris, 1908.

Kemp, Tom, *Economic Forces in French History*, London, 1971.

Keiffer, Jean-Luc, *Anquetil Duperron: L'Inde en France au XVIIIe Siècle*, Paris, 1983.

Kindleberger, Charles P. (ed.), *Economic Response, Comparative Studies in Trade, Finance and Growth*, Harvard, 1973.

Kling, B.B. and M.N. Pearson (eds.), *The Age of Partnership: Europeans in Asia before Dominion*, Honolulu, 1979.

Kumar J., *Select Documents on Indian Trade & Industry 1773-1833*, Patna, 1981.

Labernadie, Marguerite V., *Le Vieux Pondichéry 1673-1815, Histoire d'une ville colonial Française*, Paris, 1936.

Leman, G.C. (ed.), *The Ganjam District Manual*, Madras, 1882.

Lindsay, J.D. (ed.), *The New Cambridge Modern History*, Vol. VII, *1713-1763*, Cambridge, 1957.

Lis, C. and H. Soly (eds.), *Poverty & Capitalism in Pre-Industrial Europe*, Sussex, 1979.

Love, H.D., *Vestiges of Old Madras, 1640-1800*, London, 1913, 3 vols.

Lüthy, Herbert, *La Banque Protestante en France 1730-1790*, Paris, 1961, 2 vols.

Lough, John, *An Introduction to Eighteenth Century France*, London, 1960.

Malleson, G.B., *Final French Struggles in India and on the Indian Seas*, London, 1878.

Marshal, P.J., *East India Fortunes: The British in Bengal in the Eighteenth Century*, Oxford, 1976.

———, *Problems of Empire: Britain and India, 1757-1813*, London, 1968.

Martineau, Alfred Albert, *État Politique de l'Inde on 1777 par law de Lauriston*, Paris, 1913.

———, *Bussy et L'Inde Française, 1720-1785*, Paris, 1935.

Mathew, K.S. (ed.), *Mariners, Merchants and Oceans, Studies in Martine History*, Delhi, 1995.

———, *Shipbuilding and Navigation in the Indian Ocean Region, A.D. 1400-1800*, Delhi, 1996.

Mathew, K.S. and S. Jeyaseela Stephen (eds.), *Indo-French Relations*, Delhi, 1999.

Morris D. Morris, Raychaudhuri and Bipan Chandra (eds.), *Indian Economy in the Nineteenth Century: A Symposium*, Delhi, 1970.

Nightingale, Pamela, *Trade and Empire in Western India 1784-1806*, Cambridge, 1970.

Parkinson, C. Northcott, *Trade in the Eastern Seas, 1793-1813*, London, 1966.

Parry, J.H., *Trade and Dominion: The European Overseas Empires in the Eighteenth Century*, London, 1971.

Pavlov, V.I., *Historical Premises for India's Transition to Capitalism*, Moscow, 1978.

Philips, C.H. (ed.), *The Correspondece of David Scott, Director and Chairman of the East India Company relating to Indian Affairs, 1787-1805*, London, 1951.

———, *The East India Company 1784-1834*, Oxford, 1961.

Prakash, Om, *Precious Metals and Commerce: The Dutch East India Company in the Indian Occan Trade*, Aldershot, 1994.

———, *European Commercial Enterprise in Pre-colonial India*, Cambridge, 1998.

Prakash, Om (ed.), *European Commercial Expansion in Early Modern Asia*, Vol. 10 of '*An Expanding World*', Hampshire, 1997.

Rajayyan, K., *Administration and Society in the Carnatic 1701-1800*, Venkateswara, 1966.

Raju, Sharda, *Economic Conditions in the Madras Presidency*, Madras, 1941.

Ramaswamy, Vijaya, *Textiles and Weavers in Medieval South India*, Delhi, 1985.

Raychaudhuri, Tapan, *Jan Company in Coromandel 1605-1690*, Hague, 1962.

Raychaudhuri, Tapan and Irfan Habib (eds.), *The Cambridge Economic History of India*, Vol. I, Cambridge, 1982.

Regani, Sarojini, *Nizam-British Relations 1724-1857*, Hyderabad, 1963.

Rocher, Rosane (ed.), *Holden Furber, Private Fortunes and Company Profits in the India Trade in the 18th Century*, Hampshire, 1997.

Roy, Tirthankar, *Cloth Commerce, Textiles in Colonial India*, Delhi, 1996.

Scholberg, Henry and E. Divien (eds.), *Bibliographie des Française dans L'Inde*, Pondicherry, 1973.

Schumpter, E.B., *English Overseas Trade Statistics, 1697-1800*, Oxford, 1960.

Sen, S.P., *The French in India, 1763-1816*, Calcutta, 1958, rpt., Delhi, 1971.

Siddiqi, Asiya, *Trade and Finance in Colonial India*, Oxford, 1995.

Singh, S.B., *European Agency Houses in Bengal 1783-1833*, Calcutta, 1966.

Sinha, N.K., *The Economic History of Bengal*, Vol. I, Calcutta, 1965.

Spate, O.H.K., *India and Pakistan—A General and Regional Geography*, London, 1954.

Stephen, S. Jeyaseela, *The Coromandel Coast and its Hinterland, Economy, Society and Political System*, Delhi, 1997.

Stein, Burton, *Peasant, State and Society in Medieval South India*, Delhi, 1980.

Subrahmanyam, Sanjay, *The Political Economy of Commerce: Southern India 1500-1650*, Cambridge, 1990.

Subrahmanyam, Sanjay (ed.), *Merchants, Markets and the State in Early Modern India*, Delhi, 1990.

———, *Money and the Market in India 1100-1700*, Delhi, 1994.

Sutherland, Lucy S., *The East Indian Company in Eighteenth Century Politics*, Oxford, 1952.

Terrade, Jean, *Le Commerce Colonial de la France à la fin del'ancien régime*, Tome I and II, Paris, 1972.

Thurston, Edgar, *Monograph on the Cotton Fabric Industry of the Madras Presidency*, Madras, 1897.

Tracy, James D. (ed.), *The Rise of Merchant Empires, Long Distance Trade in the Early Modern World 1350-1750*, Cambridge, 1990.

Tripathi, Amales, *Trade and Finance in the Bengal Presidency 1793-1833*, Calcutta, 1956.

Varadarajan, Lotika (tr. and annotator), *India in the 17th Century: Social, Economic and Political Memoirs of François Martin*, Delhi, 1981-3, Pts. I and II.

Watson, I.B., *Foundation for Empire : English Private Trade in India, 1959-1760*, Delhi, 1980.

Weber, Henry, *La Compagnie Française des Indes, 1604-1875*, Paris, 1904.

Williams, Judith Blow, *British Commercial Policy and Trade Expansion, 1750-1850*, Oxford, 1972.

Williams, G., *The Expansion of Europe in the Eighteenth Century*, London, 1966.

ARTICLES

Ahuja, Ravi, 'Labour unsettled: Mobility and protest in the Madras region, 1750-1800', *The Indian Economic and Social History Review*, 35, 4, 1998, pp. 381-404.

Alam, M.S., 'Masulipatam—A Metropolitan Port in the Seventeenth Century', *Islamic Culture*, July 1959, Vol. XXXIII, No. 3, pp. 169-87.

Arasaratnam, S., 'Aspects of the Role and Activities of South Indian Merchants, *c.* 1650-1750', *Proceedings of the First International Conference of Tamil Studies*, Kuala Lumpur, 1966, Vol. I, pp. 582-96.

———, 'Trade and Political Dominion in South India 1750-1790: Changing British-Indian Relationships', *Modern Asian Studies*, Vol. 13, No. 1, 1977, pp. 19-46.

———, 'Indian Commercial Groups and European Traders 1600-1800: Changing Relationships in Southeastern India', *South Asia* (N.S.), Vol. I, No. 2, 1978, pp. 42-53.

———, 'Weaver, Merchants and Company: The Handloom Industry in Southeastern India 1750-1790', *The Indian Economic and Social History Review,* Vol. XVII, No. 3, 1980, pp. 257-81.

———, 'Indian Merchants and the Decline of Indian Mercantile Activity: The Coromandel Case', *The Calcutta Historical Journal,* Vol. VII, No. 2, 1983, pp. 27-43.

Bassett, D.K., 'British "Country" Trade and Local Trade Netwroks in the Thai and Malay States *c.*1680-1770', *Modern Asian Studies*, Vol. 23, No. 4, 1989, pp. 625-44.

Boulle, Pierre H., 'French Mercantilism, Commercial Companies and Colonial Profitability', in L. Blussé and F. Gaastra (eds.), *Companies and Trade,* The Hague, 1981.

Brennig, Joseph J., 'Textile Producers and Production in Late Seventeenth Century Coromandel', *The Indian Economic and Social History Review,* Vol. XXII, No. 4, 1986, pp. 333-56.

Chaudhrui, K.N., 'The Structure of Indian Textile Industry in the Seventeenth and Eighteenth Centuries', *The Indian Economic and Social History Review,* Vol. XI, Nos. II-III, 1974, pp.127-82.

Das Gupta, Ashin, 'Presidential Address', Medieval India Section, *Indian History Congress Proceedings,* 35th Session, 1974, pp. 99-111.

De, Barun, 'Early Manifestations of the Colonial Premise in the British Occupation of Bengal', *Indian History Congress Proceedings,* 38th Session, 1977, pp. 474-88.

Dermigny, Louis, 'East India Company et Compagnie des Indes', in Michel Mollat(ed.), *Societes et Compagnies de Commerce en Orient et dans L'Ocean Indian*, Paris, 1970.

Divien, Emmanuel, 'The Development of Tamil Society in Pondicherry 1706-1898', unpublished thesis, 1975, Madras University.

Dodwell, H., 'The Madras Weavers under the Company', *Proceedings of Indian Historical Records Commission,* Vol. IV, 1922, pp. 41-6.

Frasca, Richard A., 'Weavers in Pre-Modern South India', *Economic and Political Weekly,* Vol. 10, 26 July 1975, pp. 119-23.

Georgia, Sr., 'Textiles and Weavers on the Coromandel Coast with special reference to Pondicherry during the Second Half of the Seventeenth and the First Half of the Eighteenth Centuries', *Indian History Congrests Proceedings,* 51st Session, 1990, pp. 332-7.

Habib, Irfan, 'Potentialities of Capitalist Development in the Economy of Mughal India', *Journal of Economic History,* 29 March 1969, pp. 32-78.

Haudrere, Philippe, 'The French Company and its Trade in the Eighteenth Century', in Sushil Chaudhury and Morineau Michel (eds.),

Merchants, Companies and Trade, Europe and Asia in the Early Modern Era, Cambridge, 1999, pp. 287-99.

Haynes, Douglas E. and Tirthankar Roy, 'Conceiving Mobility: Weavers' Migrations in Pre-colonial and Colonial India', *The Indian Economic and Social History Review,* XXXVI, I, 1999, pp. 35-67.

Hossain, Hameeda, 'The Alienation of Weavers: Impact of the Conflict between the Revenue and Commercial Interests of the East India Company 1750-1800', *The Indian Economic and Social History Review,* Vol. XVI, No. III, 1979, pp. 323-46.

Irwin, John, 'Indian Textile Trade in the Seventeenth Century Coromandel Coast', *Journal of Indian Textile History,* Vol. 2, 1956, pp. 24-42.

Kennedy, Brian Ernest, ' Anglo-French Rivalry in India and the Eastern Seas 1763-1793: A Study of Anglo-French Tensions and of their Impact on the Consolidation of British Power in the Region', Ph.D. unpublished thesis, Canberra, 1969.

Lawandowski, Susan J., 'Changing Form and Function in the Ceremonial and the Colonial Port-City in India: An Historical Analysis of Madurai and Madras', *Modern Asian Studies,* II, No. 2, 1977, pp. 183-212.

Mitra, R.C., 'Political and Commercial Relations of the French in India before 1777', *Proceedings of Indian Historical Records Commission,* Vol. XXVIII, No. 2, pp. 67-70.

Mukherjee, Rila, 'The French East India Company's Trade in East Bengal from 1750 to 1753: A Look at the Chandernagore Letters to Jugolia', *Indian Historical Review,* Vol. XVII, Nos. 1-2, 1990-1, pp. 122-35.

Nussbaum, Frederick L., 'The Formation of the New East India Company of Calonne', *The American Historical Review,* XXXVIII, No. 3, 1933, pp. 475-97.

Perlin, Frank, 'Growth of Money Economy and Some Questions of Transition in Late pre-Colonial India', *Journal of Peasant Studies,* Vol. II, No. 3, 1984, pp. 96-107.

Prakash, Om, 'Dutch Source Material on Indian Maritime History in the early Modern Period—An Evaluation', *Indian Historical Review*, Vol. VIII, 1981-2.

Racine, J.L., 'Esquisse d'une Historie Commercial de Pondichéry jusqu 'en 1954', *Revue Historique,* Vol. 10, 1972, pp. 1-80.

Ray, Indrani, 'The French Company and the Merchants of Bengal: 1680-1735', *The Indian Economics and Social History Review,* Vol. VIII, 1971, pp. 41-55.

———, 'Journey to Kasimbazar and Murshidabad: Observations of a French Visitor to Bengal in 1743', *Bengal Past and Present,* Vol. 2, 1981, pp. 49-72.

———, 'India in Asian Trade in the 1730s—An 18th Century French Memoir', *Indian History Congress Proceedings,* 34the Session, 1973, Pt. I, pp. 271-90.

Sen, S.P., ' Franco-Mysore Relations (1785-93)' , *Proceedings of Indian Historical Records Commission*, Vol. XXXI, Pt. 2, 1955, pp. 32-9.

Sridharan, M.P., 'Tipu's Letters to French Officials', *Indian History Congress Proceedings*, 45th Session, 1984, pp. 503-8.

Stephen, S. Jeyaseela, 'Socio-Economic Role of Dubash Pedro Kana Karaya Mudaliar in the French colony of Pondicherry: A Study in Resilience', *Revnue Historique de Pondichéry*, Vol. XVIII, 1995, pp. 15-32.

Swarnalatha, P. and P. Sudhir, 'The Company and the Coromandel Weaver: Structural Change in the Short Term 1790-1820', *Indian History Congress Proceedings*, 48th Session, 1987, pp. 461-6.

Index